Russell Long

RUSSELL LONG

A Life in Politics

Michael S. Martin

University Press of Mississippi Jackson

www.upress.state.ms.us

The University Press of Mississippi
is a member of the Association of American University Presses.

Manufactured in the United States of America

First printing 2014
∞

Library of Congress Cataloging-in-Publication Data

Martin, Michael S., 1972–
Russell Long : a life in politics / Michael S. Martin.
pages cm
Includes bibliographical references and index.
ISBN 978-1-61703-974-4 (cloth : alk. paper) — ISBN 978-1-61703-975-1 (ebook) 1. Long, Russell B. 2. Legislators—United States—Biography. 3. United States. Congress. Senate—Biography. 4. United States—Politics and government—1945–1989. I. Title.
E748.L864M37 2014
328.73'092—dc23
[B] 2013030502

British Library Cataloging-in-Publication Data available

For Amy, Sam, and Alex—and Mom.

CONTENTS

ACKNOWLEDGMENTS

This book started, as I suspect many do, in a conversation. While walking across the campus at the University of Arkansas on a spring day in 1998, I discussed the Long family of Louisiana with Dr. Randall Woods. As we walked, I lamented that just about everything that could be said about Huey and Earl Long had been said (a sentiment I do not necessarily agree with anymore), to which Woods responded, "Yet not much has been done on Russell."

I immediately set about finding out what I could about Russell Long, Huey's son and Earl's nephew, and what I discovered was that, indeed, not much had been written about him by historians. To be sure, a biography existed—Bob Mann's *Legacy to Power: Senator Russell Long of Louisiana*—but it was an authorized biography and had not been done by a professional historian. Aside from that, very little had been written about this man who had risen to the highest levels of our nation's government in a political career that spanned four decades. And so from that conversation came the genesis for this book.

As the reader might suppose, my most heartfelt thanks go to Dr. Randall Woods, Distinguished Professor of History at the University of Arkansas. This book would not exist without him. To the rest of the faculty of the Department of History at the University of Arkansas during my time there—in particular, David Chappell, James Chase, Willard Gatewood, Thomas Kennedy, Charles Robinson, David Sloan, Richard Sonn, Daniel Sutherland, Elliott West, Jeannie Whayne, and Patrick Williams—I offer my gratitude for your willingness to challenge me, listen to me, and teach me.

As with any work of history, this book is constrained by its sources. Happily for me, the amount of information related to Long's career is extensive. Indeed, the sheer size of his collection of papers housed at Hill Memorial Library on the campus of Louisiana State University boggled my mind at times. Thus, I am particularly grateful to the staff at Hill Memorial, notably Emily Robison, Judy Bolton, and Tara Zachary Laver, who helped me sift through what at times seemed like mountains of files and folders during those days I spent in their beautiful reading room.

Their efforts impressed me all the more since I worked in a similar collection while a Research Associate with the Albert Gore Research Center of Middle Tennessee State University. I am indebted to Lisa Pruitt, director of the Gore Center at the time, for showing me the inner workings of such an archive and for serving as a sounding board. My work at the Gore Center focused on research for a biographical project on Albert Gore Sr., and it was through that project that I came to know and admire Anthony J. Badger, an eminent historian who worked closely with me and provided me with a model for clear thinking, rigorous research, and lucid writing. Tony helped me become the historian I am now, and for that I am forever grateful.

Over the years, many of my colleagues and friends have read over or commented on various portions of this book. Others have simply offered me words of advice and encouragement. Their insight, constructive comments, and support made this a better book. And so I send a hearty thanks to Thomas Aiello, Janet Allured, Vaughan Baker, David Barry, Carl Brasseaux, Richard Cusimano, John Kyle Day, Susan Dollar, Adam Fairclough, Kevin Fontenot, Julia Frederick, Joseph "Andy" Fry, Shannon Frystak, Edward Haas, Glen Jeansonne, Dolores Labbé, Jeff Littlejohn, Kyle Longley, Andy Moore, Charles Pellegrin, and Amos Simpson.

Although working for the state of Louisiana in the early twenty-first century can amount to a roller-coaster ride of budget exigencies and fiscal cliffs, getting to spend my workdays with my colleagues in the University of Louisiana at Lafayette's Center for Louisiana Studies and Department of History, Geography, and Philosophy sure makes the ride fun. To the staff at the Center—Mary Karnath-Duhé, Linda Garber, Jennifer Ritter Guidry, Chris Segura, John "Pudd" Sharp, Melissa Teutsch, and James Wilson—each of you make my job interesting and enlightening. Likewise, I always look forward to learning something new from Bob Carriker, Mary Farmer-Kaiser, Rich Frankel, Judith Gentry, Rob Hermann, Jordan Kellman, Susan Nicassio, Chad Parker, Tim Reilly, Carl Richard, Sara Ritchey, Chet Rzadkiewicz, and John Troutman. Each of you have inspired me in your own way. The friendships I have with Mary, Bob, Jordan, and their spouses strengthens me and reminds me that life is fuller when you can share its ups and downs with those you care about.

Finally, nothing I do would be worth the doing without my family. My mom and stepfather, Tommi and John Kent, and my dad and stepmother, Steve and Levy Martin, have given me more support and encouragement than any one person deserves. My sons, Sam and Alex, have inspired and distracted me in the very best possible ways. And my wife, Amy, has simply been the reason I do anything.

Russell Long

INTRODUCTION

When Russell Long entered the United States Senate in 1948, World War II burned brightly in American memories, and the Cold War loomed ominously. The politics of civil rights and the civil rights movement were just beginning to make inroads in the nation's public consciousness. In his home state, Louisiana, Long's uncle, Earl Long, had earlier in the year brought the so-called Longite political faction back to power. This book provides an investigation of Long's public life over the four decades that followed his swearing in to the Senate and places him within the context of Louisiana, southern, and national politics during the twentieth century.

As a member of Louisiana's most famous and influential political family, and as the son of Huey Long, perhaps the most famous Louisianian of all time, Russell Long's political career was seemingly preordained. Remarkably, he extended the political power first forged by other members of his family and attained heights of true power unknown even to Huey and Earl. The Long family pervaded Louisiana politics from the late 1920s through the 1980s and attained a notoriety rivaled only by the Kennedys of Massachusetts. A Long, particularly the eldest son of Huey, simply could not be apolitical in Louisiana. Russell's father and mother, aunts and uncles, cousins and in-laws all lived political lives, some of them very publicly and others privately. His father's assassination, the single most significant event in Russell's life, set the wheels in motion for his eventual political career. From that point on, the trajectory of Long's life pointed toward politics.

Russell Long's significance for Louisiana's political history comes from his position within the Longite camp of the Long/Anti-Long factionalism of the 1940s and 1950s, but he is also important for his attempts to transcend those political boundaries.

Particularly in the period from 1948 until 1960, Long played an active role in Louisiana politics—first as special counsel to his Uncle Earl; then as partner with two well-known Anti-Longites, Congressman Hale Boggs and New Orleans mayor DeLesseps S. Morrison in the 1951–1952 gubernatorial race; and finally as one of the major actors in the confinement of Uncle Earl to a mental institution in 1959. That last episode left Long with a distaste for Louisiana politics, and he distanced himself from the internal politics of the Bayou State for most of the rest of his career, although he continued to work for the benefit of his state from Washington.

The politics Russell Long practiced differed dramatically from that of his father and uncle. The stances he took, the legislation he sponsored, and the deals he brokered during his thirty-eight-year career point to a political philosophy rooted in practicality and pragmatism. In part that demonstrated Long's own political proclivities—he was neither as stubborn nor as ruthless as Huey or Earl—but his politics also reflected his context: the U.S. Senate from the dawn of the Cold War to the era of Reagan. Long entered the Senate with the so-called Class of '48, a group that included Lyndon Johnson, Robert Kerr, Paul Douglas, Clinton Anderson, Estes Kefauver, and Hubert Humphrey, most of whom were champions of the New Deal liberal consensus and who dominated the upper house for the following three decades. Long himself rose to a prominent position on the Foreign Relations Committee, the chairmanship of the Finance Committee, and the post of Democratic majority whip. Long can be firmly placed within the liberal consensus, but only to a certain extent, for while he was a member of the "Class of '48," he was also a member of the Senate's racially conservative southern bloc.

Those affiliations with liberalism and conservatism might seem remarkable, given the national political scene of the early twenty-first century, but for Russell Long, and indeed for some of his southern colleagues, blending liberalism and conservatism was not only the norm, it was a necessity. Indeed, for Long and other national southern politicians of the mid-century, the most practical political stance was to support liberalism's programs, which were tremendously popular and terribly necessary in their home states, while maintaining a stance of defiance on any change to the purported "southern way of life," which would have been popular with the majority of southern voters through the 1960s. As a southern politician working in the national realm, Long, from early in his career, exhibited a political penchant that mixed support for liberal social welfare programs and active foreign policy with a conservative civil rights agenda. As his Senate tenure wore on, he maintained those stances, with some minor deviations, even as he outlasted many of his southern contemporaries from the sixties and fifties. Equally important, as the South changed politically during those years, Long maintained his position of prominence in the Senate. As black voter participation increased, as a neoconservative movement spread, and as a two-party system developed in the South, Long continued to be reelected in Louisiana and to espouse virtually the same political positions as he had from his earliest days in Washington.

What is notable about Long's career within the national political context is the way in which political changes happening around him created the appearance of Long's shifting one way or the other along the political spectrum. In particular, as the Democratic Party, partly as a result of the leadership of his Senate colleagues Edward Kennedy, Hubert Humphrey, George McGovern, and Edmund Muskie, became more uniformly associated with liberal political stances and as the Republican Party became more and more the party of entrenched conservatism during the 1970s and 1980s, Long stayed the course and continued to espouse a practical political philosophy rooted more in getting things done than in following the dictates of ideological precepts. As a result, his willingness to work across the boundary of "conservative" and "liberal" at a time when that boundary was becoming more rigid made him appear to become more conservative within the confines of his own Democratic Party. The appearance was only strengthened by a changing of the old guard in the Senate, through death or retirement of the body's elder statesmen, politicians who, like Long, had often straddled the divide between liberal and conservative. But that appearance in reality reflected a leftward shift of the Democratic Party and its officeholders, not a rightward move by Long.

As a national politician, Long started his career surrounded by giants of the Democratic Party—most of them southerners—and he learned much of his politics from them, along with his Uncle Earl. Although he lost his father while still in high school, Long learned to use memories of Huey to either bolster his own stances or undermine his opponents'. Such uses of the historical Huey might be considered de rigueur for a politician in Louisiana, where even decades following his death, Huey was remembered as the first state politician to enunciate and grapple with issues that affected a majority of Louisianians, but Russell Long knew that memories of his father could be just as useful on a national stage. Long's repeated appeals to his famous father's memory, and his attempts to defend—and at times shape—that memory, form a recurring theme throughout his career.

This book is not intended to be a true biography, in the sense that it covers, in detail, Russell Long's life from birth to death. Instead, it is a political biography that, while not ignoring his personal life, focuses mainly on his public career. The first chapter examines Long's early life, particularly the political environment in which he matured, and his earliest forays into Louisiana's bifactional politics. Chapter two focuses on Long's first four years in the Senate, a time in which he developed his practical political philosophy by crossing ideological boundaries and joining a coalition of supporters of New Deal liberalism on matters of domestic and foreign policy while staking out his allegiance to the Senate's southern bloc with conservative stances relative to civil rights initiatives, particularly those put forth by the Truman administration. This early part of Long's Senate career was also marked by his maintaining a strong connection to Louisiana's internal politics, particularly during the gubernatorial campaign of 1951–1952, the outcome of which helped convince Long that high-minded idealism, rather than practical political considerations, would lose more often than win in politics. By the mid and late 1950s, as chapter three shows, Long held key posts on the Senate Finance and Foreign Relations committees, from which he enunciated liberal stances on taxation, social welfare policy, infrastructure improvements, and Cold War diplomacy. At the same time, he boosted his credentials as a conservative southerner with his public attacks on the *Brown v. Board* decision of 1954, the Supreme Court itself, and the burgeoning civil rights movement. His advocacy for Louisiana in the 1950s centered most especially on the dispute between the federal and state governments over ownership of oil deposits in the tidelands off the coast, and his last major dealing with internal state politics came as a result of his involvement in the aftermath of his Uncle Earl's notorious mental breakdown and institutionalization in 1959.

Those events of 1959 left Long with a bitter taste for Louisiana politics and reminded him that practicality should rule his political decision making. As chapter four shows, he devoted himself to rising in the ranks of the Senate during the 1960s. By the latter half of the decade, he was serving as Senate Finance chair and majority whip, and he had been instrumental in ushering in much of Lyndon Johnson's Great Society program, albeit while opposing the Second Reconstruction. Long's stances on Cold War issues hardened following the Bay of Pigs invasion, and by the time the Johnson administration was escalating American involvement in Vietnam, he had firmly placed himself within the "hawk" camp. Although he would never again involve himself in Louisiana politics as much as he had in the 1950s, Long did use his prominent position in the Senate to promote legislation and policies beneficial for the state. In 1969, Long lost his majority whip position, but through his chairmanship of the Finance

Committee, he became one of the Senate's most powerful individuals during the 1970s. He was said "to know the tax code the way the Pope knows the Lord's prayer," noted the New Orleans *Times-Picayune* in January 1980.[1] Presidents bent to his will on matters of fiscal policy, and he jousted with them over energy policy and social welfare legislation, often coming out on the winning end. The decade showed that Long's practical politics were still in full force, as he was just as likely to form a strong working relationship with Republicans as with Democrats, conservatives as with liberals. That willingness to transcend political boundaries was becoming a rarity, however, as both parties were becoming more tied to polar positions on the major issues of the day. By the election of Ronald Reagan in 1980, those poles had become further apart and had crystallized around certain ideological stances, as seen in the book's conclusion. Long lost his chairmanship of the Finance Committee in 1980, but he continued to work both sides of the political fence, engaging in a give-and-take over the Reagan administration's fiscal, diplomatic, and economic policies. This was the twilight of Long's career, however, and he retired in 1986. The conclusion offers an analysis of Long's place in the end of the New Deal liberal coalition and the dominance of the Senate's southern bloc, and it shows his place in the emergence of the twentieth century's New Right.

By the time Long retired from the Senate in 1987, memories of World War II were clouded not only by time but also by intervening conflicts. Korea and Vietnam had come and gone. The Cold War neared its end. African Americans had gained civil as well as political rights. In Louisiana, voters concerned themselves more with the political ramifications of an ongoing slump in the oil economy rather than with rival Long/Anti-Long political factions. Russell Long had taken stances and oftentimes created laws that affected all of these changes, and he had done so with a mind tuned toward practical politics. In many ways he became the antithesis of his father, Huey.

Long's role as a senior senator also places him in a much different context than the other political members of his family. Although Huey Long served as a senator for three years in the early 1930s, his direct political effect on the nation proved negligible.[2] Russell Long, however, had a positive or negative effect on most major legislation during his career. Particularly after rising through the ranks of the Senate Finance Committee to become its chair, Long wielded great influence on taxation and social welfare issues. As Robert Mann notes, "More than forty percent of all government spending was under his authority" between 1965 and 1981.[3] And as Julian Zelizer points out, Long achieved such authority at a time when Congress "retained an iron grip on all tax policies, thereby enabling committee chairmen to wield significant influence on the expansion of the modern welfare state."[4] The long tenure of his chairmanship also allowed Long to "influence the policy agenda over several decades rather than just four to eight years," and his remarkable grasp of political give-and-take, and the mechanisms by which the Senate worked, often provided him the upper hand in passing legislation he supported.[5] In the end, Long, who went to Washington bearing his father's reputation as a maverick, outsider, and troublemaker, became one of the ultimate Senate insiders, with skill and influence to match.

CHAPTER ONE

Learning the Ropes in the Long Family, 1918–1948

RUSSELL LONG was born in the booming oil town of Shreveport, in the far northwestern corner of Louisiana, on November 3, 1918. His mother, Rose McConnell Long, named him Huey Pierce Long III for his father, who, at the time of the boy's birth, was busy campaigning for a seat on the Louisiana Railroad Commission. Huey changed his son's name to Russell Biliu when he arrived at the hospital.[1]

No one knows for certain why Huey changed the name, although a couple of anecdotal accounts have been handed down through the years. One has Huey, who had been named after his own father, telling Rose, "I hated being little Huey all my life. It's better for the boy to have his own name so if things go bad for me, he can have his own name to make it on." Another acknowledges Huey's certainty that he would be a divisive figure once he won political office, and his concern that his son sharing his name would cause more harm than good. "When a man is in politics, he almost always winds up being repudiated," he supposedly said.[2]

Both of those stories point to the fact that even before he won a single elected position, Huey had understood that the career he planned for himself might create personal or political problems for his child. Huey's prescience played out over the next seventeen years, as he parlayed the seat he won on the Railroad Commission into the governorship, followed by a place in the U.S. Senate and plans for a presidential run. Along the course of his meteoric rise, Huey became simultaneously the most reviled and the most beloved politician in Louisiana's history. The name Huey Long became synonymous with graft, corruption, scandal, patronage, nepotism—even, according to some observers, dictatorship and fascism. Conversely, Long ended up revered as the first Louisiana politician to provide for the needs of the vast, unrepresented masses of his state. Had the benefits Huey provided been delivered without the objectionable tactics he used, Russell Long might have found his own life much easier, both inside and outside the political arena. As it was, however, even the name change could not shelter Russell from the storm his father had brewed.

Over the course of his first thirty years, Russell Long watched his father win offices at all levels of government, garner an immense amount of personal political power, and create a dominant political machine. Following his father's death in 1935, Russell dedicated himself to completing his education, and then serving in World War II, before setting up a law practice in Baton Rouge. At the same time, he benefited from the political guidance of his Uncle Earl, who prodded Russell to campaign for Long machine candidates and to run for office himself. By the time Russell won his first office—to the U.S. Senate in 1948—he had become a seasoned political veteran, trained by two masters, his father the Kingfish and his Uncle Earl.

The Long Family

Rose and Huey, along with Russell's older sister, Rose Lolita, had moved to Shreveport less than a month before Russell's birth. They came from Winnfield, Huey's north-central Louisiana hometown. The move to Shreveport had been made for practical purposes: the city's burgeoning oil industry promised new clients for Huey's law practice, and as north Louisiana's major urban area, it provided Huey with a broader political platform, an important consideration for a young man who aspired to much higher offices than the Railroad Commission.[3]

Huey had been born on August 30, 1893, into the moderately

prosperous family of Huey Pierce Long, known as Hugh, and Caledonia Tison Long. The Long family lived among the piney woods of Winn Parish, one of the poorest and most isolated areas of north-central Louisiana and a seedbed of political discontent. Huey was the seventh of nine remarkable children. Even in his youth, Huey clearly stood above the others. As a precocious youngster, his curiosity and intelligence foreshadowed the future heights he would attain, but his personality also displayed faults that would emerge time and again in his life. He lacked attention, focus, and patience. In school or at home, he had little self-control and refused to accept discipline from others. He wanted to be the center of attention at all times, and he tended to be argumentative and restless.

Huey's inattentiveness and arrogance led to poor showings in school, and he left Winnfield High School in 1910 without a diploma. In July of that year, at age sixteen, he took a job as a traveling salesman for Cottolene, a cooking oil company. The job suited him well and allowed him to use his greatest assets, salesmanship and communications skill, without too much physical labor. It also, inadvertently, led to his courting Rose McConnell. The two first met when Huey served as a judge for a cake-baking contest Rose had entered in Shreveport. This initial meeting led to a turbulent, two-and-a-half-year courtship, culminating in their marriage in Memphis, Tennessee, on April 12, 1913. By then, Huey was a regional sales manager for the Faultless Starch Company.

When Faultless's business faltered, Huey lost his job, and he and Rose moved back to Winnfield. The young salesman hawked patent medicines for a while, but he eventually sought the help of his older brother, Julius, who fronted tuition for Tulane University's Law School. In May 1915, after only one year of classes, Huey passed a special oral examination to become a member of the Louisiana bar. He and Rose returned to Winnfield, where he entered into partnership with Julius, who was Winn Parish's district attorney and needed a young partner to help carry his caseload. Less than two months later, their partnership dissolved. Lacking experience and clients—and confronted with dim financial prospects—Huey took part-time jobs as a newspaper reporter and, yet again, as a traveling salesman.

By early 1916, Huey had earned enough through sales and writing to focus most of his energies on his latent law practice. After the move to Shreveport, Huey also began plotting his political career. As a lawyer, he specialized in cases of on-the-job injury compensation, a fertile field given the inherent dangers of the local lumber and oil industries. Huey also began representing small, independent oil companies that most often paid him in stock. World War I created great demand for these local companies' crude, but when the war ended, the demand for local oil dwindled, and the big three oil companies—Standard, Texas, and Gulf—ceased purchasing and transporting the smaller concerns' product. The big three's actions ignited an uproar among many of the Shreveport companies, who turned to their lawyer, Huey Long. Deciding that taking on the biggest of the big might create the greatest publicity, Long trained his sights on John D. Rockefeller's Standard Oil. Huey had economic motives for doing so—he stood to gain a significant amount of wealth, either in cash or stocks, from the companies he represented—but he also understood that attacking Standard, even if he lost the battle, would lead to future political benefits. Such cases provided an initial footing for Huey's claims of protecting the commoners and downtrodden in the face of external threats from faceless big businesses and their owners, a populistic rhetoric he would use to great effect after entering politics.

Russell Long spent his early childhood in Shreveport. The family—Huey, Rose, Rose Lolita, Russell, and later, youngest son Palmer—lived initially in a respectable yet modest neighborhood, but following a settlement in a 1923 case that earned Huey a $40,000 fee, the Longs moved into a larger home in Shreveport's most upscale neighborhood. When he reached school age, Russell attended Creswell Elementary School.[4]

Huey Long and Louisiana Politics

As in other southern states, the Democratic Party dominated Louisiana politics in the early twentieth century, so that a victory in the Democratic primary was the equivalent of winning the general election. It had been consolidating power since the end of Reconstruction, but its stranglehold on the Bayou State's politics had been solidified following passage of the Constitution of 1898, which disfranchised most blacks and many poor whites through literacy tests and a poll tax and effectively killed the Republican Party. True political power, however, rested in the hands of an even smaller element within the party itself. For most of the first two-and-a-half decades of the twentieth century, New Orleans's "Old Regular" political organization controlled statewide politics with an ability to deliver up to 20 percent of the state's total vote, a direct oversight of a large number of legislative seats, and a powerful control of the Democratic Central Committee. When working in alliance with the state's planter-merchant elite, the Old Regulars could usually deliver pluralities from at least two of Louisiana's three traditional geo-cultural-political domains, which were the largely Protestant north, the largely Catholic south, and the urban area of New Orleans. A minor reform wing did exist within the Democratic Party, but it usually could not summon enough electoral strength to overcome the Old Regular-planter-merchant alliance. Even in the rare instances when the reformers did manage to win state office, usually as a result of infighting within the dominant alliance, the so-called reformers did very little to change how, and for whom, Louisiana's government functioned. Both sides, it seemed, agreed that the state government should perform within very limited confines: taxes should be low or nonexistent, individual parishes should be responsible for internal improvements, and the people should take care of themselves.

Huey Long, conversely, saw providing benefits to the people of Louisiana as a necessary state responsibility. He also saw his seat on the Railroad Commission (renamed the Public Service Commission in 1921) as a springboard to higher office. On August 30, 1923, his thirtieth birthday, Huey Long announced his candidacy in the following year's Louisiana gubernatorial election. By then, he had served not only on the Public Service Commission but also as its chair, and he had begun to reshape the board into an active political body that appeared to champion the common folk of Louisiana in the face of entrenched and enormously powerful outside entities like Standard Oil and Bell Telephone. Although he lacked a political organization that could rival the Old Regulars', had very little money for advertising and travel expenses, and received no endorsements from established politicians, Huey threw himself into the campaign with abandon, while focusing on two resonant issues for Louisiana voters: roads and education. He took the offensive and attacked his two major opponents: Lieutenant Governor Hewitt Bouanchaud, the chosen successor of sitting governor John Parker, and Angola State Penitentiary general manager Henry L. Fuqua, the Old Regular candidate. Long's chief message was the populist-inspired clarion call that Louisiana's poor and hardworking people had been ignored and repressed by the state's powers that be, especially Parker, Bouanchaud, and Fuqua, whom Long claimed pandered only to moneyed interests. Such appeals to class resentment swayed a surprisingly large number of voters, and Long might have stood a better chance if class issues had been the only ones up for debate. But the key question in the 1924 election turned out to be the resurgent Ku Klux Klan and its role in Louisiana. Long's wavering stance on the Klan proved his undoing—he did not seem sufficiently anti-Klan to appease south Louisiana Catholics nor sufficiently pro-Klan to satisfy Klan strongholds in the north. Long finished third in the first round of the Democratic primary, although he performed stronger in rural parishes than either of his opponents. He refused to endorse either of the candidates in the runoff election, which Fuqua won.

Over the next four years, Long prepared for the 1928 governor's race. On August 3, 1927, Huey stood before a throng of supporters in Alexandria and officially announced his candidacy for governor. He faced two major opponents for the 1928 Democratic nomination: Riley J. Wilson, who received much of the support of Louisiana's upper classes, and Oramel H. Simpson, who had been lieutenant governor under Fuqua and had succeeded to the governor's office when Fuqua died in 1926. Wilson and Simpson campaigned on traditional pledges of efficiency and conservatism, but Long promised improvements to the state's highways, schools, and medical services; free textbooks for schoolchildren; financial support for farmers and laborers; and a state government free of greed and corruption. Long shrewdly chose for his running mate Paul Cyr, a native of south Louisiana. As he had during the 1924 campaign, Huey alleged that wealthy interests and behind-the-scenes political powers controlled his opposition.

Huey sat in his Shreveport home with his wife Rose, their ten-year-old daughter Rose Lolita, and their two sons, nine-year-old Russell and six-year-old Palmer Reid, as the results of the Democratic primary rolled in on January 17, 1928. The returns came as no surprise to Huey, and they confirmed the worst fears of his opponents. Long received 126,842 votes, Wilson 81,747, and Simpson 80,326. Wilson eventually conceded the Democratic nomination.

Following his inauguration on May 21, 1928, Huey set about the business of gaining control of the state legislature. He personally chose members of all committees, where almost all legislation originated, and dispensed patronage freely to create or firm up loyalties. By controlling the lawmakers, he was able to fulfill many of the promises he had made during his campaigns. Over the course of the 1928 session, Long received the lawmakers' endorsements of free school textbooks, bond issues for highway and bridge construction, and small increases in funding for state educational and medical institutions. To pay for the new expenditures, the legislature increased severance taxes and issued bonds. Despite the opposition of a group of legislators that called itself the Dynamite Squad, Long also managed to place control of major state agencies, and their patronage, within his own hands.

Huey's family, meanwhile, briefly considered moving into Louisiana's antiquated Governor's Mansion, a dilapidated, termite-infested house, but thinking better, returned to Shreveport following Huey's inauguration. Huey moved into a suite at Baton Rouge's Heidelberg Hotel, from which he ordered, without proper legislative authorization, the demolition of the old mansion and the construction of a new one. Only after the new mansion was finished in 1930 did Rose, Russell, and the rest of the Long family join Huey in Baton Rouge. They lived there for the next two years.[5]

While the new mansion was being built, Huey Long called a special session of the legislature in March 1929 to place a tax on refined petroleum. The proposed tax represented a new source of revenue for the perpetually poor state, but Long also intended it to be a direct jab at his old nemesis, Standard Oil. Long drew his line in the sand when he publicly declared that any member of the legislature who voted against his proposal had been paid off by John Rockefeller. The tax plan failed to pass. At this point Long, miscalculating the recalcitrance of his opposition, made a major blunder: He called for a second special session, to meet later in March, and he reiterated that those who opposed the tax dwelled deep in the pockets of Rockefeller and his Standard Oil. As earlier, the tax plan failed, and this time Huey's opponents seized the opportunity to begin impeachment proceedings against the governor. The Dynamite Squad passed nineteen impeachment charges on March 26. By April 26, the House had approved eight articles of impeachment, with charges ranging from bribery and attempted bribery of government officials to intimidation of the press and misappropriation of state funds. Sensing that, although the proceedings presented a serious challenge to his ambitions, defeating them would only solidify his dominance of Louisiana's government, Long rallied for the fight. With the help of his younger brother, Earl, the governor cajoled, bribed, and threatened Louisiana senators and managed to secure the promise of fifteen that they would not vote for his conviction, no matter what evidence was presented, because the articles of impeachment had been approved after the special session's scheduled end date. On May 16, 1929, only two days after the impeachment trial had begun, Senator Phillip Gilbert presented a petition signed by the fifteen senators. Their signatures on the document that would be known as the Round Robin insured that the two-thirds vote needed to remove Huey would never materialize. His opposition capitulated.

Following the attempt to remove him from office, Governor Long determined to secure his political dominance of Louisiana through nepotism, patronage, and legislative action. Then, on July 16, 1930, following defeat in the legislature of a measure that would have allowed the issuing of bonds for more paved roads, Huey announced that he would run for the U.S. Senate. He declared that the race would be a referendum on the bond issue and, more generally, on his overall political leadership of the state. And if he won, he promised that he would not take office until a suitable successor—Long and his lieutenant governor, Paul Cyr, had become bitter enemies—was chosen by the people of Louisiana. The 1930 Senate race marked the first time Long instituted a system of deducts whereby state employees turned over a percentage of their pay to cover his campaign costs. These deducts provided an independent source of funding for what was becoming an efficient and energetic new political organization, the Long Machine. The vote tally showed Huey Long defeating the incumbent, Joseph Ransdell, with 57.3 percent of the vote.

The election solidified Long's political control of Louisiana. From this point on, his proposals—including more highway and bridge funding, a new capitol building, and increased money for schools—passed the legislature with minimal opposition. Long's opponents understood that not only had the governor amassed a great deal of political power, but also, if they went by the Senate election's returns, that he had won over a substantial majority of the state's voters. By 1932, the Long political machine was so dominant that it could provide a first-round Democratic primary victory in the governor's race for Huey's handpicked successor, Oscar K. Allen, who functioned as little more than a puppet. At the same time, Earl Long, Huey's most important ally and his political equal if there ever was one, split with his brother when Huey refused to back Earl for governor. The wounds created in 1932 would present political problems for members of the Long family for decades to come. At the time, however, Huey felt secure enough with O. K. Allen in office that he could head to Washington, D.C., and take the Senate seat he had won two years earlier.

After Huey took his Senate seat in January 1932, his family moved to a home on Audubon Boulevard in New Orleans. Russell, who at the time served as a class president at Baton Rouge's University High School, did not wish to transfer in the middle of the school year, so his father set him up with his own suite at Baton Rouge's Heidelberg Hotel. Two state policemen served as Russell's guardians. The teenager's situation troubled Huey's friend, Louisiana State University (LSU) president James Monroe Smith, who opened up his own home to the youngster and allowed him to live with his family until University High's semester ended. At that point, Russell joined his mother and siblings in New Orleans, where he enrolled in Alcée Fortier High School in the fall of 1932.[6]

Russell's father now performed on a larger, national stage, but the change in venue brought little change in his politics and temperament. Politically, Long's Senate tenure was defined by obstructionism—directed mainly toward President Franklin Roosevelt's New Deal legislation, which he said was woefully inadequate—and self-promotion. None of Long's bills, resolutions, or motions passed while he served in the Senate, and his political alienation was only exacerbated by his tendency to filibuster legislation offered up by his opponents.

Share Our Wealth, Long's most famous proposal as a senator, sought to redistribute wealth and realize the motto "Every Man a King." More important, from Long's perspective, Share Our Wealth provided an opportunity to attract attention for a possible presidential run in 1936. The Share Our Wealth campaign, funded by kickbacks from contractors and deductions from Louisiana state employee paychecks, became wildly popular, despite the fact that if offered very little hope of ever becoming a reality. Share Our Wealth called for a redistribution of America's wealth based on confiscatory taxation aimed at Huey's favorite scapegoat, millionaires. His plan included a tax on property valued at over $1 million that would become progressively larger until reaching 100 percent at $100 million worth of property, a tax limiting lifetime inheritance to $5 million, and a tax that limited income to no more than $1 million per year. Taxing millionaires at such extreme levels would bring enormous amounts of money to the federal government, Huey claimed, and the increase in the public coffers then could be used to provide impoverished families with necessities such as a one-time grant of $5,000 to buy a house, car, and radio; a guaranteed annual income of $2,500; free college education for qualified youngsters; old-age pensions; and veterans' bonuses.

Long's proposal became immensely popular. Share Our Wealth clubs sprang up around the nation and letters of support poured into Long's Washington office. The promises of Share Our Wealth melded perfectly into Long's penchant for populist rhetoric, and the proposed program became his ticket to national political prominence. Yet Share Our Wealth had no chance of becoming a reality, and its popularity reflected the dire social and economic straits the nation had fallen into during the 1930s more than any potential for its political success. Desperate people living through desperate times latch onto desperate measures. The fact of the matter, and economists of the day and Huey himself understood this, was that there simply was not enough wealth in America to share as he proposed.

If Share Our Wealth represented a tactic for gaining higher offices on a national level, it did not mean that Huey had decided to ignore Louisiana's internal politics. In fact, even as he served as senator, Huey focused most of his attention on maintaining—and increasing—his political dominance of his home state. In the summer of 1932, for instance, he managed the campaign of John Overton, who defeated incumbent senator Edwin S. Broussard, a former Long ally. The swearing in of Overton, who readily accepted Huey's leadership in political matters, allowed Huey to control both of the state's votes in the U.S. Senate. Then, in 1933, Long began a duel with President Roosevelt over federal patronage that eventually kept the state from receiving its share of the New Deal's federal largesse and thus prolonged the suffering of Louisiana's economically devastated population.

Beginning in 1934, and continuing into 1935, Long instituted complete one-man rule in Louisiana. He began this process in the summer of 1934, when he forced his entire legislative package through the statehouse. Although the program contained relatively innocuous and potentially beneficial enactments that did things like revoking the state's poll tax, instituting income taxes, and creating the homestead exemption for property taxation, most of the legislation was of a more ominous character and simply placed more control of state and local political power in the hands of Long's easily controlled political underlings. Long's hostility toward the Old Regular political machine reached its apex in 1934, when he and New Orleans mayor T. Semmes Walmsley engaged in a showdown over control of local elections that nearly led to armed conflict between the Long machine and the Old Regulars in the Crescent City.

The year 1935 brought even more concerted, and more successful, attempts at increasing Long's in-state power. That summer, Long ordered Governor O. K. Allen to call a series of special legislative sessions. Long himself directed the sessions, usually from the floor of the statehouse. There, the submissive legislators, whether out of fear of political reprisal or as a result of bribes and promises, simply followed Long's lead. The legislature thus became complicit in creating the closest thing to a state-level dictatorship in U.S. history. The list of powers—both statewide and local—placed under Long's authority is notable if taken point by point but extraordinary when compiled together. Public safety, taxation, and education fell under Huey's control when the legislature put him in command of all Louisiana fire and police departments, tax assessors, and school boards. Long gained the last word on local finances by taking into his own hands the right to review all loans, grants, and bonds requested by the state's parishes and municipalities. He showed that the revocation of the poll tax a year earlier had been an act of symbolism more than anything else when he forced the legislature to provide the governor, and thus himself, with control over all local, parish, and state elections by allowing him to choose election commissioners and poll watchers for the Democratic primaries; controlling the only elections that really mattered in the solidly Democratic state allowed Long to effectively disfranchise Anti-Long voters. Finally, the legislature created a State Board of Censors, which granted Long authority over all movies and newsreels shown in Louisiana and gave Huey complete command of New Orleans's powers of taxation, which killed any notion that the Crescent City could remain economically or politically independent of Long and his political machine.

On September 8, 1935, Huey Long presided over yet another special session of the legislature. During the proceedings, Long saw to it that Judge Benjamin Pavy of St. Landry Parish, one of the last notable Anti-Long politicians still in office in Louisiana, would lose his position. Huey had the legislature gerrymander Pavy's district, and he then went even further by spreading rumors that the Pavy family had black blood coursing through its veins, the single most abhorrent indictment, and by far the most politically potent, that one white southerner could make against another in the 1930s. All of this seemed a normal day's work for Huey, but he did not count on meeting up with Judge Pavy's son-in-law, Dr. Carl Austin Weiss, in a hallway of the state capitol building. Although no observer claims to know exactly what happened, at some point on September 8, Weiss, already upset about the gerrymandering of his father-in-law's district, probably learned of Huey's plans to spread the rumors. Hearing that the senator would soon besmirch not only Judge Pavy but, by their family ties, his own wife and child, Weiss decided upon a course of action that would forever change the lives of both his and Huey's families. Weiss knew where Huey could be found. The doctor drove to the capitol building, went inside, and saw Long leaving the floor of the House of Representatives. Weiss carried a small pistol when he made house calls, and he had it then. He hid behind a column in a back hallway and waited. Huey rounded a corner, and Weiss made his move. He pulled his gun and shot Huey Long. Long's bodyguards shredded Weiss's body with their bullets. The doctor died within seconds. Long was rushed to Our Lady of the Lake Hospital.[7]

Aftermath of Assassination

Russell Long fielded the phone call. It was late in the evening—just past ten—but phone calls at all hours were common in the Long household. This one was different. The voice on the other end of the line belonged to Russell's uncle, Gilman McConnell.

McConnell delivered the devastating news: Huey had been shot and was in the hospital. The family needed to get to Baton Rouge quickly.

Russell told his mother and then helped her and his siblings hurriedly pack for what they expected to be an extended stay in the capital. The family piled into their Plymouth DeSoto. Sixteen-year-old Russell took the wheel. He made his way to Airline

Highway and barreled his way to Baton Rouge at dangerously high speeds. The Long family arrived at the hospital while Huey was still in surgery.

The surgery might have saved Huey's life, but the doctors missed a torn kidney duct. By the time the mistake was caught, he had bled too much. Early in the morning of September 9, the family and friends who had gathered in the senator's bedroom faced reality: Huey was dying, and nothing could be done to save him. Just after 4 a.m., Huey died.[8]

Much has been made about the events surrounding Long's death. Theories abound as to whether or not Dr. Weiss's or Huey's own bodyguards' bullets pierced the senator's flesh, and even more questions have been raised about the motivations behind the assassination. But the theorists generally overlook the single most significant fact about the events that occurred on September 8 and 9, 1935: Huey's death.

In the space of less than twenty years, Huey Long had completely transformed the landscape of Louisiana politics. In 1918, when he first won office, Louisiana was dominated by the Old Regulars and their elitist allies, and the state government rarely responded to the needs of citizens. By 1935, Long had crushed the Old Regulars and had created an incipient welfare state that provided benefits to citizens which far outpaced most other American states. Long fashioned a political structure that centered on conflict—poor versus wealthy, rural versus urban—rather than consensus. He honed a populist political style by portraying himself as the champion of the downtrodden, and he offered a compelling, if not necessarily achievable, goal of more equitably redistributing wealth. His nonchalant attitude toward corruption became pervasive in state politics, as candidates, officeholders, and voters alike learned to turn a blind eye toward political malfeasance and spoils politics.[9]

Long's influence far outlasted his life. His political machine, funded by deducts and fueled by patronage and nepotism, functioned at varying degrees until his brother Earl's death in 1960.

Future politicians—Earl, most notably, but also John McKeithen and Edwin Edwards—would mimic Long's populist rhetoric and his flamboyant personality. Huey created a state revenue system based on oil and gas taxation that allowed administrations from the 1940s through the 1970s to continue and even expand his burgeoning welfare state, all with little financial burden to the taxpayers of Louisiana. And because the revenue from oil and gas taxation was so great, politicians felt at ease taking some of the money for themselves, while the taxpayers laughed it off because the funds did not come out of their own back pockets.

Although his influence persisted, Huey's death left Louisiana without its dominant politician. It left his allies without their provider. It left his opponents without their scourge. And it left Russell Long without his father.

Russell Long's early years were partly defined by the degree to which his father was absent from his life. Huey's passion for politics and power left the Long family with an empty spot at the table most nights, and the absenteeism only increased following his swearing in to the Senate. Before moving from Baton Rouge to New Orleans, Russell told an interviewer that although he missed his mother, sister, and brother since their move to the city, "I miss Dad the most because I do not get to see him often." When Huey was home, it was usually as a part of some political visit, and their father's cantankerous personality often kept the children at bay. Russell's sister remarked in a later interview, "When he was home, we were good and quiet and tried to be nice and not bother him. He was always obsessed, usually—not all the time—but lots of the time, with whatever was going on in political circles."[10]

In many ways, the Huey Long that Russell Long knew was very similar to the Huey Long that the public knew, and that Huey Long was not always portrayed in the best lights. Indeed, Huey's decision to change Russell's name could not prevent his eldest son—or his other children—from facing the fury of his political opponents. As much as Rose Long might have tried to keep their home life normal, Huey Long's children met with taunts at school; heard threats and accusations against their father; and even, at times, faced physical violence—all because of Huey, who was largely absent from their life. The anxiety of such a childhood manifested itself in Russell's stuttering, a condition that lessened only when he reached high school.[11]

Huey Long's assassination brought tremendous change to the members of his family. Although they initially faced dire economic straits—part of Huey's political genius was his ability to keep whatever funds his machine generated out of his own pockets—Rose Long, through a combination of business sense and sheer luck, and with the help of knowledgeable advisors, parlayed what little money they had into a series of successful oil ventures. Particularly profitable would be the interest Huey had gained, and the Long family inherited, in the Win or Lose Oil Company, which had been created by Long's cronies in the early 1930s and, even before Huey's death, was under federal investigation for questionable business practices. The Win or Lose shares would ultimately be worth millions.[12]

Besides caring for her family's economic fortunes, Rose had another, more demanding task to tend to: a seat in the U.S. Senate. Initially, Huey's replacement was to be O. K. Allen, who won the seat in a special election. Allen died before he could take office, however, and interim governor James Noe convinced Rose to fill her late husband's Senate seat. Surrounded by her children, Rose took the oath of office on February 10, 1936. She served until January 1937.[13]

While his mother worked in Washington, Russell Long enrolled in Louisiana State University. He had originally hoped to attend Princeton University, but following Huey's death, Russell felt strongly that he should attend the school his father had spent much time and energy improving. During his undergraduate years, Russell focused mostly on campus politics. He served as freshman class president, then sophomore Arts and Sciences president; chair of sophomore presidents; and after a junior year dedicated to honing his political skills on the debate team and forming his own Independent campus political party, Long won the race for senior class president.[14]

Off campus, Russell began to learn the ropes of state politics. Over the Christmas break of his freshman year, he campaigned for the Long ticket—Richard Leche for governor and Uncle Earl for lieutenant governor. Later, he worked as minutes clerk at the state senate, a job secured for him by Earl. When not politicking, Russell became a member of the Delta Kappa Epsilon social fraternity, and during his sophomore year he met a pretty, dark-haired Mississippian, Katherine Mae Hattic, with whom he fell in love. Engaged before Russell's graduation, Russell and Katherine were married on June 3, 1939.[15]

While on his honeymoon, Russell read in the newspapers about growing evidence of corruption in Governor Leche's administration. The so-called Louisiana Scandals of 1939 laid bare for the people of Louisiana and the nation the dishonest dealings that formed the foundation of Louisiana politics at this time. Following Huey's death, the leaders of the Long machine had made peace with the Roosevelt administration, resulting in a flood of hundreds of millions of New Deal dollars into the state. With those millions came temptation, and many public officials could not resist skimming a few dollars or more from the state's coffers. By 1939, some $100 million was missing and 191 indictments had been handed out. Governor Leche resigned and ultimately served five years in a federal penitentiary.[16]

Remarkably, Russell's Uncle Earl, Leche's lieutenant governor, came out of the Louisiana Scandals untainted. Earl, like Huey, knew that although money was necessary to run the Long machine, the safest way to control funding was to control the people who held the cash. Following Leche's resignation, Earl became governor of Louisiana.[17]

Russell and Katherine returned to Baton Rouge after their honeymoon, where he finished up his undergraduate career at LSU in 1941. Like his father before him, Long planned a legal career, and he enrolled in LSU's School of Law that fall. Devoting more time to his studies than he had as an undergraduate, Long showed that, when working hard, he could be a first-rate student. He ranked first in the Law School's first-year class, won its prestigious moot court trial, and received the second most votes for valedictorian. He graduated in 1942.[18]

While Russell attended law school, the United States became an active belligerent in World War II. In August 1942, Long joined the U.S. Naval Reserve and began training in New York. He later transferred to Camp Bradford, Virginia, where he received an assignment on a landing craft tank (LCT) vessel. His orders took him to North Africa, where, after spending time in Algiers, he participated in the Allied invasions of Tunisia, Sicily, and France. In October 1943, Long received command of his own LCT boat and in March 1944 earned a promotion to lieutenant junior grade. He landed among the first wave at Cavalier-sur-Mer during the invasion of southern France, and he ultimately received four battle stars before his return to Camp Bradford in September 1944. In November 1945, Russell received his discharge papers and returned to Louisiana. There, Katherine and their daughter, Rita Katherine, who had been born in March 1944, awaited.[19]

With the war over, Russell Long sought to pick up where he had left off before enlisting. He became active in Baton Rouge social and civic affairs and in 1946 established a law partnership with Gordon West, a former classmate at LSU Law School and a fellow participant in the invasion of Sicily. Things seemed to be settling down for the young family man. Then, in 1947, Uncle Earl came calling.[20]

Russell Long and Louisiana Politics in the Late 1940s

Earl Long had been itching to get back into the governor's office since losing to Anti-Longite Sam Jones in 1940. Although he had not been implicated directly in the corruption, Earl's political fortunes were tainted by the Louisiana Scandals, and

Jones, a Lake Charles oilman, capitalized on Earl's weaknesses. As governor, Jones established a governing pattern that became the model for future governors of the Anti-Longite faction. Because many of the programs created by Huey Long and his followers were so beneficial for the people of Louisiana, the antis could not dismantle them and generally chose to continue many of the policies the Longites themselves had created. There developed within Louisiana politics a consensus on the role of government in the daily lives of the state's citizens and the types of programs that government should provide to the people. State government pumped money, much of it coming from severance taxation, into schools, construction projects, and hospitals. The antis, including Jones's successor, Jimmie Davis, could not challenge that consensus, but they could promise a different *style* of government. To cut back on cronyism and patronage, the Anti-Longites removed control of state agencies from the hands of the executive branch and instituted civil service reforms, and to weaken the Long political machine's funding mechanism, they outlawed the deduct system.[21]

When his uncle first approached him in 1947, Russell Long initially refused to take part in Earl's campaign for the Democratic gubernatorial nomination. Russell had been thinking of getting into politics from the time of his father's death, but he had planned on taking things slowly and in a reasonable order: college, law degree, family, social standing, successful legal career, and *then* a foray into politics. Earl, like his older brother Huey, was not known for his patience, however, and he pushed his nephew to jump into the fray. Russell ultimately bent to Earl's arm-twisting and promised to campaign for him, but with the condition that he would work for one month only and then return to his law practice. Earl agreed.[22]

The younger Long realized that any future he might have in Louisiana politics depended to a large extent on his uncle's political fortunes that year. He also saw the campaign as an opportunity to refurbish his father's image, which had been tarnished in the years since the assassination not only by the Louisiana Scandals, but also by books and articles published by friends and foe alike. Russell's first real venture into statewide politics attracted much attention, and his month-long stint quickly turned into a commitment to campaign for Earl for the duration of the race.[23]

On the stump and over the airwaves, Russell stared down the most difficult challenge to Earl's candidacy: the memories many voters still had of Earl and Huey's bitter rift in the early 1930s. Anti-Long candidates capitalized on these memories by portraying Earl, the Longite candidate, as a charlatan. It was impossible for someone who had disagreed so strongly and so vocally with Huey to be a true Longite, they contended, and it would be incumbent upon even Longite voters to vote against Earl. It fell to Russell Long to counter these charges. "As for the differences which arose between Earl Long and my father," he said in a statewide radio address, "we know that those differences lasted less than a year before Huey and Earl patched them up, and Earl went back to helping my father and continued to do so until after Huey Long's death several years later." He added,

> When Huey Long and Earl Long made up their differences, that was the end of it as far as my family was concerned, and that is how it has been since that time. It is too bad that brothers sometimes have a quarrel or a spat; when it happens, all they can do is shake hands and forget it. That is what Huey Long and Earl Long did sixteen years ago, and my family doesn't care to hear any more about these differences.[24]

Russell proclaimed that his uncle sought to fulfill the unfinished work of his father, and he campaigned on traditional Longite platform promises: old-age pensions; teacher pay raises; highway, educational, and hospital construction; higher homestead exemptions; veterans' bonuses; and hot school lunches. Three Anti-Longites ran in the Democratic primary: former governor Sam Jones, U.S. congressman Jimmy Morrison, and Judge

Robert F. Kennon. Following the first-primary weeding out, Long faced Jones in a runoff that, aside from the outcome, mirrored the 1940 race. Despite the endorsements of current governor Jimmie Davis, U.S. senator John Overton, and New Orleans mayor DeLesseps Morrison, Jones's campaign pledges of a clean and by-the-books government failed to muster enough votes to defeat Earl. The final tally for the second Democratic primary, held on February 24, 1948, came to 432,528 for Long and 223,971 for Jones. Earl then easily dispatched his token Republican opponent in the general election.[25]

On the evening of Earl's inauguration, Russell Long joined his uncle in a symbolic acknowledgment of the Long faction's return to power. Both men stood on the grounds of the Louisiana state capitol, built by Huey and the site of his assassination. Together, Russell and Earl threw the switches of spotlights that flooded light upon Huey's monumental tomb opposite the building. Sam Jones had extinguished the lights eight years earlier, and Russell Long had called for their rekindling during the campaign.[26]

The lights represented not only a return to power of the Long faction, but also a victory for the memory of Huey Long. Russell Long had both personal and political interests in seeing his father's memory vindicated. Certainly, as a son who deeply mourned his father after his death and who revered his memory, the way Huey Long was portrayed by the media, and later by historians, affected him deeply. From a political perspective, as Russell pondered and then pursued a career in politics, the image of his father in the public's mind became vitally important. He would, after all, forever be known as "Huey's son," and that connection carried with it a great deal of political significance, both favorable and unfavorable. As Russell couched his political rhetoric in the language of his father and coaxed Huey's memory into political speeches, he became increasingly concerned with just how the portrayals reflected upon himself. Therefore, Russell Long understood all too keenly the necessity of keeping the historical Huey portrayed in the best possible light, and he played an active role in maintaining that image throughout his life.

While Russell jousted with those who promulgated negative portrayals of his father, he also entered for the first time the carnival of Louisiana government under his Uncle Earl. After some persuading, Russell agreed in 1948 to serve as executive counsel for the new Long administration. His chief job in that capacity was to persuade state legislators to agree to raise taxes in order to pay for Earl's ambitious programs to expand Louisiana's old-age pension plan, put people to work through construction projects, and generously fund education. Russell also trekked to Washington, D.C., where he convinced the federal government to match increases the state of Louisiana made to its pension program. Russell worked diligently in Baton Rouge and Washington to find the money to pay for Earl's programs, and he agreed with the overall goals of Earl in expanding state spending. On one issue, however—Earl's bitter and vengeful treatment of New Orleans—Russell strongly disagreed with his uncle.[27]

Earl's political treatment of the city between 1948 and 1952 became popularly known as "the Rape of New Orleans." It reflected little more than a resumption of spoils politics on a grand scale and the fulfillment of a personal vendetta Earl Long held against Crescent City mayor DeLesseps "Chep" Morrison. As a first step, Earl had the legislature grant him complete control over all personnel on the patronage-rich New Orleans Dock Board. He then pushed through the state house legislation that actually changed the makeup of the city's government. More councilmen were added to the mayor-council system, and changes to the election system were effected whereby councilmen would be elected from individual districts, replacing the previous citywide elections. The new districts had been gerrymandered so that the anti-Morrison/pro-Long candidates would have the majority on the city council. Additionally, Long's legislation stipulated that any appointment the mayor made had to be approved by a majority of the city council. Morrison's opponents thus took control of his appointive authority. Finally, Earl went after Morrison's ability to garner revenue by manipulating the new state taxes he had implemented. Earl made sure, for instance, that much of the new tax revenue would be distributed evenly among the state's sixty-four parishes; New Orleans, with a disproportionately large percentage of the state's population, and which paid a disproportionately large amount of state taxes, thus received a disproportionately small percentage of the tax revenue. Earl then pushed through a law that forbade any Louisiana city with a population of more than three hundred thousand—New Orleans was the only one—to create a sales tax higher than one percent. New Orleans actually had to lower its sales tax and lost $4.5 million in revenue. At roughly the same time, the legislature, at Earl's bidding, ordered the mayor of New Orleans to provide pay raises and make higher contributions to the city's pension program. Morrison and his administration ended up with less money to spend on more expenses. Despite the fact that he opposed Earl's attack on the Crescent City, the Rape of New Orleans proved harmful to Russell Long's young political career.[28]

Russell had expected to move more slowly up the political ladder than Uncle Earl allowed, and the pace only quickened in 1948, when within a week of Earl's inauguration, Senator John Overton died. Earl hoped to appoint Russell to the vacant seat in Washington. Russell, however, was only twenty-nine years old and thus did not meet the constitutional requirement that senators be thirty. After conferring with Allen Ellender, Louisiana's other U.S. senator, Earl appointed William C. Feazel, a staunch Longite, to keep the seat warm until a special election could be held later in the year.[29]

On July 2, 1948, Russell Long resigned his executive counsel position and, in a written statement, formally announced his candidacy for the unexpired Senate term. His announcement outlined broad goals of "greater federal aid to education, for highways, for social security and old age benefits and for our school lunch program." Such goals closely mirrored the traditional Longite programs that had been advertised on Louisiana election posters since Huey's campaigns in the 1920s. Earl himself stumped for his nephew, constantly reminding listeners that the younger Long was dedicated to his father and uncle's goals, and he pulled as many political strings as he could to get local politicos behind Russell's candidacy. Russell, meanwhile, played on the electorate's collective memory of his father by mimicking his populist rhetoric. "I hope to be of service to all Louisianians," Russell noted, "but above all, to the best of my ability, I intend to represent the average man and woman. It is my feeling that the small merchant, the little farmer and the laboring man seldom have a candidate in the race for public office who can be depended upon to serve their interests." Such rhetoric would serve Russell Long well throughout his career, and he clearly understood, even at such a young political age, that the words he used created connections to his father within the minds of voters.[30]

Long faced a spirited campaign waged by Robert Kennon, a former justice of the Louisiana Supreme Court and current judge for the Second Circuit Court of Appeal. Supported by all the major Anti-Long powers and controlling bulging campaign coffers, Kennon attacked Long's political inexperience and his ties to Earl's administration, which, even in 1948, had become unpopular with many voters thanks to their increased tax burden. He also charged that, as a U.S. senator, Long would support President Harry Truman, an unusual statement if taken at face value, considering that all three—Kennon, Long, and Truman—were Democrats. Yet the Democratic Party in Louisiana exhibited cracks along factional lines that were evident within the national party as well. In Louisiana, the factions reflected the Longite/Anti-Longite division; in the broader political context, the factions reflected the Truman Democrat/Dixiecrat split. Strom Thurmond's Dixiecrat presidential candidacy had just carried Louisiana in the 1948 presidential election, and the Longite faction had vigorously opposed the South Carolinian and his party's encroachment on their territory. Kennon understood that, in the minds of voters, opposing Thurmond meant supporting Truman, which meant further that Russell Long would acquiesce to the Truman administration's will and would ultimately not defend the state's Jim Crow society in the face of presidential civil rights initiatives. The charge held great potency.[31]

Russell countered Kennon's charges by embracing a platform of traditional Longite promises for Louisianians, albeit with a slight twist. His speeches and interviews reflected a single-minded devotion to the things his family and its followers had trumpeted for years; the only difference between his promises and earlier ones was the context. Long emphasized that he could do even more of these things from a seat in the United States Senate. National issues such as the burgeoning Cold War hardly entered the campaign's discourse, a reflection not only of the focus of the candidates but of their understanding that Louisiana voters, like voters everywhere, tended to be motivated first and foremost by local concerns. Where national politics did enter the fray—the Truman administration's early attempts at dealing with racial inequities in the armed forces, for instance—the candidates did their best to localize the discussions.[32]

Russell's inexperience proved to be a political liability, but not in the sense that Kennon charged. The traditional courthouse-square campaigning, still the bread-and-butter of Louisiana politics, was not Russell's forte. He had not found his campaigning voice at this stage in his political career. The populist message he brought to his listeners was at times belied by his lawyerly and "citified" tone. Russell's campaign was plagued, too, by his own concern that the unpopular tax increases he and Uncle Earl had overseen created an insurmountable political obstacle. He expected to lose and therefore, early in the campaign, began to entertain thoughts of withdrawing. Uncle Earl, however, would not hear of it. With Earl's prodding, Russell took the offensive. He stressed the tangible benefits—the roads, buildings, and bridges—that the taxes were already beginning to provide, and he argued that Kennon's denunciation of the taxes meant that the judge opposed those benefits. Long shifted the focus of attention away from his own inexperience by contrasting his World War II service with Kennon's. Long had seen combat in the European theater and had commanded his own boat; Kennon had risen to the rank of colonel in the U.S. Army but had not seen active combat. The distinction was vivid only three years after hostilities had ended, and it was used to great effect by Long and his supporters.[33]

On primary day, August 31, 1948, the Long machine went into action. The carefully woven political connections Earl, and Huey before him, had created proved crucial to Russell's chances, and its get-out-the-vote mechanisms may have made the difference in the election. Long defeated Kennon by a little more than ten thousand votes. Long then easily dispatched of Republican Clem Clark in the November 1948 general election.[34]

Russell's election numbers showed particular strength in Louisiana's rural areas, and his constituency may be safely considered to have been a political inheritance from both his father and his uncle. That bequest would remain important to him for the next four decades. Russell received solid support from poor hill farmers in Louisiana's north and west-central parishes, plus sugar farmers in the state's southern regions. Since his father's death, Uncle Earl and the Long machine had broadened that constituency to include organized laborers in urban areas, small farmers in the delta region, and after the mid-1940s, increasing numbers of rural and urban blacks who managed to surmount numerous obstacles to vote.[35]

On New Year's Eve, 1948, Senator Arthur Vandenberg swore Russell Long into the Senate. At just past thirty years old, Long was the upper house's youngest member. He was no novice, however. He had been born into a whirlwind of politics. His father, Huey, had redefined Louisiana's political structure and his Uncle Earl had expanded and refined what Huey had done. Russell witnessed it all and learned from them both. Over the course of the next thirty-eight years, he would use Huey and Earl as basic reference points for political stances, and he would attempt to model his own political persona upon theirs. But a seat in the U.S. Senate fundamentally changed those stances and created for Russell a practical political philosophy that differed from anything that Earl, or Huey, ever espoused.[36]

CHAPTER TWO

Finding His Footing, 1949–1952

ARTHUR VANDENBERG was sixty-four years old when he swore Russell Long into the United States Senate. Vandenberg had served in the Senate since 1926 and had been a colleague of Long's father, Huey, during the 1930s. Russell, for his part, had just turned thirty years old.[1]

The Senate that Russell Long encountered as a freshman legislator was vastly different from the one of Huey's prime and Vandenberg's youth. Certainly, some of the same politicos still haunted the halls, and the physical setting had changed very little. But the nature of American politics had been transformed by the New Deal and World War II, and the politics that defined the post–World War II Senate differed dramatically from those defined by the Depression of Huey's era. A new accord about the nature of American politics, referred to by some historians as a "liberal consensus," had emerged. During the first three years in which he held his Senate seat, from 1949 through 1952, Russell Long would place himself firmly within the confines of that liberal consensus, circumscribed as it was by his southern background and constituency. By the end of Harry Truman's presidency, Long had crafted a political philosophy rooted in practical considerations, tinged by the political inheritance he received from his father and Uncle Earl, and in line with most of his southern colleagues.

New Deal Liberalism and the "Liberal Coalition"

Franklin Roosevelt's Great Depression and World War II–era presidency fundamentally altered the nature of not only the executive branch but also the entire federal government. Presidents for the rest of the twentieth century used Roosevelt as a model and acted as initiators of legislation and creators of policy—functions traditionally reserved for Congress and its committee system—while also maintaining their traditional roles of commanders in chief and executors of law. This change in presidential thinking reflected the economic, political, and social crises of the 1930s and Roosevelt's method for grappling with them. His New Deal had two main goals: alleviate the suffering of Americans and cure the root cause of that distress, the Great Depression.

The most important effect of Roosevelt's New Deal policies on subsequent American politics, however, had little to do with how successful they had been at solving the problem of the Depression. What mattered instead was that voters, along with their political representatives, came to see large-scale government intervention into certain segments of American society as beneficial. This belief in government activism on a widespread scale formed the domestic component of the liberal consensus, and World War II seemed to confirm the positive side of federal vigor: the government spent enormous amounts of money on defense needs and jump-started the American economy. The war also sparked a shift in American diplomatic values, as interventionism, rather than isolationism, in world affairs came to be seen as a necessary and advantageous guiding principle for the United States. Interventionism formed the second major component of New Deal liberalism, the first being federal domestic activism.[2]

It was these new understandings about the capacity of the federal government that led to the formation of what has been variously termed the "liberal consensus" or a "New Deal liberal coalition." Roosevelt's New Deal had been paradoxically both radical and conservative, in that it fundamentally altered the methods of American government but also sought to protect and maintain capitalism. Saving capitalism meant not condoning redistributionist policies such as those of Huey Long, or even worse, those of socialism or communism. It meant a commitment to Keynesian fiscal policies, which espoused temporary tax cuts and enormous government spending during times of recession. The liberal consensus thus championed an activist government that would work to protect and improve the nation's economy along with the social welfare of its citizens, but it was limited in just how far it could go to reach those ends.

From such commitments came, according to historian Alonzo Hamby, the dominant theme in American politics until the late twentieth century, "a tradition of New Deal liberalism emphasizing welfare statism and government management of the economy; along with this came a commitment to large-scale international involvement built around the concept that American liberal values should be defended and extended in the larger world." The New Deal liberal tradition would overcome some initial conservative attacks during the late 1940s and would reign triumphant during the 1950s and early 1960s. By the late 1960s, however, divisions between older, original New Dealers and their younger, more idealistic, and anti-interventionist liberal counterparts began to emerge. The cracks grew larger in the early 1970s, and the supremacy of the New Deal liberal coalition had ultimately crumbled by the early 1980s.[3]

For Russell Long and his southern colleagues in the Senate, the liberal consensus could be at once enticing and repulsive. A federal government with expanded authority promised to bring great benefits to their home states. If one region of the nation stood to gain from the shift in political philosophy at the federal level, it was the impoverished South. Long's father and uncle had shown the real benefits of such a setup on a state level; now New Deal liberalism seemingly promised to do the same on a national scale. However, by the late 1940s it was becoming evident that an important corollary of New Deal liberalism would be an effort to provide full citizenship to all Americans, including southern blacks. When confronted with such attempts, usually from the executive branch, the Senate's southerners recoiled and retrenched.

Southern senators could appear contradictory in their policy stances, but it was a matter of political survival. Russell Long's senior colleague, Allen Ellender, provides a useful example. Ellender's most able biographer has labeled him a consensus politician, "a coalition builder, who sought common ground with a majority of his constituents, his white constituents at least." A member of the Senate since 1937, Ellender supported almost all of Roosevelt's so-called Second New Deal measures, and over the course of his career managed "to blend his own deal of New Deal liberalism with intense racial segregation." For a southern politician working at the national level, the practical political path was evident: support what is popular with the voters and oppose what they dislike, keeping in mind that the voters are white. Russell Long learned this lesson well.[4]

The Fair Deal

When Long first entered the Senate, Roosevelt's successor as president, Harry Truman, was attempting to consolidate New Deal liberalism through his domestic Fair Deal and diplomatic policies of containment. In his January 1949 State of the Union address, Truman proposed continuing or expanding most of Roosevelt's liberal domestic policies; this Fair Deal would include progressive tax reform, public power development, minimum wage increases, and expanded Social Security. Beyond that, Truman proposed repealing the 1947 Labor-Management Relations Act, commonly known as the Taft-Hartley Act, which had tempered gains earned by organized labor as a result of the New Deal–era Wagner Labor Relations Act. He also championed either creating or extending such New Deal–inspired liberal programs as federal health insurance, farm policy reform, low-income housing support, and a permanent Fair Employment Practices Commission (FEPC).[5]

Created by presidential order in 1941, the FEPC investigated discrimination complaints in defense industries and government agencies. Truman's proposal for a permanent FEPC was a thorn in the side of Russell Long and many of his southern colleagues; their opposition demonstrated the limits of the southern embrace of the liberal consensus. Although many southern politicians of the postwar era well understood the benefits that New Deal liberalism might provide, the political situation in their home states led them to remain steadfastly conservative when liberalism meant challenging the racial status quo. When that happened, southerners typically joined together with their northern allies to reconstitute a bi-partisan conservative coalition that had developed during the late 1930s. The coalition was made up of economically conservative northern Republicans troubled by the increasing power of organized labor and racially conservative Southern Democrats energized by even the most minor challenge to the southern racial status quo.

Elements of this conservative coalition opposed the Fair Deal at nearly every turn and often succeeded in stopping passage of Truman's proposals. Only two of the major Fair Deal proposals made their way out of the Capitol: an increased minimum wage and the Housing Act of 1949, which fostered urban renewal, increased funding for federal mortgage insurance, provided support for the construction of more than eight hundred thousand public housing units, and allowed the Farmers Home Administration to provide mortgages for rural single-family homes. Truman was enraged that members of his own party would scuttle his proposals. "I suppose that Presidents in the past have had hostile Congresses—but they were frankly of the opposition," he wrote in his diary. "This one—the 81st—happens to be of my own party on the surface. But the majority is made up of Republicans and recalcitrant Southern 'Democrats'—who are not Democrats." He concluded: "There are liars, trimmers and pussyfooters on both sides of the aisle in the Senate and the House. I'm sorry. I wish I had straight out opposition and loyal support. I guess it is too much to ask for!"[6]

Truman's lament that he did not have clearly demarcated supporters and opponents reflected the limitations of New Deal liberalism's political appeal to southerners. Even southerners accepted the necessity, indeed the benefits, of the new role the government played in the American economy, and as will be seen below, the new understanding of the place of the United States in the world. But they refused to embrace New Deal liberalism's commitment to expanding civil rights for blacks, no matter how slowly and piecemeal those advances may have come, and they were willing to work with members of the opposition party to make sure that such proposals stagnated.

It was logical for a southern politician, knowing that his constituency stood to benefit from much of what the liberal program provided, to support certain aspects of Truman's Fair Deal—and New Deal liberalism in general—while at the same time, knowing that his voting constituency remained almost exclusively white, to oppose other elements of that program that threatened Jim Crow segregation and disfranchisement. These conflicting political considerations are evident throughout Russell Long's tenure, especially in his early years as a senator. Long maintained conservative policy stances for much of his career, but his conservatism was tempered by tendencies toward liberalism of the New Deal variety and tended to be relegated mainly to matters of race.

So it was that, during his first years in the Senate, Long backed Truman's call for minimum wage increases; began what would be a career-long pattern of supporting increases in Social Security coverage and payments; and unlike some of his more rigidly conservative colleagues on both sides of the aisle, supported Truman's proposal for federal aid to education. Long had promised during his 1948 campaign to fight for the latter; he felt it would provide the greatest benefits to the states that needed it the most—particularly southern states such as Louisiana. "The whole idea," Long noted on the floor of the Senate, "is to help the poor States educate their children."[7] The poorer states had more children and less money, he argued. Even if they taxed their citizens more heavily than the more affluent states, the discrepancy between the haves and the have-nots would be too great to overcome. Only the federal government could provide the level of support needed to equalize educational opportunities. Long's arguments in favor of federal aid to education had a familiar ring to Louisiana's citizens; his father had championed state involvement in education at all levels, and his Uncle Earl had carried on in the same tradition. But even with the Longite inheritance in his political baggage, Russell Long knew that future battles might change his stance, and as early as 1949 he hinted that southern states would not accept federal aid if it came with requirements for desegregating educational facilities. In the end, Long and a majority of his Senate colleagues voted in favor of federal aid to education, but the legislation languished in the House of Representatives.[8]

Taking a more conservative stance, Long characterized Truman's national health insurance plan as "socialized medicine." In doing so, he allied himself with the American Medical Association and the Senate's conservative coalition. But his stance seemed to disavow one aspect of his political inheritance: both his father and his uncle had overseen dramatic increases in state funding for Louisiana hospitals; providing health care for those who could not afford it had been a hallmark of the Longite welfare state. Long's opposition to Truman's plan, however, was not absolute. His "socialized medicine" argument remained tempered by an awareness that such a stance could go too far. "Many of us," he noted in 1951, "believe that the American Medical Association is making a great mistake in taking a position against anything which would, in the long run, mean better health for the people."[9]

While Long seemingly differed with his father and uncle when it came to state-provided health care, in other realms he felt perfectly at ease using the populist rhetoric that had worked so well for them. An early example came in 1950, during debates over a bill to legalize the basing-point price system. This system allowed manufacturers to base their final selling prices on the factory price plus an additional charge for shipment to a city near the buyer. The Supreme Court had declared the system unconstitutional in April 1948 because it allowed large corporations to secure unfair pricing and thus undermine competition. Long sided with the Court. He argued that the bill would weaken antitrust laws, particularly the Robinson-Patman Act, which Congress had passed in 1936 to protect small, independent stores and suppliers from unfair competition by large conglomerates, and he presented the debates over the basing-point system as a battle to protect small businesses from large, impersonal corporations. He called the basing-point bill the "most cleverly conceived device ever invented by the mind of man" to evade antitrust law.[10]

At their most basic, Long's arguments against the basing-point bill echoed statements his father had made as a lawyer, Public Service commissioner, governor, and senator in attacking huge corporations like Standard Oil or Bell Telephone. The proposed basing-point legislation, Russell Long argued, endangered fair competition by granting enormous, faceless, external interests the freedom to trample small, familiar, local businesses. He noted during the final days of debate on the bill that he and others who opposed the legislation "do not oppose price competition; we do not oppose keen competition; we do not oppose vigorous competition. What we do oppose is unfair and destructive methods of competition which would make it impossible for small-business men to compete." Huey might not have said it better, and in the end, a majority of Long's Senate colleagues agreed with him. The legislation that he referred to as "this great loophole bill" was voted down.[11]

Maintaining fair competition and resisting monopolies would serve as themes for much of Long's career. As chair of the Subcommittee on Monopoly of the Senate's Select Committee on Small Business, Long during the 1950s and early 1960s oversaw investigations into the effects of monopolistic practices on small business, the enforcement of contemporary antitrust laws, and the possibility of strengthening those laws. Quite often, those investigations led him to criticize the Justice Department for "not actively and more vigorously pursuing the antitrust laws of this Nation." He would publicly challenge the Justice Department over other matters as well, particularly its role in redefining the southern racial structure beginning in the mid-1950s.[12]

The Politics of Race

Debates over civil rights marked one of the important ways Russell Long's experience in the Senate varied greatly from that of his father, Huey. The differences were striking. Both in Louisiana and in Washington, Huey had no reason to even think upon the matter; segregation and disfranchisement were too firmly entrenched in the South of the 1920s and 1930s for any politician to challenge them. Thus, for Huey, the question was moot, and ignoring race relations and civil rights was merely practical politics. Two decades later, however, Russell had to confront challenges to the "southern way of life" head-on, albeit for just as practical reasons.

Russell Long's defense of the southern political and social status quo began almost as soon as he entered the Senate. In early 1948, months before Long arrived in Washington, Truman sent Congress a civil rights message calling for anti-lynching, anti-poll tax, and voting rights legislation, along with laws prohibiting discrimination in interstate transportation. Such proposals flew in the face of what southern whites, and their Democratic senators and representatives, considered the southern way of life. They challenged a system of racial segregation and black disfranchisement that had existed for half a century or more. The centerpiece of Truman's proposal, however, was the permanent FEPC, which would investigate and publicize instances of discrimination within government agencies and defense industries, no small matter in an early Cold War Washington that was witnessing dramatic growth within both. Truman's proposal died when the Eightieth Congress ended in the autumn of 1948.[13]

Undaunted—and invigorated after his November 1948 re-election—Truman resubmitted his civil rights program to the Eighty-First Congress on February 2, 1949. The package met with some success in the House of Representatives, where both the permanent FEPC and the anti-poll tax legislation were approved. But the Senate was a different matter. There, southerners brought out a tried-and-true method, the filibuster, to halt any consideration of the bill. Their goal was to scuttle the whole program by talking it to death. The southerners, however, knew well that their opponents had a trump card that, if played right, could end a filibuster in its tracks—cloture, which, as provided for in Senate Rule XXII, allows for a vote to be taken on ending debate. Cloture was the sole defense against the filibuster, and Truman, for the sake of his civil rights proposals, pushed his Senate allies to change Rule XXII so as to reduce the number of votes needed for cloture.[14]

Russell Long, like all of his southern colleagues, opposed the FEPC legislation, and he fought the attempted changes to Rule XXII that would have made FEPC's passage easier. It was, in fact, during a filibuster against the proposed rule change that Long made his first formal speech on the Senate floor—a speech that would set the tone for his anti–civil rights rhetoric over the following two decades. He defended unlimited debate (the filibusters) as a protection of minority rights, but the minorities he sought to protect were of a particular type. Minority *states'* rights, in Long's formulation, were in desperate need of defense, and the filibuster and contemporary cloture rule "give the minority the right to test out the majority and to see how convinced they are of their own righteousness, and whether they are attempting to play petty politics at home." Long's voting record on civil rights, however, would demonstrate that these stances on minority states' rights did not correlate to minority *individual* rights.[15]

In defending the filibuster, Long asserted that the majority for one issue, however prominent and powerful at a particular moment in time, might easily become a minority in the future. At that point the senators calling for limits on debate would be on the wrong end of the argument. Furthermore, he argued, loosening the cloture rule would eventually, and perhaps most damagingly, remove public oversight of the government: filibusters, however specious some of the speeches within them might be, provided publicity and clarification to the public on controversial or complicated items of legislation. The filibuster, Long attested, "is the greatest protection the rank and file of our people in the United States enjoy. It guarantees them a chance to know what is going on in the Senate before something that would do great harm to them is passed."

Of course, the filibuster also provided an effective way to stall movement—either on bills or on rules changes—and the successful southern filibuster against changes to Rule XXII ultimately resulted in a measure that made cloture more difficult. From that point, cloture required a two-thirds vote of the entire Senate rather than two-thirds of senators present. The change effectively killed Truman's civil rights package, and by the next year, the Truman administration and Congress both recognized that efforts to pass meaningful civil rights legislation had become hopeless.[16]

Long, for his part, continued to voice opposition to Truman's civil rights proposals, whether they had a potential for success or not. Such resistance represented not just Long's personal convictions, but also the politically expedient course a representative of a southern state had to take. So much of Louisiana's and the rest of the South's social system was based on division of the races, and so much political power had been removed from black hands, that to even consider opening the door to such things as workplace discrimination suits could potentially create a flood of changes that would result in a wholesale shift in the dynamics of southern society and politics. Almost every voter in Louisiana was white, thanks to the state's disfranchisement mechanisms, and Long well knew that. Those voters, and the elected officials of the southern wing of the Democratic Party, held deep convictions about the necessity of maintaining segregation and black disfranchisement. Alienating them would lead to political repercussions, including potentially being voted out of office. He therefore challenged any attempt to change the system.

Therefore, even though Truman's proposals were as good as dead, Long consistently reminded his colleagues and his constituency that he firmly opposed any changes to the status quo. In May 1950, for instance, Long called the FEPC proposals "an obnoxious piece of proposed legislation" that would allow employees to run roughshod over their employers by pursuing frivolous and expensive lawsuits. As implemented, he argued, the FEPC would allow an employee who had been passed over for a promotion to take his boss to court and, at the government's expense, sue for damages. Even if the employee lost, the employer would be out the cost of defense, while the government would foot the employee's bill. More important, Long believed the legislation, "which purports to assure people of their American rights, denies them their most fundamental American rights—the right to trial by jury, the right against self-incrimination, the right to be left alone, the right to choose one's own company, the right to pick one's own employees, the right to pick one's own associates." The argument would become a consistent weapon in Long's opposition to civil rights initiatives: protecting rights for one group threatened more fundamental rights for others.[17]

Long's hostility toward civil rights legislation, however, did not lead him to engage in race baiting or black bashing. As a result, he distinguished himself from many of his southern Senate compatriots, including his senior colleague from Louisiana, Allen Ellender, who made no bones about his belief in white supremacy. At roughly the same time that Long was using legal and economic justifications for opposing the FEPC, Ellender remarked at the University of Chicago that "the Negro race

. . . will invariably go back to barbaric lunacy" without white control. Long's tempered opposition to the FEPC, and to future civil rights legislation, reflected an internal unease with certain of the tactics of the southern opposition, but he opposed the changes nonetheless, and he would continue to do so in the future.[18]

The Early Cold War

When Russell Long arrived in Washington, he possessed little acumen concerning foreign affairs, like most freshman senators before and after, including his father. Huey had never needed to formulate an opinion on foreign affairs—for all intents and purposes, he was an isolationist, but it really mattered very little in the Depression-era Senate in which he worked. However, the rapidly polarizing Cold War world of the late 1940s—and New Deal liberalism's thrust toward an activist role for the United States in world affairs—forced Russell into formulating and enunciating positions on the relationship of the United States with the rest of the world. He quickly showed himself to be, like most of his southern colleagues, an avid Cold Warrior who supported most, if not all, of the Truman administration's diplomatic policies.[19]

Those policies had been enunciated by Truman on March 12, 1947, well before Long took office, and would have long-term implications for the Louisiana senator's political career. The Truman Doctrine declared it "the policy of the United States to support free people who are resisting attempted subjugation by armed minorities or by outside pressures" and espoused a strategy of containment, which posited that Soviet expansion would be a matter of course and should be countered by both economic aid for nations facing communist threats and outright military alliances. The Soviets and their allies, in this formulation, acted as a monolithic, concerted, communist menace, bent on world domination. According to Truman and his advisors, given enough time the communist economic and social system would collapse as a result of its own internal weaknesses. The goal for the United States and its allies would be to *contain* the threat of communist expansion until the collapse.[20]

From the time he arrived in Washington, Long supported the Truman Doctrine, especially its military components. He viewed Soviet expansion as a true threat to the United States and its allies, and he firmly believed that the United States had to do all in its power to limit that expansion. He understood, too, that in the heated anti-communist political climate of the late 1940s and early 1950s, any elected official had to protect himself from charges of being "soft on communism." During his first year in office, Long urged President Truman to review and possibly increase the administration's military budget because "the people don't want to economize on their own safety." In a 1950 radio address with Senate colleagues William Knowland, George F. Mahon, and Edward Martin, Long further stoked the Cold War fires with his assertion that a Soviet attack on the United States was probably imminent, and "fifteen to thirty of our larger cities will have atomic bombs dropped on them within the first week or two." His comments were widely reported.[21]

Although Long supported the idea of containment and the general tenets of the Truman Doctrine, he occasionally voiced reservations about particular aspects of the strategy. One such instance occurred following the entrance of the United States into the North Atlantic Treaty Organization (NATO), the first of a series of mutual security alliances created by the U.S. government and its allies to contain communist expansion. Long viewed the move with satisfaction, and he generally supported the early activities of NATO, but he also expressed concerns over just how *mutual* such security pacts could be. He publicly fretted that "when the fighting breaks out, in the long run the United States [will be] called upon to do a tremendous share of the fighting." Moreover, he cautioned the administration, "We should be a little careful before we say that we are willing to take into the North Atlantic Pact every nation which is opposed to communism." Spreading containment too far and wide, Long sensed, could negate the strategy's effect.[22]

Long's doubts about containment's limits, however, disappeared when he confronted cases of outright communist aggression. In June 1950, the army of Soviet-friendly communist North Korea crossed the 38th parallel and invaded South Korea, a nation with close ties to the United States. The United Nations called for member nations to provide assistance in order to defend the south from the northern incursions, and within a week President Truman ordered American forces under General Douglas MacArthur to the Korean peninsula. Truman's executive decision left Congress without a say in the matter, but Senator Long seemed not to mind. He agreed with the Truman administration that the action was justified according to the dictates of containment policy and that this was a dramatic instance of just such "outside pressures" as the president had noted in his 1947 speech. If anything, the Louisiana senator supported a much stronger showing of force, as did most of his southern colleagues. Long publicly supported the overly aggressive MacArthur, even after Truman had dismissed the general for ignoring orders. Following MacArthur's testimony about his ouster before a joint Armed Services and Foreign Relations Committee hearing, Long, who had only recently been named to the committee and had been relatively quiet during the hearings, urged the general to "continue to speak out on foreign affairs."[23]

Long's support for the military aspects of containment did not necessarily correlate to an unquestioning approval of the strategy's economic aspects, solidified as they were only nine months before Long took office when Congress created the Economic Cooperation Act, more commonly referred to as the Marshall Plan. Economic containment worked under the assumption that an infusion of capital into weakened economies would stave off the expansion of communism. The Truman administration hoped that the Marshall Plan, which proposed funneling billions of dollars into rebuilding a Europe that lay in economic, social, and physical ruins would strengthen global capitalism while also undermining the appeal of communism for Europeans in the aftermath of World War II. Truman and his advisors further hoped such economic beneficence would weaken the economic and political structure of those places where communism had already made inroads—Eastern Europe, most notably—and the moneys were thus offered to all European nations, including the Soviet Union itself.[24]

Although the Soviets and most Eastern European nations turned down the Marshall Plan's offer, many Western European nations accepted it. The transatlantic infusions of capital required enormous shifts of wealth from the United States to those nations. That transfer of wealth sometimes alarmed Long, and during the 1940s and 1950s he often either voted against the foreign aid legislation authorizing the program or offered amendments to decrease the amount appropriated for it. Long's opinion reflected that of a sizeable and influential minority of his Dixie cohort. He aligned himself with Ellender, as well as Senators Walter George, Harry Byrd, Kenneth McKellar, Olin Johnston, and John McClellan, all of whom argued that money sent overseas would be more sensibly spent on domestic needs and that, anyway, the plan was not fiscally sound. Long tread a middle ground between these more conservative members of the southern bloc and its more Marshall Plan–friendly majority, who claimed that the money sent to Europe ultimately would be returned to the United States—and particularly the South—in the form of payments for two of the pillars of the southern agricultural economy: cotton and tobacco. Between 1948 and 1965, Long voted seven times against the foreign aid program but five times for it, and he ultimately judged the program "meritorious in general," despite instances of waste and inefficiency.[25]

The Cold War on the Home Front

The emerging Cold War redefined the foreign policy of the United States in the late 1940s, but it dramatically changed domestic politics as well. If the Soviets and their allies were intent on world domination, the reasoning went, then communist expansion could not be viewed solely as an overseas threat. The United States would be in their sights as well. Thus, there arose an intense effort led by prominent American politicians to root out real or imagined communist infiltration and to punish those who were "soft on communism." By the early 1950s, the anti-communist movement had coalesced around Long's Republican colleague Joseph McCarthy, junior senator from Wisconsin. McCarthy embodied early Cold War paranoia about communist infiltration into the nation and, more specifically, the federal government. His assaults on alleged internal communism began during the 1950 election cycle, when he assailed the Truman administration with charges of being soft on communism, but his tactics quickly took a turn toward unsubstantiated accusations and rumormongering. McCarthy soon accused Americans from celebrities to common folk with fomenting communist insurgencies and undermining American capitalism and democracy. McCarthy's obsession with rooting out alleged communists ultimately transcended his personal role in the struggle and took on the dynamics of a popular crusade. McCarthy's public support made him near sacrosanct, and his tactics temporarily garnered bipartisan support in the halls of Congress.[26]

Senator Long deferred to McCarthy's popularity, an unusual step for him to take. For decades prior, Long had stood up to very powerful and influential people who denounced his father. His courage was never dampened during such battles, and he understood the effect false accusations could have on the lives of the accused. But when it came to McCarthy and his tactics, Long followed the majority in allowing the Wisconsinite to badger, bully, and browbeat celebrities, government workers, and average Americans. Even when McCarthy attacked Long's own Democratic Party, he did not attempt to defend it. He was not alone. Most of his fellow Democrats refused to do the same. Long's stance on McCarthy is most notable for its silence. His pragmatism got the better of him, and he bent to McCarthyism's popularity with American voters.[27]

Then, in 1954, McCarthy and his Senate Subcommittee on Investigations charged that the highest levels of the U.S. Army had fallen under the control of communist subversives. Even the most reticent politicians—Long included—took notice. Calling the accusations "extremely serious," Long supported Senate hearings into McCarthy's claims. "There is nothing minor about the charge that the Secretary of the Army has been coddling Communists," he admitted. "If these charges are true, I believe the truth should be developed. If the charges are not true, then I believe the committee owes it to the Secretary of the Army to state affirmatively that the charges are not true."[28]

As the spectacle of the McCarthy-Army hearings unfolded, key senators, encouraged by President Dwight Eisenhower and his administration, began to openly resist both McCarthy and his tactics. Following four months of hearings, the opposition reached a head on July 30, 1954, when Republican Ralph Flanders of Vermont introduced a resolution to censure, or publicly condemn, McCarthy. While not as harsh as removal from office, a censure generally resulted in such adverse publicity that the senator involved saw his career left in a shambles. After consideration in a special committee, the censure resolution reached the Senate floor in November. Emboldened by recent elections that had returned them to majority control, Long's fellow Democrats led the charge.[29]

The day before the censure resolution vote, Long stood before his colleagues and pondered the new precedent that the Senate would be creating. Recalling, no doubt, accusations and allegations that had been leveled at his father, he reminded his colleagues that "it is not enough . . . to disapprove generally of the personal conduct of a Senator or the manner in which he carries out his duties." Had that been the case, Huey Long would undoubtedly have been censured at numerous points during his three years in the Senate. Instead, "Specific misconduct is essential as a basis for censure." Long sensed that censure of a colleague struck at one of the body's most revered traditions—the right to freely and openly voice unpleasant opinions, even "to impugn the motives of a fellow Senator or a senatorial committee."[30]

McCarthy had failed to produce evidence to support his charges. "Therefore," Long concluded, "I shall vote in favor of censure. In view of all the circumstances, I do not see how I could do otherwise." His conscience was not entirely eased, however, and he still feared "that I am establishing a precedent which can be used in the future to enforce uniformity in our conduct as individual Senators and representatives of our respective States." He concluded by warning that "the right to challenge must be undisputed and, equally so, the burden of proof must rest with the challenger when his challenge is accepted." On December 2, 1954, the full Senate voted 67 to 22 in favor of censure. McCarthy, once among the most powerful and infamous of senators, began a descent into alcoholism and shame that only ended with his death in May 1957.[31]

The Louisiana Governor's Race of 1952

Russell Long kept closely connected with politics inside of Louisiana even as he established himself in the Senate. Much like his father, Long understood that the Bayou State and the city on the Potomac constituted two parts of a political whole. Especially during the first decade of his political career, Long's interest in Louisiana revealed itself in a penchant for directly dabbling in state politics.

Long's most pressing Louisiana concern during the late 1940s was his campaign for a full Senate term. The task turned out to be less daunting than he had initially supposed. In spite of the opposition of such powerful political personalities as New Orleans mayor DeLesseps "Chep" Morrison and Plaquemines Parish boss Leander Perez, Long handily defeated Anti-Longite Malcolm Lafargue in the July 1950 Democratic primary. Lafargue had attempted to capitalize on growing Cold War fears of communist infiltration by labeling Long a practitioner of "creeping socialism," but his contentions fell on deaf political ears. Long received 68 percent of the state's Democratic vote. The November general election only confirmed the primary decision.[32]

In order to help Russell win reelection to the Senate, his uncle, Governor Earl Long, had backed off from some of the heavy-handed spoils politics that had defined the first two years of his term. After the July primary, however, Uncle Earl returned to his previous political ways. In August 1950, for instance, he called for a constitutional convention that he hoped to control through his own factional underlings. He managed only to alienate supporters and embolden opponents. Led by Leander Perez and Chep Morrison, those opponents publicly contended that the governor would use the convention to garner even greater control over New Orleans (only two years after the Rape of New Orleans), to extend his term in office, and to keep the Long machine running smoothly and powerfully. The opposition's denunciations stoked a backlash among the public, and Governor Long eventually revoked the call for the convention.[33]

Earl's heavy-handed attempt at manipulating the proposed constitutional convention, plus the substantial tax increases that had been required to pay for many of his expanded social welfare programs, left the race for the next Democratic gubernatorial nomination wide open. Earl could not run for reelection; the Constitution of 1921 provided that no governor could succeed himself. And the public backlash against his policies meant that the nomination was no shoo-in for whomever Earl would run on the Long ticket. Thus, candidates who otherwise might not have run in the January 1952 primary rushed into the political arena.[34] Among the relative oddities of that primary was that Kermit A.

Parker, a New Orleans druggist, campaigned as the first black man to run for a statewide office in the twentieth century. Lucille May Grace, the state land registrar, entered the fray as the first woman to make a gubernatorial run. And an unlikely trio of young, dynamic, up-and-comers—Russell Long, Hale Boggs, and DeLesseps Morrison—teamed for a try at political dominance through control of Louisiana's most important local, state, and national offices.[35]

Boggs possessed the most political experience of the three. He served as a U.S. representative for Louisiana's Second District from 1941 until 1943, when he was defeated for reelection. After a period service in the U.S. Navy from late 1943 until early 1946, Boggs won election to the seat he formerly held and had retained it without interruption. He made a name for himself as an avid Anti-Long politician. In 1939, he teamed with Morrison to form the Anti-Long People's League of Independent Voters in 1939. He supported Morrison's successful bid to unseat Longite Robert Maestri in the 1946 New Orleans mayoral race, and he participated in the creation of the Anti-Long Crescent City Democratic Association. By 1952, Boggs was well on his way to becoming, as one knowledgeable observer would later tag him, "the class of Louisiana politics."[36]

Senator Long let Boggs know during the spring of 1951 that, should the congressman decide to run for governor, he would actively support the candidacy, even over the Long machine's own candidate. The proposed alliance would be mutually beneficial. Boggs would receive the endorsement of the popular and well-known senator, and Long would establish his independence from Uncle Earl, possibly setting himself up for a gubernatorial run of his own in 1956. Situated in Washington, where their social and political lives frequently intersected and where the bitter and often petty factional squabbles of the Long/Anti-Long rivalry seldom reached, Long and Boggs had established a cordial personal friendship. They were well-regarded among their

Washington colleagues, and their political stances on national issues closely paralleled one another.[37]

An alliance between Boggs and Morrison might have seemed natural, but the thought of DeLesseps S. "Chep" Morrison associating with Senator Long would have conjured images of oil and water. As mayor of New Orleans, Morrison had been mired in the factional muck of Louisiana politics since the mid-1940s, and he had developed a deep-seated political and personal hatred for Earl Long. The alliance of Boggs and Morrison with an actual Long would require a delicate balance of political necessity, high-minded ideals, and shrewd salesmanship.[38]

The Boggs candidacy needed the backing of Mayor Morrison and his Crescent City Democratic Association if it was to have any chance of winning, but the mayor was reluctant to endorse the congressman. Anti-Longite Robert Kennon had been courting Morrison even before Boggs decided to run, and the mayor had also seriously considered running for the position himself.[39]

So when Boggs came to Morrison to ask for his support, the mayor was initially conflicted. Like Long, Morrison believed that supporting a winner in this race would possibly set the stage for his own triumph in a later governor's race. He therefore did not like having to choose between two candidates, Kennon and Boggs, who might split the Anti-Long vote. Also, Morrison—who had consistently and vehemently opposed the Longs since the late 1930s—had to consider the political ramifications of throwing his lot in with a candidate supported by Russell Long.[40]

On June 16, 1951, Boggs formally announced his candidacy in the 1952 governor's race. Long would be his campaign manager. Endorsements from an impressive array of Louisiana's political bigwigs poured in. Sam Jones, former reform governor and an influential leader of the Anti-Long faction, gave Boggs's candidacy an early endorsement, as did U.S. congressman Jimmy Morrison. William Feazel, a Longite who kept John Overton's Senate seat warm until Russell Long could win the 1948 special election, had encouraged Boggs to enter the race, and he now offered his public endorsement.[41]

Mayor Morrison, however, still could not decide. After months of deliberation, on September 8, 1951, Morrison, acting on the counsel of public relations consultant David McGuire, finally announced his support for the Boggs candidacy. In a long and detailed memo to the mayor, McGuire had made the case for supporting Boggs. Longism and the Long/Anti-Long paradigm was dead in Louisiana, he wrote. Factionalism had become passé, and voters in the 1950s would make their decisions based on issues, not labels. Such themes would form the foundations of the Boggs campaign team's rhetoric in the months leading up to the Democratic primary.[42]

The Boggs-Long-Morrison team stressed that it would work to undermine the old political categories, divisions that shifted the focus of politics and government away from doing good for the people of the state. They would instead create a new, progressive state government. Two days after Morrison announced his support for the Boggs candidacy, Russell Long wrote to Boggs that "the active participation of Mayor Morrison in your campaign is extremely encouraging to those of us who believe that you will give the state sound progressive government honestly administered." He added, "It is becoming abundantly clear that there are many in Louisiana who agree that it is high time we put behind us the blind prejudices of the past and work unitedly for a better day in our State." The very same day, Morrison addressed a statewide radio audience. "I am convinced," the mayor said, "that the people of Louisiana . . . will demand, and will get, a 'new era' in Louisiana—an era with young progressive leadership moving to the front—not confounded and burdened with *bigotry, dogmatism*, or *old hates and antagonisms*."[43]

Mayor Morrison understood only too well that any politician with the name Long would naturally bring to mind those "old hates and antagonisms," and thus he took great pains to distinguish between Senator Long and his Uncle Earl. To complicate matters, Morrison had to justify his partnership with Russell—despite previous opposition—and his continuing hostility toward Earl. "I have opposed Senator Long," he said in his radio address,

> mainly because of my consistent opposition to the administration of Governor Earl K. Long. Despite this opposition, I have consistently stated then, and do *now* state, that Senator Long has been a sincere and a capable public official. In the three years he has served us as U.S. senator, I am glad to acknowledge that he *has* worked for New Orleans and has vigorously supported *our vital projects* regardless of our political differences.[44]

Boggs faced a diverse array of opponents in the Democratic primary. The Anti-Longites included Boggs, Parker, and Grace, plus the French-speaking, patent-medicine-hawking Cajun state senator Dudley J. "Coozan Dud" Leblanc; the state legislature's sergeant at arms, Cliff Liles; central Louisiana cattle rancher James "Cadillac Mac" McLemore; and former Louisiana Supreme Court associate justice Robert F. Kennon. On the Longite side of the political divide sat Baton Rouge district judge Carlos G. Spaht and Lieutenant Governor William Dodd. Spaht was the official Long machine candidate. Although he possessed few of the traditional attributes necessary for victory—he was nondescript and had very little political experience—"Earl's boy," as many Louisianians called him, was guaranteed a spot in the Democratic runoff election thanks to the Long machine's support and Earl's active campaigning.[45]

The real race would be for the other runoff slot. Dodd probably best fit the model of a Longite politician, yet he did not receive the support of Earl or the Long machine. Of the Anti-Long candidates, Kennon had the best prospects for getting into the runoff. Since waging a vigorous campaign as Russell Long's opponent in the 1948 special Senate election, he had built statewide support and recognition. Raised in Webster Parish in far northern Louisiana, Kennon had been an LSU football player, a World War II lieutenant colonel, a mayor of Minden, and a district attorney before entering the judiciary. The judge ran in 1951–1952 on a platform of fiscal conservatism, and he promised to limit corruption and cronyism within state government. "Cadillac Mac" McLemore could also count on receiving a share of the vote, but his share, like Dodd's, would not amount to enough to make it to the runoff. McLemore did receive the endorsement of the New Orleans *Times-Picayune*, and after focusing on segregation and states' rights issues late in the campaign, he earned the support of Plaquemines Parish boss Leander Perez. But he ultimately took a back seat to the two major Anti-Long candidates, Boggs and Kennon.[46]

The candidates differed little on the issues. All opposed tax hikes. They advocated pay-as-you-go highway construction, continuation of social welfare programs, a professional civil service, home rule, pay raises for state employees, and state control of Louisiana's oil-rich tidelands. With a nod toward Louisiana's strong support for the Dixiecrat ticket in the 1948 presidential election, the candidates paid lip service to anti-Trumanism. The lack of policy differences did not mean, however, that the candidates did not portray themselves as distinct from one another, nor did it mean that the Louisiana voters themselves would not create distinctions within their own minds. But these differences were matters of style rather than substance. All candidate said that they could most efficiently and most ably administer the state, even if their policies were the same.[47]

In addition to the enormous difficulty of convincing Louisiana voters that the Long/Anti-Long distinctions no longer mattered, the Boggs campaign team had to counter assaults from both the Longites and the Antis. A notable attack came from minor candidate Lucille May Grace and her powerful political benefactor, Leander Perez. Perez, who controlled Plaquemines and St. Bernard parishes in southeastern Louisiana in a fashion even more dictatorial than Huey Long's, waged a two-front attack on the

Boggs campaign. First, the Perez faction filed a formal complaint with the Louisiana Democratic Party. The complaint argued that according to the party's own rules, Boggs could not legally run for one office, the governorship, while simultaneously holding another, his congressional seat. If the party disqualified Boggs and thus did not allow him to run in the Democratic primary, the congressman's candidacy in a state so solidly Democratic would be dead. Second, Perez and Grace publicly charged that during his college years at Tulane University, Boggs had joined the American Student Union, an organization subsequently singled out as subversive by the House Un-American Activities Committee. The Plaquemines Parish boss knew the deadly force carried by accusations of subversion in the early 1950s, and he well understood that, even if the Democratic Party allowed Boggs to run, the insinuations would wreak havoc on his candidacy.[48]

The Democratic Central Committee ultimately dismissed the accusation that Boggs could not run for one office while holding another and dropped the subversive activity charges against him, but not before Earl Long and Perez engaged in a bitter give and take over the congressman's right to run for office. Earl's defense of Boggs would have major implications later in the governor's race.[49]

Leander Perez and Lucille May Grace could not match Russell's Uncle Earl when it came to destroying an opposition candidate. Earl Long understood Louisiana politics better than anyone else, and when he saw an opportunity to damage the Boggs campaign, he seized it. The governor realized that Boggs faced three major hurdles—his Roman Catholic faith, his big-city background, and his alliance with Russell Long—and he used his own political acumen to raise those hurdles to heights that could not be surmounted.

In the largely Protestant central and northern Louisiana parishes, a candidate's Catholicism was a surefire way of alienating voters. Earl Long knew this, and while campaigning in those areas for Judge Spaht, he made certain to emphasize that the archbishop of New Orleans, the preeminent Catholic cleric in Louisiana and a man with direct ties to Rome, had seen fit to come to Boggs's defense in the face of the Grace-Perez accusations. And in a state that, despite growing urbanization during the middle of the twentieth century, remained populated mostly by ruralites, Earl understood the unease voters would feel about a candidate from the big city of New Orleans. The governor therefore consistently stressed in speeches and interviews that Boggs called the Crescent City home. What's more, he had allied himself with the one person many Louisianians considered the biggest city slicker of them all: Mayor Morrison. Both of these ploys went over well outside of New Orleans; they exacerbated voter fears of not being represented in Baton Rouge and played upon the populist themes that Earl and his brother Huey had so consistently trumpeted.[50]

At the same time, Earl carefully cultivated the fears of Anti-Longites by hinting that Boggs might be under the covert control of the Long machine. The connection between Boggs and the Longs already existed, given the campaign role of Russell. And many Boggs supporters still viewed him as a Longite in Anti-Longite clothing. Earl knew that linking Boggs to Longism through Russell would only harm the congressman's chances among his own longtime supporters.

In the face of such challenges, Russell Long had to walk a political tightrope, soothing both Longite and Anti-Longite alike, calming fears while extolling the virtues of his candidate. It was no easy task. Boggs, when confronted with questions about his own political independence, could draw on his long history of opposing Earl and the Long political machine, but Russell had been part of Earl's administration and had helped implement his policies. In the days leading up to the election, Senator Long had to alleviate the apprehensions of both Boggs's supporters and his own. Doing so meant proclaiming that "Hale Boggs is a sincere conscientious independent for governor, and that when he is elected he will [not] be and cannot be controlled by Russell Long, Earl Long, Sam Jones or anybody else." Anti-Longites feared control by the Longs; Longites feared reformers like Sam Jones. Russell had to calm both sides.[51]

Long's strongest case in support of Boggs's candidacy revolved around their similar stances in Congress. He reminded traditional Longites, most of whom had voted for him in both 1948 and 1950, that during those campaigns "I pointed out that many people who were opposing me were hypocrites, because many of them had endorsed Hale Boggs for reelection to Congress on the ground that he had made a wonderful record in Congress. At that time, I argued that Congressman Boggs had made almost exactly the same record that I have made as a Senator." Boggs's policy stances mirrored his own. The perceived differences mattered very little. Long and Boggs were the same sort of politicians, he argued, and their supporters could feel free to transcend Louisiana's Longite/Anti-Longite political divide. Jumping the gap would be even easier if it was to support a candidate like Boggs: "His record in Congress is the kind of record our Long Congressmen are supposed to make," he wrote one long-time Longite. If the mark of a true Longite politician was how well he fulfills the promises Huey made, "We don't have an old-fashioned share-our-wealther up here whose record of voting for those things [that] would help the poor, the aged, the farmer, and the working man is any better than [the record of] Hale Boggs."[52]

What Long stressed more than anything else during the campaign season of 1951–1952 was that the Long/Anti-Long factional rivalry in Louisiana had become decrepit, outmoded, and counterproductive. The rivalry had served a purpose at one time, and it had brought important changes to Louisiana politics, but by the early 1950s it needed to be replaced. "Our State is suffering badly from this civil war that has been going on within Louisiana for the last generation," Long wrote one of his supporters. That suffering could be alleviated, however, with an infusion of new political blood. "We younger public officials," he continued, "should do what we can to help to stop this bitter feud and attempt to bring all of our people together[,] working for something that is good in Louisiana." Discarding the old labels and encouraging unity "may not be popular, but I know myself it is good and right, so, personally, I would be willing to sacrifice myself in having a try at giving our State better leadership than it has known in recent years." Ultimately, Long believed that the people of the state would best be served if both sides "should now unite for the good of Louisiana behind a conscientious man of high principles," Hale Boggs.[53]

Despite the Boggs-Long-Morrison rhetoric of reconciliation, the old Long/Anti-Long rivalry continued, and Louisiana's voters still responded to those labels. The politicians understood this. As a result, they committed themselves to defining each other with the very labels they proposed eliminating. Boggs and Morrison were forced to argue—although not always explicitly—that Russell Long was an Anti-Longite, in spite of his surname. Long, for his part, could do little to refute this characterization without jeopardizing Boggs's candidacy, and therefore he could not reassure his own Longite supporters of his allegiance to them. The team thus championed a political tactic that stressed discontinuity with the previous Louisiana political structure yet implicitly acknowledged a continuity of political labels.

The characterizations had to work both ways, though, if Boggs expected to win the governorship. Russell Long had to convince his own supporters—who usually backed his Uncle Earl—that Boggs (and, to a lesser, extent Morrison) avowed the sorts of policies that Longites politicians always had. "If we Long people are what we claim to be," he wrote, "then we should support Hale Boggs, because he has stood and fought for what we believe in. If we judge him on his record, he is one of the best Long men to ever serve in Washington." In the senator's formulation, Boggs would perpetuate the positive benefits of Longism—particularly such programs as old-age pensions and hospital and highway construction—without Longism's political baggage of corruption, patronage, and authoritarianism.[54]

Probably the most potent weapon Russell Long held in his political arsenal—his father's memory—was largely impotent amid the promises of creating a new mode of Louisiana politics. But Long did not hesitate to lace his rhetoric with Huey's memory, for he knew that his father's image remained vivid—both positively and negatively—for much of the Louisiana electorate. He therefore sought to capitalize on that memory for the political benefit of Hale Boggs, whose election, Long wrote to one supporter, "means the continuance of all of those things for which my father and for which I have fought." Tying Boggs and Huey Long together was tricky business, and Russell Long took great pains to distinguish between his father's political era of the late 1920s and early 1930s and the contemporary bi-factional, Longite/Anti-Longite period. In doing so, the senator argued that, yes, Boggs opposed the Long political machine, but such opposition did not necessarily translate into opposition to Huey or his ideas. Boggs "was only 21 at the time of my father's death in 1935. I see no reason to involve him in the political battles that occurred while he was a mere boy and in which he did not participate." What's done was done, and "I believe it is time that those of us who share the same beliefs in the needs of our people work together rather than fight about issues of the past."[55] Shedding the past would not be so easily done.

On the campaign trail, Earl Long bitterly denounced his nephew as a turncoat and a political amateur who had become too big for his britches. Russell did not back down from his uncle's volleys, and indeed, as the campaign wore on, the two men became increasingly vituperative in their attacks on one another. George Long, Earl's older brother, also assailed his "unfortunate, misguided nephew" who had sold out his political heritage to "team up with Sam Jones and his young protégé, his political godchild Hale Boggs." For Uncle George, as for most Louisianians, the Longite/Anti-Longite demarcation lines remained clear, and his nephew had turned his back on family and friends and embraced the vile Antis. "You show a very lamentable ignorance of history," George scolded Russell in a campaign speech, "when you say that out of peace at any price in Louisiana will come progress, advancement[,] and prosperity for our state and it's [*sic*] people." His words revealed a sentiment widespread among the state's voters.[56]

It was that sentiment which doomed the Boggs campaign. And it was the governor who sealed its fate. A mere two weeks before the primary election, "Earl Long began telling people that if they couldn't vote for his candidate . . . they should 'vote for Boggs.'" This was a certain way to bring to the surface fears among the Anti-Longites that Boggs was nothing more than a secret Long candidate, ready and willing to answer the Long machine's every beck and call.[57]

Louisiana's voters sent a resounding message to Russell Long, Hale Boggs, and Chep Morrison on January 15, 1952. That day, Judge Carlos Spaht, with the support of the Long machine, came in first in the Democratic primary with 173,987 votes. Anti-Longite Robert Kennon ran a close second with 163,414. Spaht and Kennon would face one another in a runoff election. Boggs came in a disappointing third place, with 142,542 votes; he won New Orleans and little else. In the runoff, Kennon—endorsed by every defeated candidate following the first primary—trounced Spaht, 482,302 to 315,179, and then moved on to victory over his Republican opponent in the April general election.[58]

Russell Long refused to endorse either of the candidates in the 1952 Democratic runoff. Both represented the factions he had fought so hard to transcend. Both symbolized his inability to wield his own growing political influence in a practical manner. The failure of the Boggs candidacy showed that the voters of Louisiana had either found Long's arguments unconvincing or that they had simply doubted his sincerity, and this made a lasting impression on the young senator. In the future, he would walk the Longite line.

• • •

By the end of President Harry Truman's presidency, Russell Long had established himself as a senator with a bifurcated political identity. On a national level, he exhibited voting tendencies that reflected affiliation with the so-called liberal consensus, particularly on matters of social welfare and foreign policy. Yet when that affiliation contradicted his standing as a member of the Senate's southern bloc, the southern affiliation triumphed. Both aspects of Long's politics reflected the practical considerations of a southern senator at the time. The welfare statism of New Deal liberalism stood to benefit the region and its constituents; the activist liberal foreign policy being developed during the early Cold War reflected their very real concerns with Communist aggression on the world stage. But the feelings of supporters back home—the almost exclusively white voting population that elected them—could not be ignored without jeopardizing future electoral chances. Challenging those voters could cripple a career.

The 1952 governor's race in Louisiana taught Long that lesson well. The state's voters would not so easily throw off the old political labels of Longite/Anti-Longite, just as they would not so easily allow challenges to segregation and disfranchisement. Long took a calculated risk in that campaign, and his ploy failed. Supporting Hale Boggs might have been the ideal thing to do—the congressman was, after all, eminently qualified and politically talented—but the ideal had obscured the pragmatic. In the future, Long would take a more practical approach to Louisiana—and national—politics.

CHAPTER THREE

On the Outside Looking In, 1953–1960

IN JULY 1952, Russell Long ventured to Chicago as a member of the Louisiana delegation to the Democratic National Convention. Long hoped Georgia senator Richard Russell would receive his party's presidential nomination, but it was not to be. "Had Richard Russell not come from a Southern state," Long later stated, "and remained loyal to the view of the people of the state that he represented . . . he probably would have been president." But Senator Russell *did* maintain his loyalty to "the view"—a view that included the maintenance of racial segregation and black disfranchisement and that would pervade the politics of all southern senators for the next decade and half—and the Democrats instead nominated Adlai Stevenson, the smooth, sophisticated governor of Illinois and darling of the party's liberal wing. Although he had suggested that he would have liked another Illinois liberal, Senator Paul Douglas, to receive the nomination, Senator Long approved of Stevenson as the party's choice, and he kept more conservative elements among the Louisiana delegation from bolting the convention over the nomination. Exhibiting a penchant not only for being a good party operative but also for supporting liberal presidential candidates, Long campaigned for Stevenson in Louisiana, Texas, and Arkansas.[1]

Who earned the Democratic nomination mattered very little when the votes were cast that November, because the Republicans ran World War II hero Dwight D. Eisenhower, who handily won. Eisenhower's victory ushered in a period of relative budgetary restraint on the domestic front and a new variation of containment on the diplomatic. For Russell Long, it brought the first chance of his young career to function as a member of the opposition party.[2]

During the Eisenhower administration, Long refined his philosophy of practical politics. Committed to relatively liberal stances on social welfare and foreign policy, he also held to conservative—even reactionary—postures on matters of southern race relations and racial politics. In both instances, Long was rather typical of southern politicians, and particularly southern senators, of his day.

To the chagrin of the Republican Party's more conservative elements, Eisenhower and his administration maintained many of its Democratic predecessors' economic and social welfare policies. Although not committed to *expanding* the New Deal/ Fair Deal programs, the administration *maintained* the liberal welfare state. Indeed, during the first two years of his presidency, Eisenhower appeared committed to following in Truman's footsteps by revising the Taft-Hartley Act, promoting national health insurance, and backing federal aid to education. As during the Truman administration, however, the congressional conservative coalition wanted no part of most of these reforms. Following the 1954 election cycle, in which Democrats gained control of Congress and liberal Democratic legislators began to wield more influence, the administration managed to gain some increases in Social Security.[3]

For Russell Long, those minor gains in Social Security were scarcely enough. Expanding the compass of the Social Security system formed one of the major themes of Long's early career, and it reflected a political inheritance he had received from his father and his Uncle Earl. During the few months in 1948 that Long had served as his uncle's special counsel, his chief mission had been winning legislative approval for increases to the state old-age pension and gaining federal matching funds for the program. He took his support for such programs to Washington. In 1950, Long had pushed for a major extension of the national Social Security system, but Senate conservatives on both sides of the aisle wanted nothing of it. When Eisenhower assumed the presidency, Long hoped progress might be made: in an early State of the Union address, the president called for increases in both the number of people receiving Social Security payments and the size of those payments. By Eisenhower's second term, however, Long understood that the president's more conservative commitments tempered his dedication to expanding such liberal programs. Long's disillusionment with the administration's lack of movement on Social Security translated into opposition stances on other issues.[4]

Long's appointments to important Senate committees during the 1950s placed him on a path to national influence that, although not fully realized until the 1960s, would have long-term implications stretching into the 1980s. In 1953, he was named to the Senate Finance Committee, and two years later, he was appointed to the Foreign Relations Committee. As a member of Finance, Long began to sharpen his understanding of the nation's tax codes and soon began to champion fiscal causes that sometimes flew in the face of the Eisenhower administration. When inflation broke out in the 1950s, Long enunciated a "loose-money," low-interest rate stance. In a May 1956 exchange with Treasury Secretary George M. Humphrey, Long charged that rapidly rising interest rates the preceding year had cost the federal government huge sums in interest payments on the national debt and, even worse, had discouraged home ownership among middle- and lower-class Americans. The following year, he argued for lower interest rates to spur the housing industry, and in a televised interview called for a congressional resolution to urge the Federal Reserve Board to lower rates. In 1958, he offered an amendment to the Emergency Housing Bill; the amendment called yet again for lower rates and explicitly indicted the

Eisenhower administration's tight-money policies as the cause of what by then was a general recession.[5]

Long's Finance Committee duties also granted him a forum for his continued support of increased funding of programs such as Social Security and unemployment coverage, in addition to pushing for more benefits for the working elderly. In a slight reversal of his opposition to national medical coverage, but in line with his states' rights tendencies, Long supported a joint federal-state medical plan for the disadvantaged co-authored by Robert Kerr of Oklahoma, a Democratic colleague on the Finance Committee, and House Ways and Means chairman Wilbur Mills of Arkansas.[6]

The Tidelands Dispute

The Eisenhower administration brought a glimmer of hope to senators like Long who represented states with offshore oil deposits. These senators, pitted in a so-called tidelands dispute, stood on the front lines of a battle being waged by their states against the federal government. The dispute, centered on basic notions of state and federal sovereignty and growing in intensity since the mid-1940s, raised two fundamental questions: which government controlled the billions of barrels of offshore crude oil that had yet to be accessed, and which would receive the economic benefits of that control?

The dispute reached back to 1945, when President Truman, by a presidential proclamation, had asserted federal jurisdiction over the continental shelf and its resources, including oil. In a 1947 decision, the Supreme Court confirmed the proclamation's jurisdiction in California's tidelands. On December 21, 1948—only ten days before Long took the oath of office as a freshman senator—the United States sued Louisiana and Texas in the Supreme Court for a ruling on those states' jurisdictions. The Court heard the Louisiana case in March 1950, and on June 5 it ruled that the federal government had "paramount rights" to the submerged lands. The Court later ruled the same regarding Texas's claims.[7]

The potential loss of revenue for Louisiana, Texas, Florida, California, and other similarly situated states ranged into the billions of dollars. Long and senators from those states—particularly his Democratic colleague from Florida, Spessard Holland—therefore introduced legislation to counteract the Court's rulings. Although they initially hoped for a quitclaim bill, which would have forced the federal government to return paramount rights to the states, they eventually settled for a Senate resolution that legalized state leases from before the Supreme Court's 1947 California decision and allowed the states to receive 37.5 percent of the post-1947 royalties from the disputed area. The remaining 62.5 percent would be put into escrow until Congress reached a final settlement. From 1950 until 1953, Long and Senator Holland led the battle against the federal government's paramount rights.[8]

Long reveled in the rhetoric surrounding states' rights versus federal prerogatives when he felt such a stance necessary or practical. The tidelands dispute was one instance; the battle over civil rights would be another. Using such tactics, he strengthened his commitment to mid-century southern political ideals. In the debates over the tidelands issue, Long insisted that history justified the stances of the states: the tidelands had always been considered state jurisdiction, and the Supreme Court's arbitrary decision could not change that fact. The Court had based its paramount-rights doctrine on the idea that the national government existed before the state governments and therefore held jurisdiction over offshore lands. Long found this argument wrongheaded and, basing his counterargument on the wordings of the Declaration of Independence, the Articles of Confederation, and the Constitution, suggested that "it is strange . . . that we should ever find ourselves arguing over the question of whether the States of this Nation were ever independent and sovereign, individually and in their own right." Calling forth arguments similar to those his southern forebears had made a century before to justify maintaining slavery, Long insisted that simply acknowledging the fact that the states existed before the federal government—"a basic point in American history" by his reckoning—undermined "the entire case for the claim of the Federal Government to own this property."[9]

Long's case thus rested on the fundamentally conservative notion of the predominance of states' rights when in dispute with federal prerogatives. When necessary, he also espoused a strict constructionist viewpoint of the Constitution to reinforce his tidelands arguments, as when he challenged Senator Paul Douglas "to find in the Constitution where the States ever gave the Federal Government that property or the right to claim it." The fact that the Court previously had ruled in favor of the states fifty-two times in such matters only bolstered Long's arguments, and he concluded that the Court was setting a dangerous precedent that potentially opened the door for massive encroachments on the rights of the people. "We have a dangerous thing," he noted, "in these vast new powers of the Federal Government if our Government continues to take from the States and local government their functions and their rights. It will injure ordinary American citizens in ways that I cannot at this moment anticipate."[10]

On March 26, 1952, Senator Holland offered an amendment substituting the Senate tidelands resolution with a quitclaim bill. Over the course of the following week, Long and Holland defended the bill from attack. On April 2, the full Senate voted to approve Holland's substitute. Following House and conference committee deliberations, the Senate passed the final form of the bill on May 16. Less than two weeks later, President Truman vetoed the legislation.[11]

In 1953, Senator Long supported yet another tidelands quitclaim measure. The new bill proposed overturning the Supreme Court's ruling but did not determine exact boundaries between state and federal control of offshore underwater lands. As supported by Long, it allowed for negotiations to take place that would ultimately define the limits of state and federal control. In contrast to the previous year, the tidelands-state senators had a new ally in their corner, the recently elected President Eisenhower.[12]

On May 22, 1953, Congress passed and President Eisenhower signed into law the Submerged Lands Act, which codified the quitclaim proposal. Over the following decades, the tidelands states and the federal government bickered over boundaries. Louisiana contended that it should control three marine leagues from its coast; the federal government wanted to allow only three nautical miles, a much shorter distance. In October 1956, the two sides reached a compromise whereby control over the offshore lands would be divided into four zones: the closest to land would be owned by Louisiana, the middle two would be jointly held, and the furthest out would be controlled by the federal government; moneys from the disputed areas between three nautical miles and three marine leagues would be held in escrow until the dispute was settled. Resolution came on May 31, 1960, when the Supreme Court ordered that Louisiana's control would extend only three nautical miles.[13]

Infrastructure Programs of the Eisenhower Era

Although President Eisenhower was reluctant to interfere with what he considered state prerogatives in the tidelands matter, he did not hesitate to use the power and economic might of the federal government to engage in public works programs that might be defined as Keynesian. In particular, the Republican administration spent enormous amounts of time, effort, and money developing the nation's infrastructure through projects like the joint Canadian-American St. Lawrence Seaway and the Federal Aid Interstate Highway System. Russell Long theoretically supported such projects and their infusion of jobs and money into the American economy. After all, such programs had been shown to bring great benefits in Louisiana under both his father and his uncle. Ironically, however, Long opposed the final legislation that created both of the federal projects, mainly due to their financing methods.

As passed by the Senate on January 20, 1954, the St. Lawrence Seaway legislation created the St. Lawrence Seaway Development Corporation, authorized to borrow up to $105 million from the U.S. Treasury. Those funds would be used to build and operate a navigable waterway connecting the Great Lakes with the Atlantic Ocean, thus spurring economic development deep into the interior of the United States and providing easy maneuverability for naval vessels to carry out defense missions. The borrowed money would be paid back from tolls collected. Senator Long believed borrowing the money in a lump sum from the Treasury was economically irresponsible and instead offered an amendment that would have guaranteed annual appropriations from Congress for repayment of the construction funds with interest. His amendment was rejected, however, and following House approval, President Eisenhower signed the bill into law on May 13, 1954.[14]

Long did not oppose the bill because of the amount of money the federal government was committed to spending. His concerns with the fiscal responsibility of the project reflected, rather, a way of paying his dues to the Republican branch of the conservative coalition, still a force to be reckoned with in 1954 and still opposed to what it considered unwarranted spending and government intervention into the economy. Ever the practical politician, and coming to understand the importance that conservative connections would have in matters near to any southern politician's heart and mind, Long played along. Just as important in his thought process, however, was a deeply held principle that allowing substantial amounts of money to be borrowed and spent by an agency of the federal government required congressional oversight of the project.

Two years later, Long opposed amendments to the Federal Aid Interstate Highway System that would create an interstate highway network to crisscross the nation. Sponsored by the Eisenhower administration as a way of making national defense more efficient while also bolstering internal trade, the legislation called for the creation of forty-one thousand miles of superhighways connecting all of the nation's major cities. The project was so large in scale that it held the promise of producing thousands of jobs over two or three decades, and with an expected cost of $51.5 billion spent over the course of thirteen years, the system would be the largest public works project ever undertaken by the United States. The federal government would provide 90 percent of the funding, an enormous federal outlay of capital that rivaled that of the world wars and the New Deal.[15]

Long understood quite well the positive economic benefits that two of the highways written into the original plan, Interstates 10 and 20, could have on Louisiana, and he did not argue against the creation of the system. Rather, Long contested the highway legislation for the same reason he had opposed the St. Lawrence Seaway project: he disagreed with its funding method. He thought that the one-cent-per-gallon "pay-as-you-ride" tax on gasoline that the conference committee had written into the bill was simply unnecessary; current tax revenues were sufficient to pay for the construction. Long's thoughts on funding for the interstate highways changed over time, particularly as both he and the Eisenhower administration realized that the system's construction would cost more and take longer than expected. In 1959, for instance, when the administration proposed funding the plan from general revenues, Long argued that, instead, the best way to fund the program was to repeal the tax credit granted to those taxpayers who earned dividends from investments. Using the sort of populist rhetoric favored by his father and uncle, the senator contended that the removal of this "completely unnecessary, unjustified tax advantage" provided to a select and elite group of individuals would produce enough extra revenue to pay for the highways.[16]

The Long-Morse Report and the Formosa Resolution

Long's concerns about funding such major infrastructure projects reflected his growing worries about potentially wasteful, inefficient spending by the federal government. For much the same reasons, during the 1950s he also began to publicly express misgivings about the way the containment strategy was being used to handle Cold War foreign affairs. He had harbored doubts about the economic aspects of the Truman administration's policies—particularly of the foreign aid appropriations made annually by Congress—and those misgivings continued into the Eisenhower era.

Long's negative perceptions filtered into his views of the *military* component of containment beginning in August 1952, when he and Senator Wayne Morse of Oregon, as part of their Armed Services Committee duties, made an inspection tour of American military installations under construction in the North Atlantic, Western Europe, Turkey, and North Africa. Long and Morse described "waste and extravagance" in the construction and equipping of the installations and reported that the bases were both too numerous and too widespread. In their final report, the senators suggested that *mobility* of forces might provide a better deterrent against "the threat of Communist aggression at remote points [rather] than an attempt to station and maintain enough American boys at sparsely settled outposts to defeat a major enemy assault upon such points." Long told his Senate colleagues that, although the American people "want to be prepared . . . want us to be strong," they will not—and should not—"support waste and extravagance in the name of preparedness. They want their dollars to go into fighting strength, not into elaborate trappings and trimmings. They want their drafted sons usefully occupied, not sitting idly in some Arctic wasteland or sand desert."[17]

The Long-Morse official report came out on the heels of Eisenhower's first inauguration. The new president entered the

Oval Office having pledged to both reduce the federal budget and "roll back" communism. The commitment to roll back proved illusory, however, and the new administration's Cold War strategy turned out to be a variant of Truman's containment. Rather than placing conventional combat forces on the ground in potential hot spots, as the Truman administration had done, the Eisenhower administration proposed a "New Look." Under the New Look most U.S. defense dollars went toward the Air Force's Strategic Air Command, which could deliver nuclear weapons over long distances and which, because of U.S. superiority in delivery systems, would guarantee deterrence of communist expansion. Long's stance on creating a more mobile strategy of response to potential communist expansion, and his belief in making military containment more cost efficient, might have made the New Look agreeable to him. Surprisingly, though, his support for military containment under the Eisenhower administration waned as the 1950s wore on.[18]

Long's misgivings became apparent in January 1955, when a joint meeting of the Senate committees on Armed Services and Foreign Relations proposed granting Eisenhower permission to use U.S. forces if necessary to defend Taiwan and related territories. The joint meeting had been called following actions on two tiny Taiwan Strait islands, Quemoy and Matsu, at the center of increasing friction between the Taiwan-based Republic of China, the United States, and the mainland communist People's Republic of China. Since September of the preceding year, the People's Republic had been shelling the islands in what American observers suspected was an initial probing of the limits of containment, if not a prelude to an all-out assault on Taiwan. President Eisenhower had asked Congress for a resolution authorizing him to use American forces, if necessary, in defense of Taiwan.[19]

Senator Long had reservations about the so-called Formosa Resolution. What alarmed him most was that it provided a blank check for the commander in chief to make preemptive strikes against China, and he worried that a vote in favor of the resolution might be misinterpreted as granting the president the opportunity "to attack the Chinese mainland prior to the time that our opponent could launch any amphibious invasion." It "could serve as justification for heavy bombardment of Red Chinese ports." Such uncertainties, however, could not dissuade Long from ultimately voting in favor of the resolution. "This resolution," he stated, "serves notice upon Communist China that she has taken all of the territory by force of arms which she will be permitted to take." Containing communism, in this instance, trumped Long's worries about expanding the president's war-making powers.[20]

The Brown Decision and the Emergence of Civil Rights as a National Issue

If Long was concerned that President Eisenhower might overstep the bounds of his authority, he was absolutely convinced that the Supreme Court was doing the same thing by the mid-1950s. During debates on the tidelands dispute, Long intimated that the Court of his day had lost all respect for the time-honored principle of precedent. The Court's decision in *Brown v. Board of Education of Topeka, Kansas* (1954), which declared segregated public educational institutions unconstitutional, only confirmed and reinforced his contention.[21]

The day after the Court announced its *Brown* decision, Long declared that the Court had become politicized and had given up any pretense of abiding by the rules of precedent. He reminded his Senate colleagues that "some of us argued in view of the language of the tidelands cases, anyone who was relying upon . . . earlier decisions was leaning upon a broken reed." The *Brown* decision "demonstrates what many of us have felt, namely, that the Court today feels that prior decisions . . . were unwise, and perhaps do not conform to what the Court today thinks is sound public policy." Previous decisions, whether in regard to ownership of offshore oil deposits or segregation, "have been entirely correct and completely in pursuance of the legislative intention both of those who wrote the Constitution and its amendments and those who have enacted laws of the Congress." Yet the contemporary Court, according to Long, simply disregarded its own precedents. In short, the Louisiana senator, like most of his southern colleagues, held to a staunchly strict constructionist approach in this instance: the Constitution may be amended, new laws may be created, and the Court may rule on those laws, but the meanings and intentions of those amendments, laws, and rulings do not change.[22]

Long was not alone in his critical assessment. Southern senators and congressmen—and their local and state counterparts—lambasted the *Brown* ruling and sought means to effectively ignore it. By early 1955, Louisiana's legislature had passed a constitutional amendment granting the state the right to use its police force to maintain segregation as a matter of public health, morality, peace, and order; the state's disproportionately white voting population approved the amendment by 5 to 1. The legislature had also passed a law granting school superintendents the power to assign students to schools on an individual basis; thus, local school administrators could technically segregate students without its being mandated by law.[23]

While the legislature and voters of Louisiana dug in their heels, Long went to work on what he considered the source of the problem: the Supreme Court justices themselves. Long argued that the *Brown* decision, and the Court's 1955 *Brown II* enforcement ruling, undermined not only segregated southern society but also public faith in the Court. He therefore introduced, on May 9, 1956, a joint resolution calling for term limits of twelve years for Supreme Court justices. At the same time, he introduced a bill that would have required all Court justices to possess at least six years of on-the-bench experience—a deliberate swipe at Chief Justice Earl Warren, who had been confirmed to the Court with no prior judicial experience. Upon submitting the resolution and bill, Long reiterated his strict constructionism;

he was "not one of those who believe that the clear intention of the Constitution or the meaning of the laws passed by Congress change with the times." Constitutional philosophy aside, Long well knew that term limits and prior experience qualifications might be used to place onto the Court justices who were more amenable to the segregated "southern way of life."[24]

At the same time, Long also predicted that southern whites would challenge the Court's decision both in the streets and the statehouses. "These minority groups would do well to remember," he stated, "that the rights which they enjoy in this Nation could be endangered if the majority of the people should turn against them." Long might not have realized the irony of such a statement. In his unswerving defense of the cloture rule, he had always portrayed himself as defending the minority from the trampling might of the majority. But here the tables were turned. In reality, Long's defense of minority rights only went so far as minority *states'* rights. Minority *individual* rights were another matter. Long could defend southern states from what he perceived as northern or western or federal encroachments, but defending minority populations within those southern states fell outside the purview of his practical political convictions. Allusions to the rise of what would later be called massive resistance were common among Long and his southern counterparts, and their public statements about majority backlashes against minority populations most likely encouraged those contemplating just such actions.[25]

If the *Brown* decision engendered backlash among southern whites, it emboldened many blacks to quicken the pace of their challenges to segregation's status quo. On December 1, 1955, Rosa Parks, a politically active black seamstress, refused to yield her seat on a Montgomery, Alabama, bus to a white man. Parks was arrested and spent the night in jail; her plight sparked the Montgomery Bus Boycott, which lasted until December 21, 1956. Directed by the Montgomery Improvement Association (MIA) and its charismatic young leader, the Reverend Martin Luther

King Jr., the bus boycott engendered such white opposition, including the bombing of King's home in early 1956, that the MIA sought legal recourse. In November 1956, the U.S. Supreme Court ruled bus segregation in Montgomery unconstitutional.[26]

The Montgomery Bus Boycott set the pattern for southern civil rights activity over the next half decade: local black protests directed at local discrimination typically led to a white backlash that created national publicity and ultimately forced national policy changes. The boycott also set the trajectory for King's career as a leader of the black freedom struggle. He would come to personify the civil rights movement for many Americans, and his strategy of nonviolent civil disobedience, which evolved over the few years following the bus boycott, granted his followers significant media attention while maintaining the upper moral hand, at least in the eyes of many outsiders. Russell Long and most of his southern Senate colleagues saw King and his strategy differently, however.

At the time, Long practically ignored the Montgomery Bus Boycott, just as he had disregarded a bus boycott two years earlier in Baton Rouge. Later in his career, however, he would trace the riots that plagued American cities during the summers of the mid-1960s back to King's notion of civil disobedience. Civil disobedience, in King's formulation, entailed willfully breaking immoral laws. King married civil disobedience with nonviolence, which granted his philosophy a moral authority that was only enhanced when local or state police forces used violence to enforce the laws. For Russell Long, however, the ends of King's means were the "senseless riots which have seriously scarred scores of our already ailing urban communities." Though speaking in the late 1960s, Long argued that the urban unrest could be traced back to the "morally corroding 'civil disobedience' demonstrations of a few years ago." To Long, white backlash did not create the violence and rioting. Rather, King himself deserved the blame. While locked up in the Birmingham jail King, in Long's formulation, "wrote an inflammatory letter which gained wide recognition in its pleas for Negroes to disobey laws they felt to be unjust. Many negroes reacted to this dubious leadership by setting a string of racial demonstrations throughout the United States."[27]

The *Brown* decision and direct action campaigns like the Montgomery Bus Boycott stimulated massive resistance in the South. White southerners expressed their opposition to both *Brown* and to black assertiveness through various means. Politically, they endorsed the theory that state governments could interpose themselves between the federal and the local. Legally, they sought litigation to stop desegregation from occurring. Socially, they increasingly turned to intimidation and, at times, outright violence.

Southern politicians in Washington, in a show of support, approval, and encouragement for massive resistance, affixed their signatures in March 1956 to the Declaration of Constitutional Principles. More commonly known as the Southern Manifesto, the document, signed by Russell Long and all other southern senators but three, vowed to support interposition and massive resistance against the "unwarranted decision" of the Supreme Court in *Brown*. The Manifesto further stated that the Court, "with no legal basis for such action, undertook to exercise their naked judicial power and substituted their personal political and social ideas for the established law of the land." The signatories pledged "to use all lawful means to bring about a reversal of this decision . . . and to prevent the use of force in its implementation."[28]

The year Russell Long signed the Southern Manifesto was an election year. As he had four years before, Long campaigned for Democratic presidential nominee Adlai Stevenson in Louisiana. But this time Long's own reelection, and campaigning for his Uncle Earl, with whom he had patched up his differences, took time away from his presidential stumping. Stevenson lost the state to Eisenhower, but the Longs emerged triumphant. Uncle Earl trounced Chep Morrison with a first-round primary victory, and Senator Long faced little opposition and returned to Washington for his second full term.[29]

The Civil Rights Act of 1957

On a national level, the Republicans, in particular those within the Eisenhower administration, noticed a slight shift in voting patterns. As they analyzed the 1956 election results, GOP leaders found that blacks voting for Republicans had increased dramatically, following twenty years of black support for Democrats. Republicans hoped to capitalize on that increase by solidifying their position as the party of Lincoln and civil rights. But they were not alone. On Capitol Hill, Democratic majority leader Lyndon Johnson understood that making a stand on civil rights could garner national attention, ingratiate himself to liberals outside of the South, and prime the pump for his own presidential bid in 1960. Johnson expected that he could steal black votes outside of the South from the Republicans if he could beat them to the punch and negotiate a civil rights bill, but he had to figure out a way to please both sides of the contest: a bill too strong would repulse racially conservative southern senators; a bill too weak would alienate their more liberal Democratic party mates.[30]

The administration beat Johnson to the legislative punch. Under the direction of Attorney General Herbert Brownell, the Department of the Judiciary crafted a civil rights bill consisting of four titles. Title I created an independent Civil Rights Commission charged with investigating problems of race relations in general and voting rights in particular. Title II created a Civil Rights Division within the Justice Department. Title III, which would become the most controversial portion of the bill, gave to the attorney general's office the power to bring injunctions for general civil rights violations. This third title was particularly obnoxious to southern senators because, if taken to the extreme, it potentially allowed the federal government to use the U.S. military to enforce civil rights laws. Title III also reiterated and bolstered the *Brown* decision by making segregation of schools and other public places illegal. Finally, Title IV gave the attorney general's office the authority to bring injunctions when voting rights complaints were filed.[31]

Introduced into the Senate as S. 83 and into the House as H.R. 6127, the Eisenhower administration's civil rights bill faced numerous obstacles. In the Senate, the bill became bottled up in the Judiciary Committee, where the notoriously racist chairman James Eastland of Mississippi used delaying tactics to keep it from reaching the floor for debate. Thus sequestered, the Senate bill eventually died. The House Judiciary Committee, chaired by New York's Emmanuel Cellar, approved the Eisenhower bill and sent it to the floor, where the full House approved the bill on June 18, 1957. The bill then moved to the Senate, where, civil rights proponents used Senate Rule XIV, which allows bills to be sent straight to the Senate floor for deliberation, to place it directly on the calendar for consideration. Thus, while the original Senate bill languished in Eastland's grips, the House-approved bill bypassed the Judiciary Committee graveyard. The full Senate voted to begin deliberations on July 16, 1957.[32]

Along with almost all of his southern colleagues, Russell Long found the Eisenhower administration's 1957 civil rights bill politically impractical, if not personally unpalatable, and the arguments he formulated against it would set the pattern for his opposition to such legislation for more than a decade into the future. Long felt the authority granted to the attorney general and the Justice Department in Titles III and IV were particularly inflammatory. These powers, he and his southern brethren argued, allowed the attorney general to use in civil cases methods usually reserved for criminal ones. The use of federal injunction, too, could lead to jail sentences without trials for individuals accused of denying civil rights to others. Long and the other southerners ultimately argued that Title III allowed for the use of federal force to integrate southern educational institutions and for the circumvention of jury trials. Southern members of the House of Representatives had tried to implement a provision granting trial by jury in place of the attorney general's injunction powers, but these attempts had failed, and the bill under Senate deliberation contained no such provisions. The senators from Dixie states considered filibustering, but Lyndon Johnson convinced them—early on, at least—that the legislation's supporters might actually have enough votes to invoke cloture. If that happened, the bill could be passed in substantially the same form as it had been introduced.[33]

Johnson needed insurance, however. He knew that if the House bill had any chance of passing in the Senate, he would have to devise multiple ways of keeping southerners from filibustering. The threat of cloture was one, but another possibility was to weaken the bill by dropping Title III completely and adding a jury trial amendment to Title IV. Title III's injunctive powers and so-called forced integration provisions had elicited the most indignation among the southern bloc, and removing them would clear a major hurdle for the bill. However, granting jury trials for those accused of impeding a person's voting rights virtually guaranteed acquittals in a South, where jury pools, determined by voting rosters, almost uniformly excluded blacks. All-white jury pools meant sympathetic jurors, and sympathetic jurors meant acquittals. The jury trial amendment would almost completely undermine Title IV. With these changes made, Johnson hoped that his southern colleagues would not filibuster. If he played his cards right, Johnson could get the bill passed.[34]

On July 16, 1957, the first day of full Senate consideration, New Mexico Democrat Clinton Anderson and Vermont Republican George Aiken cosponsored an amendment to completely delete Title III. Both Anderson and Aiken generally supported civil rights, and both hoped that by removing what southerners considered the most egregious portion of the legislation, they could obtain passage of the bill in some form. At the same time, southern senators took to the floor with the purpose of showing exactly how Title III would not only increase federal interventionism but also would allow outsiders to punish the South for its socially, economically, and politically stratified racial order. They hoped, as a first step in the battle against the overall legislation, to persuade enough of their nonsouthern colleagues to vote to approve the Anderson-Aiken amendment.[35]

Russell Long weighed in on July 22. Not content to train his sights exclusively on Title III, he claimed that both it and Title IV were simply unnecessary. The rights they proposed to protect fell not under the federal government's purview but rather were "rights created under State laws." Further, should Title III be passed, and should its powers be used to force integration, "whether troops are used or not used, whether Federal marshals are used or are not used, there will be great difficulty in obtaining that objective." Long cautioned that "that type of thing was attempted previously by force in the South, and it was unsuccessful even when minority groups were in the seats of government in those States, and Federal troops were there to support such minority rule." What failed once was bound to fail again, Long warned.[36]

As for Title IV's enfranchisement provisions, Long contended "the truth is that the colored citizen is obtaining his voting rights without the bill." For proof, he pointed to his home state of Louisiana, where blacks had been voting in increasing numbers since the end of World War II, and where, as Long was quick to point out, these increases had occurred without the federal government's involvement. Long had a strong case. His father, Huey, had outlawed Louisiana's poll tax in 1934. Following the Supreme Court's 1944 *Smith v. Allright* decision, blacks could no longer be excluded from participating in the Democratic primaries that determined southern office holding. And blacks across the South after World War II were becoming more willing, and more able, to challenge literacy qualifications in order to register to vote. The South, and Louisiana in particular, seemed to be changing. "At the present time," he noted, "about 15 percent of the electorate of [Louisiana] is composed of colored voters.

The colored population is only about 30 percent of the entire population of the State." So it seemed that "more than half of the job of enfranchising the colored in the State of Louisiana has already been accomplished." How would federal intervention do any better?[37]

A month later, on July 24, Long joined his southern colleagues—and their conservative northern and western allies—in voting to approve the Anderson-Aiken amendment, 52 to 38. Those northerners and westerners who voted for the Anderson-Aiken amendment did so with the understanding that they should expect just enough southern opposition to the rest of the legislation to placate voters below the Mason-Dixon Line but not a full-fledged filibuster. For their part, the southerners recognized that their colleagues agreed to significantly weaken the legislation in exchange for votes in support of federal control of power projects being developed in Hells' Canyon of the Snake River Valley, a western project that the southerners had long opposed for a variety of reasons. Thus, Title III was dropped from the civil rights bill.[38]

The southerners next turned their attention to weakening Title IV's enfranchisement provisions. Although blacks were voting in increasing numbers in the South, as Long had noted in his July 22 speech, he and his cohort well understood that their own reelection hopes lay in the hands of whites who wished to maintain the South's political, social, and racial status quo. For practical political considerations, therefore, the southerners could not accept a challenge to white voters' supremacy lying down. Long and his southern compatriots realized that their opposition to desegregation could be defended much more easily than opposition to voting rights. They could portray segregation as a venerable social tradition, a divinely ordained state of affairs, or a natural proclivity among both races. Conversely, disfranchisement—the taking away of the right to vote—seemed to fly in the face of American constitutional principles.

To challenge Title IV of the civil rights bill of 1957, the southern bloc hoped to attach a jury trial provision to the bill. The right to trial by jury was a defining principle of the American legal system, respected just as much, if not more, than the right to vote by most Americans. But jury trials had a near-fatal weakness when it came to protecting African-American civil rights in the mid-twentieth-century South: juries were almost exclusively white, and they almost exclusively found in favor of whites. Southern whites were not likely to convict fellow southern whites who disfranchised southern blacks. Civil rights advocates understood this, and they viewed those sorts of trials as rigged apparatuses for getting around the Fifteenth Amendment's stipulation that "the right of citizens of the United States to vote shall not be denied or abridged by the United States or by any State on account of race, color, or previous condition of servitude." For voting rights advocates, the answer to the dilemma came in the form of federal injunctive powers: the possibility of punishment without resort to jury trial would be more threatening and, therefore, more effective as a deterrent.[39]

The Eisenhower administration had included Title IV's injunctive powers section partially in response to occurrences in Long's Louisiana. Despite the fact that the number of blacks on voting rolls there had swelled since the mid-1940s—or perhaps reflecting that trend—recent events in the Bayou State pointed to a white backlash. In the far northern parishes of the state, White Citizens' Councils systematically challenged black voting rights. Beginning in March 1956, the Ouachita Parish Citizens' Council, with the cooperation of the parish registrar of voters, had successfully challenged and removed more than three thousand black names from the voting rosters. The purges had been orchestrated by Anti-Longite state representative Willie Rainach, an aggressive and unrepentant white supremacist from Claiborne Parish, as a means not only of reasserting white dominance of the franchise but also of taking votes away from the Long machine's base. Almost all blacks in Louisiana voted for Earl Long or his candidates, and Rainach and Earl despised one another. The voter purges in Ouachita and other northern Louisiana parishes attracted the attention of the Federal Bureau of Investigation and resulted in the empanelling of a federal grand jury in Monroe, Ouachita Parish's seat. While the FBI half-heartedly investigated, and while the grand jury failed to return indictments, the Eisenhower administration used the voter purges to justify federal legislation.[40]

The Louisiana situation placed Long on the defensive in debate over Title IV. While other southern senators could simply argue that the proposed injunctive powers denied the constitutional right to a trial by jury, Long had to do so while simultaneously responding to the fact that voter purges had occurred in his home state. On July 25, he admitted to the Senate that challenges had taken place—and that black voters had been removed from the voting rolls—but he maintained that the deletions had been legal because "the person who was challenging the qualifications of another voter was challenging them entirely in accord with the laws of the State." Regarding the Ouachita Parish purges specifically, Long equivocated and said that "I personally disapprove of the incidents in which certain persons were challenged as voters [there] who should not have been challenged." Some of the purges had been mistaken, but "that is the only case, to my knowledge, in which persons had been challenged when there was no basis for challenging them as voters."[41]

It was just those sorts of mistaken or unfair purges that civil rights proponents hoped to eliminate with Title IV's injunctive powers provisions. But an impasse loomed if southerners would not budge from their jury trial stance. In an effort to produce a compromise, Wyoming's Joseph O'Mahoney and Tennessee's Estes Kefauver, both Democrats, offered an amendment to Title IV granting jury trial rights for criminal contempt proceedings, and their party mate, Idaho's Frank Church, then offered to their amendment an addendum that granted all voting-age U.S. citizens the right to serve on federal juries. In essence, the O'Mahoney-Kefauver-Church amendment allowed for jury trials in place of some of Title IV's injunctive powers and offered a means of integrating federal juries in southern states. It made concessions to both sides of the argument: southern conservatives could say they voted for jury trials while civil rights supporters could say they kept injunctive powers for criminal contempt proceedings.[42]

Yet for Russell Long and many of his southern colleagues, the O'Mahoney-Kefauver-Church amendment did not go far enough. Long considered Title IV unacceptable without jury trial provisions for both criminal *and* civil contempt cases. If trial by jury is correct in one instance, he wondered, why not the other? Long stated that civil rights advocates did not care about the trials one way or the other, however. During an exchange with New York's Jacob Javits, one of the Senate's most liberal members on the issue of civil rights, Long remarked that "the Senator [Javits] is making his argument for eliminating trial by jury. . . . He believes that trial by jury might acquit, and because the Senator wants to be sure of conviction; therefore he argues for the elimination of trial by jury." Long did not explain that, according to the amendment under consideration, juries might be made more representative of their communities and how that might make their decisions more equitable.[43]

Long later remarked that the proponents of Title IV, even as amended by the O'Mahoney-Kefauver-Church offering, either misunderstood or disregarded American constitutional history. He found it "particularly significant" that "their purpose in denying trial by jury relates to the very reason which caused the authors of our Constitution to guarantee trial by jury three times." Title IV threatened to take determinations of guilt or innocence from a collection of the accused's peers and place them into the hands of a single individual—the attorney general. Even if this were applied only in civil contempt cases, Long thought that such a step should not be taken lightly, if it were taken at all. When pressed to take such a change seriously, Title IV's proponents still sought to deny the right to trial by jury because, he contended, "they fear that if a man were to be given those rights which the Constitution intended him to have, he would be acquitted." Civil rights proponents were using the ends to justify the means, according to Long.[44]

Ultimately, southern senators, despite their rhetoric about protecting the right to trial by jury, wanted to please the people who elected them, the vast majority of whom were white and did not want more blacks voting. And in the end, they understood that the removal of Title III had extracted the heart of the bill and made any substantive, wide-ranging changes to southern segregation nil. Long and his colleagues therefore calculated that a filibuster against the remainder of the bill would be unwarranted. When the O'Mahoney-Kefauver-Church amendment came to a vote on August 1, 1957, the Senate approved it, 51 to 42. A week later, on August 7, the Senate approved H.R. 6127, the Eisenhower administration's civil rights bill, minus Title III and with the amendments to Title IV.[45]

Despite the serious weakening of the bill through the amending process, Russell Long still felt politically compelled to vote against it. From the Senate, the bill returned to the House, where it was only slightly modified; notably, the House revised Title IV to include jury trials in contempt cases where potential punishments exceeded three hundred dollars in fines or forty-five days in jail. The changes were weak enough that southern senators again decided not to filibuster for fear of sparking a cloture ruling, which might have allowed Title III to be reinstituted. Just before the Senate vote on the final draft of the legislation, Russell Long stated "for the Record that so far as the junior Senator from Louisiana is concerned, I personally raised the issue of an organized filibuster by the southern Senators, recognizing that gag rule would undoubtedly be applied to us, and that the bill would pass under a cloture rule." On August 29, the Senate approved the revised House version of the bill by a vote of 60 to 15.[46]

Russell Long said that he voted against the bill because, even as revised, it still granted the attorney general and the courts the right of injunction in certain cases. Ironically—given his signing the Southern Manifesto, which produced much the same effect—Long justified his vote by saying the precedent would only lead to widespread disregard of court decisions. "Once the Attorney General and the courts of the Nation undertake to rule citizens by the contempt powers of the courts," he asked, "does it not stand to reason that over a period of time the people will have contempt for the courts?" The danger, he noted, was that "it will not be long until the courts will be able to place people in jail, for any crime, by contempt proceedings, and there will not be any respect left for the courts."[47]

But Long's true motivations resulted from an understanding that voting *for* civil rights legislation just might have meant career suicide. He therefore made certain that there could be no mistake about his stance on a bill that some had labeled compromise legislation. "I was no party to that compromise," he said from the floor of the Senate, and before the final vote, he reiterated that "during the past two-months my opposition to the so-called civil-rights bill has been made amply clear to the Senate and to the Nation."[48]

Aside from its place as the first step in a long stream of civil rights legislation that Congress would enact over the next decade, the Civil Rights Act of 1957, signed by President Eisenhower on September 9, did little to advance the civil rights cause. Toothless and weak without Title III and the injunction provisions of Title IV, it had very little effect upon the civil rights struggles then coalescing in the South. Even within the voting rights sphere, as covered by Title IV, the act prompted very little change. The 1957 legislation did, however, show proponents that the possibility existed for the passage of future civil rights legislation, and it granted the leaders of the Senate's southern bloc an opportunity to formulate their arguments against all such initiatives.

The Eisenhower Doctrine

Russell Long's position within the southern bloc, and his keen awareness of the practical political implications of the matter, placed him within the most conservative of contexts when it came to civil rights. His conservatism was by no means absolute, however, and his stances on foreign affairs bore that out, as by the late 1950s, the Eisenhower administration—and Long, from his Senate Foreign Relations Committee perch—began contemplating the spread of the Cold War's containment policy into the Middle East.

The spark for a more active American interventionism in that region came from Egypt. There, the government of President Gamal Abdel Nasser hoped to provide an agricultural and economic boom for his nation by building a gigantic dam at Aswan on the Nile River. The Eisenhower administration promised Nasser $56 million in loans to help with the construction costs; the British government made a smaller pledge as well. But when Nasser shopped around for better terms from the Soviet Union while at the same time establishing ties with other communist bloc nations, the United States revoked its offer. Nasser then nationalized the Suez Canal, intending to use toll receipts to offset the lost funds.

Nasser's actions caught Britain and France off guard; both relied on the canal as a vital supply route for raw materials. The canal seizure also unnerved Israel, which viewed the Egyptian move as a precursor to an outright invasion. In late October 1956, the Israeli army began moving troops toward the canal. Britain and France warned both Egypt and Israel to stay away, and—when neither side did—sent in paratroopers to guarantee that the waterway remained open. The situation threatened to erupt into a superpower confrontation when the Soviet Union offered to send military help to Nasser, and the Eisenhower administration countered that the United States would use force to stop any Soviet intervention. With the situation rapidly escalating, the United Nations stepped in to broker a compromise, whereby Egypt retained its ownership of the canal and was granted the right to administer it.[49]

In reaction to the Suez Crisis, President Eisenhower proclaimed in January 1957 that the United States would come to the aid of any Middle Eastern nation under attack by the Soviet Union, and he asked for a congressional resolution affirming the statement. The resolution, as presented to Russell Long and his colleagues in the Senate, granted the President "authority to cooperate with and assist any nation or group of nations in the general area of the Middle East in the development of economic strength dedicated to the maintenance of national independence." It further gave to the president authority to undertake "military assistance programs with any nation or group of nations of that area desiring such aid." Most significantly, the resolution provided the president with the authority "to employ the Armed Forces of the United States as he deems necessary to secure and protect the territorial integrity and political independence of any such nation or group of nations desiring such aid against overt armed aggression from any nation controlled by international communism." Later termed the Eisenhower Doctrine, the proposed resolution formally extended the Truman Doctrine's containment policies to the Middle East.[50]

Long's seat on the Foreign Relations Committee provided him an outlet for some of his sharpest criticism of the Eisenhower administration during the hearings on the Eisenhower Doctrine. Although he had voiced some doubts about the Formosa Resolution, Long had supported Eisenhower's earlier Cold War declaration. The 1957 resolution, however, found Long in a different political position. Eisenhower's fiscal policies aggravated Long, as did the administration-sponsored legislation that would become the Civil Rights Act of 1957. Furthermore, President Eisenhower had not pressed for the stronger social welfare programs that Long repeatedly endorsed. Too, Long had become embroiled in the factional party politics that intensified during Eisenhower's second administration, and his criticism of the president became outspoken and frequent.[51]

Although many of Long's southern colleagues supported passage of the Eisenhower Doctrine, key Democratic members of both the Senate Foreign Relations and the Armed Services committees balked. Arkansas's J. William Fulbright called the administration's resolution "a blanket transfer to the Executive of the Constitutional right vested in Congress to declare war." Wyoming's Joseph C. O'Mahoney contended that President Eisenhower himself did not understand the full implications of his resolution, and Oregon's Wayne Morse argued that approving the resolution would lead to an American police state.[52]

On the floor of the Senate, Long stated that the Eisenhower administration had shrouded its proposal in secrecy and vague terminology because it sought to undermine the Senate's constitutional responsibility to offer advice and consent to the president in matters of foreign relations. "When we ourselves," he argued, "walk into the legislative boobytrap of granting the right to the President to declare war not even knowing against what nation we are going to war, and then to let the President take the wealth of America and distribute it across the globe, not knowing for what projects or purposes the money will be used . . . we are doing something which is very foolish." The military and economic powers asked for in the administration's resolution were so mighty and so potentially dangerous that Congress could not simply defer to the president's will. Like Fulbright, Long believed that the resolution also jeopardized the Senate's authority by undermining its own constitutional obligations. If the resolution passed, he added, "it seems to me we ought to pass a resolution to forego our salaries. What are the people paying us for?" If the Senate gives up its power to declare war, it should then "surrender the power of the purse strings, surrender the power of appropriations, surrender our right to know what the administration proposes to do. If we pass one or two more resolutions like this, it seems to me that we should just retire on our pensions and be done with it." On March 5, 1957, Long joined nineteen other senators, including nearly half of his fellow southern Democrats, in voting "nay" on the Eisenhower Doctrine, but their votes were not enough to stop it from passing. The doctrine became a mainstay of American diplomacy through the remainder of Long's Senate tenure.[53]

Earl Long's Breakdown

While he tilted with the Eisenhower administration and Senate colleagues over foreign policy and civil rights, Long kept a close eye on the political situation in Louisiana. There, Earl Long's third tenure as governor was remarkably similar to his previous ones: he attempted to undo the reforms of his Anti-Longite predecessor, Robert Kennon, while simultaneously promoting traditional Longite welfare-state policies. Over the course of Earl's final governorship, Louisiana's state spending increased from $471 million to $566 million yearly; most of the new expenditures went toward programs that placed Louisiana at the forefront of social spending among southern states. By 1960, old-age pensions had increased by roughly 30 percent and teacher pay by 28 percent. All of the new expenditures were paid for by the continued growth of Louisiana's oil and gas industry and the subsequent increases in funds brought to the state by severance taxation.[54]

The ways Earl's third term as governor resembled his previous ones were overshadowed, however, by the reemergence of racial politics in the Bayou State. Although anxieties about race relations had simmered just below the political surface—and had occasionally bubbled dangerously near the rim—since at least the 1890s, and although states rightists had been influential in Louisiana since the Dixiecrat rebellion of 1948, the politics of race had not boiled over until the *Brown* decision. Following the Supreme Court's ruling, White Citizens' Councils sprouted in communities around the state, and the Louisiana legislature created a Joint Committee on Segregation, chaired by Senator

Willie Rainach, to devise ways to derail implementation of the Court's decision.[55]

The approval and encouragement of politicians like Rainach had inspired the voter purges in Louisiana, the implications of which Russell Long had to deal with during debates on federal civil rights legislation. The problem of the voter purges was much more serious for Uncle Earl, however, as they posed a threat to his own political power. His electoral success, and that of his Longite supporters, depended to varying degrees on the votes of black Louisianians. The purges undermined their chances. In May 1959, therefore, Governor Long introduced into the state legislature two bills designed to halt the purges. He had a twofold motive: to counteract the political effects of the purges and to thwart Senator Rainach, a longtime bitter rival. When the bills failed to make headway in the statehouse, the governor took it upon himself to simply force the bills through.[56]

On May 26, 1959, Governor Long appeared before a joint session of the state legislature, ostensibly to apologize for an outburst before the House Judiciary Committee while defending his voting rights bills. Although his aides had prepared a speech for the governor, he quickly tossed it aside and launched into an impromptu tirade. Nursing a whiskey-filled juice bottle, Governor Long bitterly and personally attacked his political opponents. He cursed, screamed, shouted; the speech degenerated into an illogical ramble. The harangue lasted almost an hour and a half before friends escorted the governor, by this time on the verge of collapse, out of the chamber.[57]

Thus began what journalist A. J. Liebling termed "the second chapter of Long-family martyrdom: following the assassination of Huey, the crucifixion of Earl." Television cameras had recorded the governor's outburst, and newspaper and radio reporters quickly filed reports. Uncle Earl, meanwhile, was whisked away to the Governor's Mansion. With the angry, agitated, and increasingly irrational governor confined to a bedroom, his closest family, friends, and political allies decided upon a course of action.[58]

Russell Long was already in Louisiana when his uncle had his breakdown. The senator had returned from Washington, D.C., to deliver a commencement address at Loyola University in New Orleans. Using notes hastily scribbled onto the back of the commencement program, he addressed his Uncle Earl's behavior during the speech. The words he wrote placed the blame on Earl's being overworked while at the same time being investigated by a Washington nemesis, the Eisenhower administration, which had "put their F.B.I. and teams of Income agents to work on him." Earl had asked Russell to keep the investigators "off of his back at least until this session was over. Their answer was to bear down all the harder. They won. They broke the man. It breaks my heart to see it happen." Expressing heartfelt thoughts of a sort he rarely allowed himself to voice in public, Long lamented that "that governor's job is enough to kill a man in one term much less three of them. The man just broke under the constant strain. Anyone who thinks the man was weak should try to take as much pressure as the man went through." Russell Long, who had contemplated his own runs for governor and had witnessed his father's tempestuous two-year governorship firsthand, probably understood such pressures more than anyone at the graduation ceremony.[59]

As he had after hearing the news of his father's shooting some twenty-four years earlier, Senator Long then sped up Airline Highway to Baton Rouge. At the Governor's Mansion, he met a throng of family members, doctors, and political allies. That night Earl's wife, Blanche, along with Russell and Dr. Arthur Long (a cousin to Earl), decided to commit the governor to a psychiatric institution. After ruling out several possibilities, Dr. Robert Bernhard, who had traveled with Russell Long from New Orleans, determined that the Titus Harris Clinic of Galveston, Texas, was the best place for Earl to receive treatment. The decision made, the family turned to the even more daunting task of telling the governor.[60]

The next day, Russell, Blanche, and other family members cautiously explained their decision to Earl. The governor, unreceptive to the family's assurances that they acted for his own good, raged against them. Russell in particular bore the brunt of his uncle's abusive wrath: the governor accused his nephew of using a medical emergency for political gain. Russell was, according to Earl, a contemptuous turncoat, seeking control of Louisiana and the Long machine while his political mentor desperately needed medical, not psychiatric, attention. Earl's behavior, which had already been violent, became only more threatening after he learned of his impending hospitalization. "We put him to bed," Senator Long later wrote, "and informed him that he must stay there and rest . . . or that we would be forced to take whatever measures were necessary to save his health even if he refused to agree to it." Earl "was outraged that we dared attempt such a thing."[61]

Long made the arrangements for moving his uncle from Baton Rouge to Galveston. During the flight to Galveston, and even earlier while confined at the Governor's Mansion, Earl Long repeatedly accused his wife and nephew, among others, of conspiring to kidnap him. Earl's contentions concerned Russell Long enough that he contacted the Federal Bureau of Investigation to confirm the legality of the family's actions.[62]

In an effort to quell any rumors and in the interest of keeping the state's political leaders informed, on Sunday, May 31, 1959, Senator Long ventured to the capitol building that his father had built and delivered a speech justifying the family's decisions. The speech brought to the minds of many observers memories of Huey and Earl orchestrating the legislature's actions for their own political ends. Almost as soon as Russell began speaking, opposition erupted: the senator had not been invited to address the legislature, and certain members of that body felt it an affront for him to appear under such circumstances. In the face of such opposition, Russell three times started to storm out of the chamber, only to have his anger soothed by friends and allies.[63]

When he finally began, Long laid out the reasoning behind the family's decisions. "The duties and burdens of this great office have been more than he could stand," he said of his uncle. Deciding to send him to Galveston had been difficult, but "if he was to be spared the duties of his office while he received the necessary rest and treatment, it was necessary for him to leave the state." The senator then cautiously, yet forthrightly, assessed the Louisiana political situation. "State legislation is not a part of my responsibility. It is yours," he told the legislature. "However, I am a citizen of this great and wonderful state and I believe I am entitled to say to you what I believe most citizens are thinking at this moment. This state is in a serious and political governmental crisis." But he saw hope, if only "you lay aside political expediency and refuse to follow those who will not do the same thing." He added, "So long as you exercise your responsibility wisely, and I know that this group of men will, I believe I speak for most of our citizens when I say that we have nothing to fear and good results to anticipate."[64]

Long had probably expected the none-too-favorable reception that greeted him, and he ended his speech with an assurance that he would not use the situation for his own political benefit. "As soon as I have reasonable assurance" that Governor Long is receiving the best possible treatment, he concluded, "I am returning to Washington. Meanwhile, I do not propose to step beyond the responsibilities of my office in matters affecting government." The *appearance* of overstepping political boundaries, however, had been made already.

The next month, Long traveled to Galveston to attend Uncle Earl's habeas corpus hearing. In the courtroom, Earl passed his nephew a note: "Russell, I will be in [New Orleans's] Ochsner Clinic no later than Wednesday. [signed] Earl K. Long." The message was more prophetic than Russell might have thought. The very next day, Earl's wife revoked his committal with the understanding that he would voluntarily enter Ochsner's in exchange for a signed statement that he would not hold liable any persons involved in his confinement. That afternoon, he arrived in New Orleans.[65]

Governor Long stayed at Ochsner's Clinic only a few hours. Breaking his word to his wife, he then rushed back to Baton Rouge, where he planned to seize the reins of government. Instead, he was met with an impromptu sanity hearing, hastily arranged by Blanche Long and East Baton Rouge Parish coroner Dr. Chester Williams and held in the Baton Rouge courthouse's parking garage. After a forty-five minute examination, Dr. Williams and Dr. Sparkman Wyatt, a local psychiatrist, urged that the governor be committed, yet again, to a mental institution. Anti-Longite judge Fred Leblanc signed the necessary court orders, and the governor of Louisiana was taken to the Southeast Louisiana Hospital in Mandeville for treatment.[66]

By this point, Russell Long had tired of his uncle's escapades and, more especially, of his Aunt Blanche's wavering over her husband's hospitalization. Russell decided that there was simply nothing more for him to do. The senator issued a statement to the press in which he said that "I have done my duty as I saw it for the welfare and in the interest of the governor, his family, and the State of Louisiana. This matter was taken completely out of my hands, and it is now in the hands of the courts and the legal authorities, who will undoubtedly discharge their responsibilities as they feel their duties require." He had given up on resolving the dilemma and decided that "it is neither my right nor my responsibility to do anything more about this situation." Long later told supporters that he had not "'washed my hands' of my uncle's situation" and acknowledged that "I will respond immediately if I am called upon or if it looks like I can do something to help restore my uncle to health or help in any way as far as the State of Louisiana is concerned."[67]

Russell Long's activities in Louisiana in 1959 brought to the minds of some observers his father's memory. This time, however, the memories he brought forth were inadvertent. Certainly, Senator Long understood the political benefits of calling to mind his father and his father's politics, particularly within the state of Louisiana. But Huey's memory was a two-way street: He had been the most divisive politician in all of Louisiana history, and it was just as likely that people thought of him as a buffoon or a dictator rather than as a populist champion of the "little people."

Long's actions in the aftermath of Earl Long's breakdown—especially his appearance before the state legislature—conjured up the not-so-flattering imagery of his father. During the last years of his life, Huey had spent much of his time shuttling between Louisiana and Washington, D.C., leaving the nation's capital for the state's in order to direct the special sessions called by his puppet, O. K. Allen. Now, Huey's son had come to Louisiana from Washington, had been involved in removing his uncle from office, and had gone, uninvited, to speak to the legislature.

In the words of *New York Post* writer Stan Opotowsky, who covered the breakdown and later wrote a family biography of the Longs, "the Ghost of Huey rose up to haunt his son. In any other state Russell's appearance under the circumstances would be unusual but understandable, and no one would search for ulterior motives." But in Baton Rouge things were different: "this was Louisiana. In too many minds there still burned the memory of United States Senator Huey Long coming down from Washington to harangue the legislature from the podium." Particularly for the Anti-Longites, Russell's actions recalled a historical Huey that they wanted no part of and that they could not stomach. These suspicions that the son might have inherited some of his father's hunger for political domination of the state turned out to be unfounded. Based on the collective memories of Huey's former opponents, however, the fears were both very real and significant.[68]

Longites, and particularly those closely associated with Earl Long, generally saw nothing to fear from Russell's appearance before the legislature, although some considered it poor form.

They also wondered about the senator's ambitions: Was this an attempted coup, as Earl had implied? Or was Senator Long being honest when he said he was only trying to help? "Russell's petulance and his disagreeable manner in insisting that he be allowed to speak," wrote one onlooker, "together with the arbitrary manner in which he presented himself, combined to work to his political detriment. Long after Earl returned to Louisiana and reassumed his office, rank-and-file voters were denouncing Russell's poor showmanship and the part he played in Earl's confinement." The evening after Long's speech to the legislature, New Orleans television station WDSU, in an on-air editorial, seemed to affirm that judgment. "There were some elements of politics about the Senator's talk," the WDSU news anchor stated. "He may not have intended it this way, but he is the son of Huey Long and the nephew of Earl Long. And there were many persons in Baton Rouge last night who were looking for reassurance from Senator Long that he was available to provide leadership, if necessary, for the Long faction." Whether good or bad, those assumptions were in the political air. "These political overtones perhaps should not be blamed on the Senator himself," the TV editorial concluded. "It's simply a fact that it's impossible to separate Russell Long, as a member of the Long family, from Russell Long political leader."[69]

From his hospital room at Mandeville, Uncle Earl orchestrated a plan that would set him free. Less than an hour before a scheduled habeas corpus hearing on June 26, Earl's political allies on the Hospital Board voted to remove the board's director, Jesse Bankston, and to replace him with Charles Rosenblum, a close personal friend of the governor. Rosenblum then led the board in firing the superintendent of the Mandeville hospital and replacing him with Dr. Jess McClendon, another of Earl's old friends. McClendon immediately declared the governor completely sane and ordered his release. Upon hearing of McClendon's declaration, Judge Robert Jones dismissed the habeas corpus hearing as unnecessary.[70]

After a brief sojourn at his Pea Patch Farm outside of Winnfield and a few days of politicking around the state, Earl Long hit the road. On July 11, he flew to Fort Worth, Texas, the first leg of a western tour that would include stops in El Paso, Texas; Juarez, Mexico; Albuquerque and Taos, New Mexico; Denver, Colorado; Kansas City, Missouri; and Hot Springs, Arkansas. The vacation's hectic pace and unusual diversions left the governor reinvigorated and ready for new political battles back home in Louisiana. Earl was determined to win reelection to the governorship in the 1960 election, a nearly impossible thing for him to do as Louisiana's constitution directly stated that a sitting governor could not succeed himself. After toying with the idea of resigning his governorship before the end of his term, and thus not technically running for reelection, Earl chose to run as lieutenant governor on a Longite ticket with Jimmie Noe for governor. He expected that once the election was won, he would have the newly sworn-in governor resign, allowing Earl back into the governor's office. The Noe-Long ticket did not make the runoff, however, and Earl instead ran for a seat in the U.S. House of Representatives. He won the race but, before he could take office, died of a heart attack on September 5, 1960.[71]

For Russell Long, the events of May, June, and July 1959 left a lingering political distaste. He had indeed considered running for governor in the 1960 election, but the backlash against his appearance before the legislature, and the cantankerousness of Uncle Earl, pushed him away from state politics. Those factors, combined with a rapid ascent up Capitol Hill's power structure during the 1960s, led Long to focus more on national politics and to be less directly involved in Bayou State politicking. Outside of his own reelection campaigns in 1962, 1968, 1974, and 1980 and his campaigning for cousin Gillis Long's gubernatorial bid in 1964, Senator Long generally stayed out of Louisiana's internal political affairs until his retirement from public life in 1987.[72]

The Civil Rights Act of 1960

Removing himself from the realm of state-level politicking did not mean that Long could safely ignore political issues that dominated Louisiana. Some issues, such as racial politics and its constitutive parts, segregation and disfranchisement, transcended political boundaries.

The passage of new federal civil rights legislation became more likely in 1959. Early in the year, the Senate amended Rule XXII, the cloture rule, to state that cloture could be instituted by a vote of two-thirds of those present, as opposed to two-thirds off all senators. Thus, civil rights proponents would have an easier go of curtailing southerners' talk-it-to-death filibuster strategy. Then, in September, the federal Civil Rights Commission issued a report detailing what progress had been made and, more important, just how much remained to be done. Advances had been few. The Commission instead found that voting purges had increased and that efforts at enfranchising black voters had failed. The report concluded that the federal government had done little to promote change in the racial status quo, even with the legislation of 1957 in effect.[73]

Senator Long challenged the Commission's report—particularly its chapter titled "Louisiana Roadblock"—insisting that "it is obvious that its recommendations are not the result of factual analysis, but simply a rehash of preconceived ideas in race relations." Long joined other southern senators in a failed attempt to do away with the Civil Rights Commission altogether; it was instead granted a two-year extension by Congress.[74]

Congressional liberals, Senate majority leader Lyndon Johnson, and the Eisenhower administration all proposed civil rights legislation in 1959, but none of the bills passed before the end of the year. On February 15, 1960, Johnson introduced into the Senate a bill that focused mainly on guaranteeing voting rights. To keep the bill out of James Eastland's Judiciary Committee, Johnson had his measure attached to a bill leasing army property at

Fort Crowder, Missouri, to a local school district. On February 29, Johnson announced round-the-clock sessions to consider his amendment. Russell Long and seventeen other southern senators began a vigorous filibuster. Organized by Georgia's Richard Russell, the southerners worked as three teams in twenty-four-hour shifts: six of them spoke for four hours stretches each, then rested while their twelve compatriots spoke for the next two days. Long's senior colleague from Louisiana, Allen Ellender, coordinated one of the teams.[75]

Long and Ellender had good political reasons to oppose any civil rights legislation. Less than two months before, the dominance of race as a political factor in their state had been made clear when former governor Jimmie Davis defeated New Orleans Mayor Chep Morrison in a race for the governor's seat. Both candidates had pandered to such devout segregationists as Leander Perez and Willie Rainach, and even Morrison—who had always projected an image of moderation on race—made broad pronouncements about using the governor's office to preserve segregation at all costs. Davis, however, had used even more strident rhetoric and had won. With the Louisiana political ramifications evident, and with his own reelection campaign coming up two years down the line, Long's practical political proclivities superseded whatever personal or moral inhibitions he may have had about withholding voting rights from black Americans. He opposed the civil rights legislation of 1960 with just as much, if not more, vigor than he had earlier proposals.[76]

Long's antagonism toward the 1960 bill, however, reflected political expediency more than his personal attitudes. On more than one occasion, he had privately told Senate colleagues that he could not justify denying any American citizen's voting rights. According to Howard Shuman, who served as an administrative assistant to one of the Senate's civil rights champions, Illinois Democrat Paul Douglas, Long had even offered tactical advice in the late 1950s. "He advised Mr. Douglas that the critically important thing on voting rights was to send registrars into the South,"

Shuman recalled. "He told him that was the way it had to be done." The Louisiana senator knew that he could never go public with such sentiments, however, and he "said he would deny it if Douglas ever said he told him that." Shuman added that "in 1960, as a result of that Russell Long conversation, Mr. Douglas and Jacob Javits put forward the voting rights bill of 1960, which would have sent registrars into the south to register blacks in those states where fifty percent of them otherwise eligible were not allowed to vote." The Douglas-Javits bill ended up tabled in favor of Johnson's, but its proposals would be resurrected in the legislation that eventually became the landmark Voting Rights Act of 1965. It is one of the great ironies of his career that Russell Long publicly opposed both the Douglas-Javits bill and the 1965 Voting Rights Act.[77]

Long's 1960 speeches against what he called "A Bill to Crucify the South" focused on themes that had become, and would continue to be, well-worn justifications for opposing almost any form of civil rights legislation. To begin with, Long complained that Johnson's introduction of the legislation directly onto the Senate floor undermined proper Senate procedure. Bypassing the committee "leaves those of us who are opposed to civil rights legislation in an embarrassing position," he said, "because we do not know what we are likely to be called upon to vote on, or how the amendment will read when we do vote." Of course, Long and his colleagues knew only too well that had the legislation been presented to its proper committee—Judiciary—Chairman Eastland would have kept it bottled up indefinitely.[78]

Long argued that "passage of this civil rights legislation will nullify the orderly progress that has been made, in the same manner that reconstruction nullified the progress made between the end of the Civil War and the advent of the Reconstruction period." Like most white southerners, Long thought of Reconstruction as a blight on southern history that resulted in a prolonged retrogression in all facets of southern society—particularly in the area of race relations. Outsiders, he affirmed, had forced Reconstruction upon southerners; the civil rights legislation under consideration, promulgated and promoted from beyond the bounds of Dixie, would lead to the same result and would turn back the clock on race relations. "When the well-intended and understanding people of the South undertake to help the colored man to improve his conditions," Long contended, "they are constantly confronted with actions by extremists from the North, seeking to make the colored man feel bitter and resentful toward his neighbor, and, in turn, stirring violent counterreaction from the more prejudiced and unreasoning whites who for the most part do not represent the prevailing Southern leadership." Troublemakers from the North begat troublemakers in the South, Long concluded, and southern white incendiaries are given an excuse to "resort to all sorts of measures to discriminate against the colored man."[79]

Although Long was fond of saying that "if the people up North would quit sending down agitators to stir up trouble, there would not be this difficulty," his arguments went further than simply blaming northerners for igniting southern troubles. Like many of his southern colleagues, he berated northern senators who condemned the South while turning a blind eye to racial discrimination in their own backyards. In an exchange with Arkansan John McClellan, Long asked his colleague if he realized that "there are approximately 500,000 former citizens of Puerto Rico who are unable to vote in that great state [New York] because they speak Spanish rather than English?" The query was a direct prod at New York senators Jacob Javits and Kenneth Keating, two staunch civil rights proponents. Would it not make sense, Long asked, for "those who believe in letting down the bars to permit people to vote, and who believe in forcibly increasing registration rolls in Southern States, that they should first set their own house in order and give the Puerto Ricans the right to vote in New York State, in view of their feeling that universal suffrage might be the wave of the future"? The senators from New York appeared as nothing more than outright hypocrites in Long's formulation.[80]

The hypocrisy went to another level, however, when Long turned to Chicago, home to Senator Douglas. Long relished the fact that the Windy City had the highest percentage of de facto segregation in the nation. He argued, in fact, that de jure segregation, as practiced in the South, actually was fairer to blacks than was de facto segregation. "A colored man should be a better adjusted person, and should feel more kindly toward his neighbor," he maintained, "if it were explained to him, as folks do down South, 'Look, we think it is better that your children should go with their kind of folks, and our children should go with our kind of folks, and we will set the schools up just that way.'" Otherwise, black Americans faced the frustration of being told, "as they do up there in Chicago, 'Fellow, you can just go anywhere; there is not segregation,' then they find they cannot live in a white area, that is all. So his children go to school near their home, and they wind up in a segregated school." Long maintained that, aside from the fact that northerners "just do it by hypocrisy and fraud, whereas down South people do it openly and frankly," the differences between segregation in the South and segregation in the North simply did not exist.[81]

Long maintained as well that the 1960 legislation's voting rights provisions were simply unnecessary. After all, he noted, "The Civil Rights Act of 1957 is obviously sufficient to do the job that was sought by those who advocated its passage." Of course, he and his southern allies had disarmed that act's most effective weapons for enfranchisement. Long said he harbored suspicions about why such unnecessary new legislation might be called for: "the only possible benefit in having such laws would be the political benefit." Pro–civil rights legislators supported needless civil rights legislation in order to gain or maintain pro–civil rights constituencies.[82]

Even in the nation's capital, efforts at school integration had resulted in the unintended consequence of white flight. "In Washington, D.C., where integration has certainly been encouraged as far as it is possible to encourage it," he noted, "there has been a tendency in this liberal community, cosmopolitan as it is, for the white to move to Virginia or to settle out in Maryland, and to settle in neighborhoods of whites." Such moves result in "segregation by residential effect," and white parents were only too willing to undertake such an exodus "rather than have their children go to schools which have more than token integration."[83]

If anything, the reaction in Washington, D.C., reinforced Long's contention that "people much prefer to be among those of their own kind than with other races. . . . It shows that a robin will make its nest with a robin, and a redbird with a redbird." This notion that the races naturally separate from one another formed a lynchpin for Long's defense of de jure segregation: forcing desegregation by law only meant attempting the impossible. "Let us not deceive ourselves," he maintained. "We cannot change attitudes by law. If the civil rights advocates do not like the attitudes of the southern people, they should attempt to change the attitudes by persuasion and education." Furthermore, when it comes to segregation, Long said, "Some of us think that there is nothing evil about it. We think it is right. We think that is how the good Lord intended it to be."[84]

In the end, Long asserted that the bill at hand would not lead to any greater benefits for disfranchised southern citizens: southerners were already handling the matter themselves. He contended that registration *had* occurred in the South and "particularly in Louisiana—because we understood our situation very well before any voting rights bills were introduced to create Federal registrars or Federal voting referees." Increased registration in his home state "occurred because the white people of Louisiana were satisfied that the colored people could qualify and should be permitted to vote." Long's paternalistic turn of the phrase belied another of the pillars of his thought on race relations and racial politics: southern whites knew what would be best for southern blacks.[85]

Changing race relations and their political ramifications too quickly presented immediate and incendiary dangers, according to Long. If southern whites understood what was best for all races in their region, as he maintained, then as the federal government became more and more involved in southern race relations—whether through court decisions or legislation—the white backlash that already had developed would inevitably get worse. "If much of the so-called civil rights legislation were to be enacted," Long warned, "and if an attempt were to be made to enforce it in the South, where the majority of the citizens strongly believe in segregation, I believe there would be general disregard of the law and, to some extent, contempt for all other Federal laws along the same lines." Any sort of legislation that forced desegregation would only widen the separation of races and would "drive a wedge between the colored and the white man . . . a wedge of fear, hatred, and misunderstanding." In the end, these proposals to *expand* rights would only lead to "a loss of rights that already existed." The potential problems, should federal civil rights legislation pass, seemed, in Long's depiction, both insidious and insurmountable.[86]

Long and his southern colleagues—and their filibuster—encountered a new hurdle when, on March 24, 1960, the House of Representatives passed its own civil rights bill and sent it to the Senate for consideration. The House bill allowed judges to appoint referees to aid in voter registration, and it created new penalties for bombings, bomb threats, and mob actions. Majority Leader Johnson sent the House bill to the Judiciary Committee only after a Senate majority voted for a requirement that the committee report it back no later than March 29. With the five-day limit in place, Chairman Eastland could not keep the bill frozen in committee.[87]

The Judiciary Committee reported out a watered down and weak bill. During full Senate deliberations, however, civil rights proponents pushed to add amendments to institute the 1957 act's deleted Title III, equal employment provisions, recognition of the Supreme Court's school desegregation decisions, and federal assistance to schools undergoing desegregation. All attempts to broaden the bill failed. On April 8, 1960, the Senate approved the bill; Long and his seventeen filibustering compatriots voted nay, but not before he expressed his "fervent hope that we are forever closing the door against force legislation that can only harm those it is supposed to help."[88]

Long's public statements and voting positions on civil rights legislation, and on the civil rights movement more generally, remained consistently conservative—at times even reactionary—throughout the 1950s and into the 1960s. Although certainly a reflection of the political realities of his time and place, the senator's racist politics did not necessarily match his personal beliefs. In many ways, Long's personal demeanor toward blacks was much more respectful than many of his southern colleagues. He seldom, if ever, used the racial epithets that his father or Uncle Earl consistently voiced, and many of his contemporaries described him as forward thinking and open-minded. George Smathers of Florida, who served with Long in the Senate for most of the 1950s and 1960s, said in a later interview that Long was "not anti-black at all. Russell Long is one of the most open-minded guys you ever saw."[89]

Black associates, such as Jesse Nichols, the Senate Finance Committee's government documents clerk and librarian for more than three decades, recalled Long as being fair and supportive. Upon assuming the Finance Committee's chairmanship, for instance, Long immediately saw to it that Nichols received Senate floor privileges, which granted the black man the right to enter the Senate's chamber and deliver documents or books directly to senators and their staff members. Before then, senators would "call for me to bring such and such a thing over," Nichols recalled, and, because he was black, "all I could do was take it to the door and get a page to take it in. Senator Long didn't like that." The system of de facto segregation in the Senate had filtered its way into unequal pay for black staff members as well, but Long made certain that Nichols's pay was equal to the other clerks of similar experience.[90]

Long had grown up and lived in a southern society dominated by the social theme of separation of the races. That separation, and the inherited beliefs that went with it, led to a sense for Long and other southern whites that most, if not all, blacks were innately inferior. Such an understanding of the races and their relationship undergirded many of Long's public statements, even when he claimed to be doing what was best for all southerners, both black and white. Long's statements also belied a paternalistic viewpoint toward blacks that implied white superiority. These prevailing assumptions among southern whites—which shaped the dominant southern social milieu of his time—do not excuse Long's oft-stated conviction that segregation was correct, but they do help explain his political postures on both segregation and voting rights.

If the ways Long thought of blacks as citizens or associates on a personal level might have been viewed as either progressive, for a southerner of his day, or ambivalent, for a Democratic senator, his *political* attitudes were neither. His postures on the floor of the Senate can only be classified as racist. Publicly, Long exhibited somewhat less strident opposition than some of his southern-bloc colleagues on the issue of voting rights, probably a reflection of his understanding that providing more votes to Louisiana blacks would mean more votes in his column when elections rolled around. Nonetheless, he stood firmly against voting rights legislation and consistently voted against it through the first two decades of his Senate tenure. Long's unwavering opposition to any form of anti-segregation legislation placed him in line with the strongest of the Senate's segregationist voices, including those of his Louisiana colleague, Allen Ellender; South Carolina's Strom Thurmond; and Mississippi's James Eastland.

Senator Long's position on civil rights was politically practical; supporting integration and voting rights might have spelled political suicide. Perhaps more than any other Dixie-state senator, however, Long might have challenged the southern political mindset and come away unscathed, thanks to two main factors: first, the substantial number of black voters in Louisiana, almost all of whom consistently voted for the Long faction; and second, the fact that he was a member of a political family that seemed untouchable at times. The Long family name carried with it a great deal of political weight, and the name itself often seemed an insurmountable obstacle for the senator's opposition. Furthermore, both Huey and Earl, while prone to racist comments and beliefs in their personal lives, were remembered inside and out of Louisiana as racial moderates by the standards of their day. Earl, in particular, was seen as downright liberal on the issue by some outside observers. Russell Long knew that his family name equated to a certain number of votes *regardless* of his stances, and he understood just as well that his political forebears had set the stage for him to act as a maverick on certain political matters. He likely understood as well that, should he support any sort of civil rights legislation—enfranchisement legislation in particular—while he might lose a substantial portion of his white votes, they would likely be replaced by black votes. He might have found it within the realm of possibilities to challenge the South's political landscape.

He *might* have, but he did not. In the end, Long's political stances never mirrored his personal attitudes. He consistently opposed any federal legislation designed to improve the lot of blacks in the South.

As a Democratic senator under a Republican administration, Long's stances and voting record between 1953 and 1960 reflected the general, although not complete, consensus that had emerged over New Deal liberalism. Indeed, his politics at the national level during the Eisenhower era affirmed continuity with the practical political trail he had blazed under Truman. Such practical politics entailed liberal stances on *most* domestic policy and a sincere, though at times skeptical, belief in American interventionism and containment. The practical course had also led him to attach himself to his cohort of mid-century southern senators and to model many of his stances on his senior southern colleagues; they, too, understood the benefits New Deal liberalism had brought their constituents and they, too, attempted to obstruct all challenges to the "southern way of life."

The practical course for Russell Long in Louisiana was a two-way affair. It is expected of all senators in the U.S. Congress that they will protect the interests of their home state. Long had done just that during the tidelands dispute, and he had supported and pushed various bills during the Eisenhower years that held great benefit for most Louisianians. Of course, Louisiana's black citizens had been roundly ignored, if not harmed, thanks to Long's obstructionism on civil rights. Too, as a Long, Russell knew that his family name and his political career choice placed him in the forefront of Louisiana's internal political scene. Thoughts of following his father and uncle into the governor's office were never far from his mind during the late 1940s and most of the 1950s. Uncle Earl's 1959 breakdown and its aftermath, though, changed the circumstances. During the coming decades, Long would take a decidedly hands-off approach to Louisiana's internal politics and would focus much more of his energies on the national political arena.

CHAPTER FOUR

In Ascent, 1960–1969

When the battle over the Civil Rights Act of 1960 ended in April of that year, Russell Long said he hoped "we are forever closing the door" on legislation to force change upon the South's racial setting. He likely knew that the door was not completely shut, but with that year's threat out of the way, he could then turn his attentions toward the upcoming presidential election. The campaign that year promised to be interesting for Long, from both a political point of view and a personal one. Of the major candidates, Long had worked alongside three—Republican Richard Nixon and Democrats John Kennedy and Lyndon Johnson—in the Senate. He initially harbored hopes that Johnson, a fellow southerner, would be his party's presidential choice, and he directed the Louisiana delegation to vote that way at the party's convention. Once Kennedy won the nomination, however, Long took to the campaign trail for his colleague from Massachusetts. Despite concerns about Kennedy's civil rights platform, Long championed his fellow Democrat while denouncing Vice President Nixon, the Republican candidate, as both ineffective and even corrupt. When election day arrived, Kennedy carried Louisiana on his way to narrowly defeating Nixon. After an eight-year Republican reign, the executive branch returned to Democratic control.[1]

American politics altered dramatically over the ensuing decade. Long was not immune to the changes. Already an eleven-year veteran of the Senate in 1960, the relatively young Louisianian would ascend to the highest ranks of political power by decade's end. His increasingly demanding responsibilities within the Senate—first as chair of the Senate Finance Committee and then as majority whip—led him to devote much more attention to his work in Washington and much less to the internal politics of Louisiana. As a strong supporter, and sometimes driving force, of the domestic and diplomatic programs of John F. Kennedy and Lyndon Baines Johnson, Long carried on his commitment to a practical political philosophy rooted in New Deal liberalism. As earlier, though, his dedication to such liberalism was tempered by his stance on race relations.

The New Frontier in Domestic Politics

In the months leading up to the November 1960 presidential election, John Kennedy campaigned on a platform promising vigorous, active, and purposeful government. He pledged a New Frontier in domestic policy and foreign relations that would refine—if not perfect—the brand of American liberalism first offered by Franklin Roosevelt's New Deal. Although the new president seemed bold, youthful, and vigorous, he had barely defeated Nixon for the presidency, and Kennedy's term would be marked more by political potential than productivity. In Congress, Kennedy faced strong and organized opposition that stalled many of his domestic proposals, including those designed to bolster civil rights and alleviate poverty.[2]

Senator Long supported most of the new president's initiatives. The key elements of Kennedy's early domestic agenda included a minimum wage increase; hospital insurance for the elderly; and federal aid for education, housing, and impoverished areas. On the floor of the Senate in 1961, Long voted for the twenty-five cent increase to the minimum wage, which Kennedy's administration hoped would, in conjunction with its other economic proposals, spur the American economy from the doldrums that had begun during the late 1950s. Long also supported and voted for the Area Redevelopment Act, which appropriated $394 million for programs to foster job growth and emerging businesses in areas of the nation scourged by chronic unemployment, and the Omnibus Housing Act, which put forth almost $5 billion to aid lower- and middle-class homeowners.[3]

Long's enthusiasm for the Kennedy administration's domestic agenda was not all-encompassing, however. He denounced the administration's program of federal aid to education, although he had backed similar proposals in the past. The political climate of the day forced Long's hand: with rising tensions over the black freedom movement, white backlash, and civil rights legislation, Long and his southern colleagues questioned whether federal aid to schools would be tied to those institutions' record at implementing the Supreme Court's *Brown* ruling. School systems that followed through and ended educational segregation might be rewarded with the money; those that did not could find their pockets empty of federal funds. The southern senators were determined that the federal government would not hold such leverage over their states' educational institutions. The federal aid-to-education legislation never made its way out of committee.[4]

Long continued to oppose programs for universal hospital insurance for the elderly. Like many of his colleagues in the Senate and much of the American public, he feared that federal involvement in health matters might be veering too close to "socialized medicine." Furthermore, Long felt that that the Kerr-Mills program Congress had approved in 1960 provided sufficient assistance to those who needed such aid. Switching to universal coverage would be extraordinarily costly, Long maintained, and could potentially undermine the correct relationship between the individual, the states, and the federal government that he and his fellow southerners held in such high esteem.[5]

Long's opposition to universal hospital insurance for one group of Americans, the elderly, did not, however, dissuade him from supporting Kennedy's proposal to help another, the mentally disabled. In 1963, he supported the president's proposals for a Mental Retardation Facilities and Community Health Centers Act, which provided grants for the construction of hospitals, clinics, and other facilities and authorized funding for the training of health-care professionals to work with disabled youth.[6]

Also in 1963, Long served as floor manager of Kennedy's proposal for major individual and corporate tax cuts. Long was a logical choice to guide the bill in the Senate. He had supported Kennedy's earlier tax reforms and was next in line to head the Senate Finance Committee. Chairman Harry Byrd was in a lengthy health decline, and it was natural for Kennedy and his advisors to assume that Long would soon rise to the chairmanship, in which case he would wield a tremendous amount of control over the nation's tax policy. Long also agreed with the Kennedy administration that the nation absolutely needed the $14 billion tax cut. The cut would allow American consumers to spend more and, with the support of additional government activity, would spur economic output and the creation of new jobs. Such long-term growth would protect the American economy from recessions of the type it had encountered in the late 1950s.[7]

Economic growth would also help alleviate the nation's social problems while providing a leg up in waging the Cold War. In keeping with the fiscal understandings of the liberal consensus, both Long and the Kennedy administration held that the tax cuts would provide such enormous social benefits that they would head off calls for redistributionist economics of the sort Long's father had espoused some thirty years before. Long did not uniformly support the administration's proposals, however, as he believed the package's tax reforms, which would have implemented austere new rules on claiming credits and deductions, unfairly singled out lower-income taxpayers while easing the burden on the wealthy. The tax cut legislation was sent to the Finance Committee for hearings before the full Senate acted upon it; it was still in committee when Kennedy traveled to Dallas, Texas, in November 1963.[8]

The Cold War and Cuba

Kennedy campaigned in 1960 on promises of energetic, yet flexible, ways of dealing with communist threats around the world. He was presented with opportunities to put those promises into action almost as soon as he took office.

From an American perspective, the most ominous Cold War developments of the late 1950s and early 1960s occurred in Cuba, less than a hundred miles from home. In 1959, the pro-American government of Fulgencio Batista crumbled, and Fidel Castro, a young, charismatic guerrilla revolutionary assumed control of the Havana government. Although for a few months the Eisenhower administration considered Castro's government benign, Cuba's activities during the Castro-proclaimed "year of the revolution," 1959, and the "year of agrarian reform," 1960, quickly alienated the American public and political leaders.[9]

Long, like most of his southern colleagues, came to despise Castro. In March 1960, Long called him "a fellow who would drink our blood, if he could." "Under previous governments in Cuba which were friendly to us, it could be said we had some interest in Cuba," he said, but now, "in view of the fact that Cuba says she is independent of us and appears to be devoting herself to a propaganda and ideological battle against the United States, there is no justification for extending any form of economic aid to Cuba." As a result, Long contended that Cuba's favored status as a sugar exporter to the United States should be revoked. Changing the provisions of the Sugar Act would have greatly benefited south Louisiana farmers who produced enormous amounts of sugar cane, of course.[10]

By 1960, Castro had begun making overtures to communist powers, and the potential threat of a communist foothold so close to the U.S. mainland prodded Eisenhower to action. In January 1961, Eisenhower withdrew U.S. diplomatic recognition; by then, his administration had already begun secretly training Cuban exiles to invade the island and topple Castro's regime.

Kennedy, who had said on the campaign trail that he favored the possibility of such an assault, inherited the situation from Eisenhower and proceeded with plans for an April 1961 invasion. What became known as the Bay of Pigs invasion ended in a dismal failure for the American-backed invaders. The botched assault turned out to be one of President Kennedy's greatest embarrassments.[11]

The Senate Foreign Relations Committee, chaired by Arkansas Democrat J. William Fulbright, investigated the failure. As a member of the committee, Long criticized the Kennedy administration's actions for being weak and insufficient. "It is fairly clear," he said, "that the advice given the President was awful. The entire operation had no chance of success." Drawing on his own experiences as an amphibious corps officer, Long contended that "the landing phases were clearly lacking in the basic essentials which were a part of every American landing in World War II."[12]

For Long, the Bay of Pigs fiasco was a turning point in the Cold War. His stances hardened. The failure of the American-backed forces, combined with the close proximity of communist Cuba, seemed to confirm his resolve that military containment must be not only sustained but also strengthened. "Whether we like it or not," he said in May 1961, "we are at war—a cold war, to be sure, but a war, nevertheless." The opposition was dangerous, and the threat imminent. "We are confronted with a brutal and calculating enemy who is willing to pay the price of victory," he said. "We must be willing to make equal sacrifice." The Cold War had developed into a new type of conflict in which the United States could not expect to win solely "by overwhelming superiority of weapons. In the future, indispensable elements of our victory will be those which sustained us in the wars which occurred early in the existence of our Nation." Those included "devotion to the ideals for which we are fighting [and] willingness to pay a high price, in blood and sacrifice, for victory."[13]

Although Cuba commanded much attention during the early

1960s, Long and most other Americans viewed their next-door neighbor and its leaders as little more than extensions of a broader communist network whose true nerve center could be found in Moscow. In September 1962, Long articulated his views on the Soviet Union, and particular on its premier, Nikita Khrushchev. Responding to a *Washington Post* editorial that quoted Khrushchev as saying the United States was "too liberal to fight," Long told his Senate colleagues that "whenever Mr. Khrushchev wants to start world war III [*sic*], we are ready to blow his nation to kingdom come, with a firm reliance that the next world will be better than this one." He asked, "Inasmuch as Mr. Khrushchev does not believe in God or the hereafter, where does he propose to go after we and the Russians blow this planet to bits?" A few weeks later, Long joined eighty-five other senators in voting for Senate Joint Resolution 230, which expressed "U.S. determination to prevent the spread of communism from Cuba to the rest of the Western Hemisphere, by any means necessary, including the use of arms."[14]

Long probably did not know how near to fruition his comments about blowing "this planet to bits" would come. Within a month, the U.S. determination mentioned in the Senate Joint Resolution 230 would be tested. In early October 1962, American U-2 spy planes photographed nine missile launch sites under construction in Cuba. On October 16, President Kennedy convened a meeting of the executive committee of his National Security Council to determine how to respond. A consensus gradually developed around the idea of quarantining the island. Kennedy announced the quarantine to a nationwide audience on October 21. In the Senate, Russell Long and many of his southern colleagues, including Foreign Relations chair Fulbright, advocated a more drastic show of force. Two days after Kennedy's announcement, nineteen U.S. ships confronted and forced the retreat of Soviet convoys, which American intelligence images showed carrying items that looked very much like loosely concealed missile components. Although the showdown at sea enforced the quarantine of Cuba, it did not solve the problem of missiles that might already be on the island. After nearly a week of frayed nerves fueled by fears of imminent nuclear annihilation, the United States and the Soviet Union finalized a deal whereby the Soviets would give up their missile sites in Cuba in exchange for promises from the United States to refrain from invading the island and to remove missile installations from Turkey.[15]

Less than a year later, Cuba and other Cold War difficulties would be placed in the hands of a new president. On November 22, 1963, John Kennedy was assassinated in Dallas, Texas. Senator Long, who had been visiting New Orleans, rushed back to Washington, D.C. On the floor of the Senate, he noted that "to one who at the age of 16 suffered through an assassination 28 years ago, the weight of the calamity that took place November 22 fell not totally unfamiliarly, but just as heavily." And he wrote a heartfelt note to Kennedy's widow, Jacqueline, in which he offered her his ruminations upon his own father's assassination and provided glimpses into his own faith. "There is no way to explain such a thing unless one has faith in God and believes in the teachings of Jesus Christ," he wrote. "If it is true that there is everlasting life beyond this place of toil and tears, then we can take solace in the fact that God called a good man to a higher reward. It is hard to believe that God knows about all these things and that he has planned it to be that way. Yet in time we may come to see that all of this is part of a master plan."[16]

The Great Society

Kennedy's successor, Lyndon Johnson, was much more adept at manipulating Congress than his predecessor had been. Johnson had mastered the art of politics to a degree nearly unmatched in the twentieth century and for most of the 1950s had been Senate majority leader. Using his own political prowess in tandem with Kennedy's memory, Johnson succeeded in garnering congressional approval for many of the New Frontier proposals—most notably the 1964 tax cut. And he coopted some of Kennedy's programs and combined them with his own to formulate a new domestic reform package, the Great Society.

As implemented in the mid-1960s, the Great Society marked the pinnacle of twentieth-century American liberalism. It included a multitude of elements, all of them rooted in the assumption that the federal government could confront and solve the major problems of American society. The Great Society's chief elements included a plan for poverty eradication known as the War on Poverty, a series of civil rights initiatives known as the Second Reconstruction, a collection of environmental laws, and proposals to improve both education for American youth and health care for the elderly. As a southern senator, Long's practical political nature would not allow him to support the civil rights initiatives embodied in the Second Reconstruction. He did, however, support almost all of the other Great Society programs, and he would play a major role in ushering through most of those proposals.[17]

Johnson won a landslide victory in the 1964 presidential race. His opponent, conservative Republican senator Barry Goldwater, had called for less federal government involvement in the lives of citizens, more power for the individual states and localities, and repeal of civil rights legislation. The distinctions were easy to see, and American voters overwhelmingly chose liberalism over conservatism. Johnson's massive victory brought with it Democratic majorities in both houses of Congress and seemed to be a mandate for implementing the Great Society.

Russell Long's role in the creation of the Great Society reflected a long-standing personal and political relationship with President Johnson. Both had entered the Senate in 1948—Long as a relative political novice, Johnson with a long career in national politics already—and both had exhibited a fundamental belief in most of the basics of New Deal liberalism during their time together in the Senate. As majority leader, Johnson had cultivated a relationship with Long that reflected not only their backgrounds from contiguous southern and oil-rich states, but also their commitment to the populist ideals of their mutual hero, Huey Long. Long supported Johnson's push for the presidency in both 1956 and 1960, and he campaigned for the president in 1964.[18]

The Long-Johnson relationship was not based solely upon Long's political fealty toward Johnson. Johnson understood that by 1965 Long had attained a level of such great Senate power as majority whip, as chair of the Finance Committee, and as a high-ranking member of the Foreign Relations Committee that he absolutely needed Long in his corner for almost every political battle to be waged. Larry O'Brien, Johnson's special assistant for congressional relations and personnel, recalled that Long's support could be "very elusive" but that he "was an important target for us and whatever the President could do . . . he endeavored to improve the relationship, all aimed at his ultimate support." Long "worked that floor and his colleagues extremely well," O'Brien later added. "There was nothing passive about Russell Long." Such an ally was of the utmost necessity to the Johnson administration in the fights over the Great Society.[19]

Strong ties with Johnson were fostered as well by Long's commitment to the successes of the national Democratic Party. Also helpful was his ability to look past political differences at times and to place the interests of the party above his own. "Long's loyalty to the party was such that when he was chairman of the Senate Campaign Committee—in a position to be the source of some very significant fund-raising—he made sure that those funds were distributed to senatorial candidates, incumbents or otherwise, on a very fair and equitable basis," O'Brien noted. "I never saw any indication that he would adjust his support on the basis of the senator's position, conservative, moderate, or liberal." Such evenhandedness reflected an ability to build bridges to Democrats of different philosophies, a useful skill in fostering consensus within the party and, again, an absolute necessity for the passage of Johnson's domestic reform agenda.[20]

The new president tabbed Long to continue as floor leader for the Kennedy tax bill that had been mired down in Finance Committee hearings. Although not the legislation's originator, Johnson viewed the tax cuts as crucial components of the Great Society. Pegging the tax package as a political and economic memorial to the fallen president, Long guided the bill to Senate approval and then oversaw a joint House-Senate conference committee that endorsed it and issued a final report. Signed into law by Johnson, it became the Revenue Act of 1964.[21]

Five months later, Long firmed up his support for Johnson's domestic agenda by voting in favor of the Omnibus Anti-Poverty Bill of 1964, more commonly known as the Economic Opportunity Act. Among the bill's most notable provisions were the implementation of the Job Corps, work-training and work-study programs, Community Action Programs, Volunteers in Service to America, and business loans for the hiring of unemployed workers. Long's vote placed him firmly in the liberal camp, and it distanced him from many of his southern colleagues—only Florida's George Smathers, Georgia's Herman Talmadge, and South Carolina's Olin Johnston voted the same way. The Senate's other southerners viewed the legislation as either too much of a federal encroachment on state and local prerogatives, as offering too much assistance to black Americans, or as too much of a combination of the two. But Long, who had politically inherited from both his father and his uncle a sense that government, if working correctly, could alleviate the burdens of the impoverished, willingly provided his backing for what would become the first foray in the War on Poverty.[22]

On January 4, 1965, Long's fellow Democrats elected him assistant majority leader, a position more commonly known as majority whip. As such, he served as the number two senator in the Democratic Party, after only Majority Leader Mike Mansfield. From his new post, Long oversaw what has been called "the legislative high point of late-twentieth-century liberalism." During his early years as whip, Long helped push through amendments to the Economic Opportunity Act that doubled funding for the administration's antipoverty programs and an Appalachian Aid Bill that provided more than a billion dollars to fund construction, health, and social welfare projects in the nation's most perpetually impoverished area. In spite of his previous stances, Long shepherded through the Senate the Elementary and Secondary Education Act, which implemented federal aid to education. He guided to passage the Water Quality Act, which required that the states maintain standard levels of water purity in interstate streams, and he garnered support for the Immigration Act, which removed the old, discriminatory system of immigration quotas and replaced it with a set of hemispheric quotas.[23]

Long supported the creation of Medicare in 1965 despite his consistent opposition to similar proposals dating back to the Truman administration. As recently as 1964, he had opposed a bill sponsored by New York's Jacob Javits and New Mexico's Clinton Anderson that would have implemented a program to provide hospitalization insurance for the elderly under the rubric of Social Security. In July 1964, Long expressed concerns that the Javits-Anderson proposal would tax the young for the benefit of the elderly, that it would mushroom into a universal program of socialized medicine, and that the greatest burden of taxation would fall on the poor. He maintained at the time that the previously implemented Kerr-Mills state-federal program of providing health care to the needy was "adequate."[24]

Yet scarcely half a year later, Long announced his support for the Johnson administration's Medical Care (Medicare) Act, which would implement substantially the same program as the Javits-Anderson bill had proposed. What's more, Long, as majority whip, served as floor manager of the legislation, calling it "the largest and most significant piece of social legislation ever to pass the Congress in the history of our country." In addition to creating a universal program of hospital insurance for the elderly, the Medicare program created a supplemental insurance program for nonhospitalization needs; it also revamped the older Kerr-Mills program into Medicaid, which covered hospitalization and other medical costs for the poor or otherwise needy. Given his political inheritance from both his father and his uncle, Long's stance should not come as a surprise. What is astonishing is that he changed positions so quickly. Probably part of that shift had to do with his new prominence within the Senate's Democratic Party machinery and with the perceived mandate for Johnson's proposals reflected in the 1964 presidential election, but a further clue to his motivations came from the coverage granted by the legislation. Unlike the earlier proposals, the 1965 bill included an increase in the matching formula for the needy, aged, blind, and disabled, groups that, Long said, had always "been very close to my heart." It provided coverage for tuberculosis and psychiatric patients, both of which he had called for when the Kerr-Mills program had been created in 1960.[25]

The Coming of the Second Reconstruction

Long felt comfortable switching sides from opponent to supporter of universal health insurance for the elderly, but if he ever thought of making such a switch on civil rights, he never hinted at it publicly. Events in Louisiana saw to that. The governor's race of 1960 had been the first statewide campaign since the 1930s in which the old Longite/Anti-Longite paradigm was overshadowed by another issue: segregation. Jimmie Davis maintained a hard line against public school integration and rode that stance to victory. Events in New Orleans soon put his campaign pledges to the test.[26]

It took six years for the city of New Orleans to take seriously the Supreme Court's *Brown v. Board* desegregation mandate. And had it not been for U.S. district judge J. Skelly Wright, the city leaders and school system might have dallied much longer. In early 1960, however, Wright, among the nation's most liberal federal district judges, ordered the New Orleans school system to submit to him a plan for integration by May of that year.

When the Orleans Parish School Board refused to do so, Wright created his own plan for the gradual integration of the schools, to begin in September.[27]

Wright's order put Long on the defensive. The senator suggested in a televised interview that the people of New Orleans "don't have to open those schools at all in September," and he stated that "when the people are faced with a complete salt and pepper integration . . . they are not going to go along with it. I wouldn't and I do not think the average person of New Orleans will." To Long, the ruling was a mistake, and although he had no evidence for it, he blamed the decision on Judge Wright's ambition. The integration order, Long wrote, "is an irresponsible and extreme act by a man . . . attempting to dump an impossible situation on the people of Louisiana in the hope that it might help him achieve eventual promotion to the Supreme Court."[28]

That June, in an effort to stave off Wright's integration order, Louisiana's state legislature placed control of the New Orleans school system into the hands of Governor Davis, who ordered that the schools remain segregated. Judge Wright then declared Davis's order unconstitutional and again ordered the schools integrated; this time the judge pushed the date back to November 14. Despite more delaying tactics on the part of the state legislature and Senator Long's ominous warnings about the dangers of "a complete salt and pepper integration," four black students entered two white schools on the appointed date.[29]

Before the actual desegregation, Long had warned New Orleanians not to engage in "unsightly demonstrations," and he had cautioned that "bad manners and angry gestures hurt rather than help our cause." His statements apparently fell on deaf ears, however, for on the day after the first black students attended the white schools, an audience of more than five thousand heard Citizens' Council leader Leander Perez declare, "Don't wait for your daughter to be raped by these Congolese. Don't wait until the burr-heads are forced into your schools. Do something about it now!" The next day, white mobs wandered through the city's streets, randomly attacking blacks. Blacks retaliated, and a near riot ensued. Russell Long addressed the Louisiana state legislature that Wednesday, asserting that the state government was in the right on the issue of desegregation and lamenting that he and his fellow southern senators did not, unlike Louisiana's legislature, have "all the votes you need to pass anything you desire" to preserve the racial status quo. Belatedly, New Orleans civil and business leaders attempted to control the situation. Mobs in the streets, vitriolic language, and violent protests only hurt the Crescent City's image as a safe place to do business and to visit while on vacation. These leaders, along with Mayor Victor Schiro, pushed for public acceptance of Wright's order. By September 1961, six more schools were integrated, and thanks largely to the leadership of the mayor and the city's business owners, the overt discontent so evident the year before was absent.[30]

The New Orleans school integration crisis pointed to the continued hostility of Louisiana whites toward any cracks in segregation's façade. But it also revealed an increased readiness among blacks to stand up to the backlash. Their willingness to persevere in the face of white intransigence placed more and more pressure on the federal government to pass meaningful and enforceable civil rights legislation. The results came to be known as the Second Reconstruction.

The Civil Rights Act of 1964

The Johnson administration sensed that rising expectations among blacks and increasingly violent confrontations between the races made civil rights initiatives absolutely necessary. In 1964, therefore, the administration reintroduced a Kennedy administration civil rights bill that had died in the Senate the preceding year. The bill's most notable provisions, and those most likely to arouse southern ire, included stronger enforcement of earlier voting rights enactments, the prohibition of segregation at public facilities, the extension of the Civil Rights Commission, the banning of discrimination in federally funded programs, and the creation of an Equal Employment Opportunity Commission. The bill passed by a large majority in the House, but in the Senate, where southern senators still dominated committee chairmanships and still had the filibuster at their disposal, its chances were slim.[31]

The initial phase of Senate debate revolved around whether or not the bill should be sent to Senator James Eastland's Judiciary Committee. As in 1960, the Judiciary Committee had been bypassed by civil rights proponents, and Long and other members of the opposition argued that proper procedure had not been followed. Skipping committee hearings meant, according to Long, that the Senate's vote would not be based on evidence but instead "would be a matter of blind prejudice, a true lynching party on the South and on our American freedoms of privacy and free enterprise." The only good thing about keeping the bill out of Judiciary, Long later said, was that "the committee system on this side of Congress is perhaps better off without the smell of this sort of proposed legislation on its hands." After the Senate voted not to send the bill to the Judiciary Committee, Long said "that any uncompromising proponent of this bill must get it through the Senate before he is forced to face the fact that the majority of his constituents are opposed to it—or would be if they knew what was in the proposed legislation."[32]

The debate over whether or not to send the bill to committee granted Long time to point out the "noxious nature of this legislation." In a key speech on March 24, 1964, he argued that the constitutional bases of the bill's equal accommodations rules—the Fourteenth Amendment's equal protection clause and the Constitution's interstate commerce clause—had been misrepresented by the bill's proponents. The equal protection clause, he maintained, "speaks only in terms of State action," therefore it could not be applied to cases of discrimination by individuals or privately owned businesses. And the interstate commerce clause, which allowed Congress to regulate commerce "among the several states," in his estimation, could not be applied to exclusively intrastate business activity. "The commerce clause, which came into our law like a lamb, has now assumed the character of a ravenous wolf . . . threatening to swallow up many of our rights of free enterprise, privacy, and property," he asserted.[33]

Long contended that a clear distinction existed between rights and conveniences, the former being protected by the Constitution and the latter not. This distinction was especially important when it came to public accommodations. "Certainly, I could list at great length the constitutional rights which belong to the people of this country," he said. "There is the right to trial by jury. There is the right to freedom of speech. There is the right against improper search and seizure." By his reckoning, these "are not mere conveniences; they belong to a select classification known as constitutional rights." On the other hand, "the convenience of stopping at a certain hotel or theater or restaurant, even though understandably important to people," had been granted no special place in the Constitution, and, "While the Government has the unquestioned authority and duty to enforce the protection of constitutional rights, the Government has no duty with respect to conveniences."[34]

Placing rights and conveniences on the same level and using the mechanisms of the national government to enforce that leveling would, Long predicted, lead to a backlash among southern whites "so adverse that the process of voluntary acceptance will be set back a decade or more." Moreover, forcing business owners and private citizens to accept the integration of public accommodations and the enforcement of equal employment measures would "blunt the initiative of our successful and competent citizens and thus destroy the capitalistic system." He stated flatly, "It is as if we were helping to fulfill Nikita Khrushchev's fateful prophecy that communism will 'bury us.' The provisions of these forced integration bills provide an opportunity to bury ourselves, and proponents seem to be intent on just that goal."[35]

The proposed legislation also threatened to trample personal freedoms, Long charged. He pointed to the white participants in the March on Washington of August 1963 as examples: "Those white people believed in integration. They believed in mixture. Let them mix." They were not forced to mix, however, and therein lay the problem. "If someone does not wish to mix, he should not be made to mix," he said. Ignoring the fact that such choices did not exist for blacks in the South, Long concluded that "a man should have complete freedom to decide whether he wishes to mix or not. If he wishes to do so, that is all right. If he does not wish to, he does not have to. Federal compulsion one way or the other should not coerce him."[36]

On March 26, the Senate voted 34 to 50 against a motion to send the bill to the Judiciary Committee. Thus, like the civil rights legislation of 1960, this bill escaped the clutches of Mississippi's James Eastland. Debate on the bill's specific provisions began four days later. Russell Long's Louisiana colleague, Allen Ellender, slept and cooked meals in his office as he headed up one of three teams of southerners engaged in a filibuster that would last through mid-April.[37]

Long played an active role in the filibuster, and he rehashed many of his well-worn anti–civil rights arguments. "Is not the entire bill," he asked on April 14, "predicated on the theory that the people are incapable of running their own State governments; that the people are dishonest, corrupt, and morally incapable of doing the decent things for themselves and their neighbors?" Southerners could decide for themselves how to handle the issues brought up in the civil rights bill. If majority rule were allowed in those eleven southern states, the dilemma would be resolved. His other arguments focused on the hypocrisy of outside agitators—"some fellow who does not even know what a poor colored man looks like, because he has never even seen a Negro"—trying to restructure southern society while ignoring problems in their own backyards. According to Long, "it is better politics to talk about civil rights, if one come [*sic*] from the North or the East, and makes the southerners do something instead of talking about civil rights in terms of setting one's own house in order." Civil rights proponents, in Long's interpretation, either missed or ignored the log in their own eyes while focusing on the speck in the South's.[38]

Because the contempt provisions of the Civil Rights Act of 1957 had been written into the 1964 bill, Long stated that the right to trial by jury might be discarded if the bill passed. The 1957 legislation provided that persons held in contempt of court for violating voting rights would be punished without the input of a jury and, if the punishment for contempt amounted to less than forty-five days in jail or a three hundred dollar fine, they could not demand a *de novo* jury trial. The 1964 bill lowered the jail time to thirty days—Long referred to the provision as "the 29-day amendment." Twenty-nine days or less meant no jury trial. He contended that this amounted to little more than an ends-justifies-the-means scenario and stated that "if we feel that citizens should be accorded jury trials in contempt cases under this bill, then it should be done without regard to the severity of the sentence involved. When a man approaches the jail door, possibly because of a violation of his rights to trial by jury, his residence behinds [*sic*] bars is just as real and just as burdensome if it is for 29 days as it would be for 31 days." The distinction was arbitrary, as would be the enforcement of the provisions, in Long's estimation.[39]

Long said that the denial of jury trials in these cases presented to the Senate a situation in which, "in the name of haste, in the name of false expediency, and in fear of what the extremist mobs might do, we are being asked to discard a substantial portion of one of the most cherished rights in our system." Because of the expanded injunctive powers written into the 1964 bill, Long prophesied the creation of a tyrannical government that ruled by injunction in the place of law. Therefore, on May 11, he offered amendments to the bill that he said would rectify the problem. The amendments gave a defendant the right to ask for a jury trial; but if he did so, he would "subject himself to greater penalties that could be imposed for criminal contempt than if he declined to ask for a jury trial." The idea was to allow defendants to have some say in whether they wanted a jury trial or not and "in so doing protect himself [*sic*] from the severe penalties that could be imposed for contempt of court."[40]

Although some of the arguments put forth by Long and his southern colleagues might have had true legal or constitutional merit, their extended statements were really nothing more than another attempt at delaying a vote. The filibuster ended on June 10, 1964, however, when the full Senate voted 71 to 29 for cloture. The cloture vote meant strong legislation would be enacted. It was what southerners had feared most in 1957 and 1960; under cloture they could not control or manipulate the bill's final version. The Senate passed the civil rights bill with no major changes and sent it to the House, where no modifications were made. The legislation that Russell Long had called "this nefarious forced integration bill" and had warned would "storm the gates of our traditional American freedoms" became the Civil Rights Act of 1964 when President Johnson signed it into law on July 2.[41]

On July 20, Long met with Johnson at the White House, and their discussion turned to the matter of civil rights. Johnson defended his stances to his fellow southerner. "I'm doing what I can to carry out my oath of office and at the same time not be ugly and vicious and mean—and be as considerate of my fellow man as I can and still try to lead the nation," Johnson told Long. "I can understand how this thing is in Mississippi and Alabama and Louisiana and East Texas, Georgia. . . . I've spent fifty-six years in it and I'm trying my damnedest to walk the tightrope that I got to walk." Long replied that "I think if you can just play it low-key from here until November, it's going to get better for you." The Louisiana senator then surmised that "this thing [the Civil Rights Act] had to pass sooner or later."[42]

Although Long had advised the president to "play it low-key from here until November," Johnson could not hold out that long, and in October he told a New Orleans audience that the Civil Rights Act of 1964 was only one piece of the Second Reconstruction puzzle. Speaking before a segregated audience—blacks at the rear of the hall, whites, including Russell Long, in the front—Johnson departed from his prepared text and explained his belief that so long as racism divided the South, the region would be doomed to economic, political, and social failure. The New Orleans speech turned out to be Johnson's major civil rights address of the 1964 presidential campaign, and it signified his commitment to see the Second Reconstruction through to its conclusion.[43]

In March 1965, Johnson spoke before Congress about "an American problem": the denial of voting rights to hundreds of thousands of black voters based upon the color of their skin. Johnson asked Congress to pass legislation to provide voting rights to those who had been disfranchised, and he concluded his remarks by declaring, "We shall overcome," the mantra of the civil rights movement. Historians later termed it "Johnson's greatest speech." Contemporary southern senators, however, expressed dismay. The day after Johnson's address, Louisiana's Ellender said, "It is my intention to filibuster against it and talk against it as long as God gives me breath." Strom Thurmond of South Carolina said that "the president betrayed the southern cause." Georgian Herman Talmadge said Johnson's remarks made him "sick."[44]

The Johnson administration's voting rights legislation took aim at discrimination in registration practices in two ways. First, it outlawed literacy tests and other means of stopping voters from registering. Second, it allowed the federal government to send voting examiners into state and local jurisdictions to actively register black citizens. Those examiners would work specifically in areas where less than 50 percent of eligible voters had cast ballots in the 1964 presidential election; the assumption was that such low voter turnout resulted from discrimination against a large portion of the electorate. At the time of the congressional debates on the bill, its provisions for federal examiners would have applied to seven states, six of which were in the South, plus various counties within three others.[45]

Senator Long initially voiced support for the president's legislation. He had always claimed to support equal voting rights for blacks, and he admitted that problems existed, even in Louisiana. "In some parishes, there have been cases in which only a small percentage were registered," he acknowledged, "and where efforts were made to intimidate people from voting. Also there have been cases in which they were denied the right to vote, not as a matter of intimidation but as a matter of registration." Long had even asked President John F. Kennedy "to recommend this kind of voting rights bill to the Senate, although I was a Senator from Louisiana and could not very well vote for it." Yet, when the actual legislation reached the Senate, Long felt it politically necessary to challenge the bill due to its enforcement mechanisms. Long directed his opposition toward the bill's all-encompassing nature and its targeting of, in his formulation, the wrong problem. He charged that the bill was unfair in that it punished the many for the crimes of the few: it would have applied to all parishes in Louisiana even if discrimination against black voters had actually occurred in only two or three. His opposition, however, was neither as loud nor as stringent as it had been toward earlier civil rights legislation. Long refused to filibuster against the bill and urged his Democratic colleagues "to vote for cloture on that bill, although my colleague [Allen Ellender] was leading the filibuster, because I felt that the bill should have been passed and made applicable to Louisiana."[46]

Long's protests may have been subdued, but many of his fellow Dixie senators felt little compunction in vociferously opposing the voting rights bill. Thurmond said the ever-mounting demands of the civil rights movement, of which voting rights was but one of a litany, amounted to "a war against society and the existing political order—in short, an insurrection." Talmadge said the bill "was conceived by an unholy alliance of lawless mob actions on the one hand and murder and mayhem on the other."[47]

Their attacks were to little avail, and the southern senators understood that they would lose the battle. The Senate passed the Voting Rights Bill by a 77 to 19 vote on May 26. On July 9, the House passed a slightly amended version of the bill, and it then went to conference committee for a hashing out of differences. Finally, on August 4, the Senate approved the conference report, and two days later, President Johnson signed into law the Voting Rights Act of 1965.[48]

The Voting Rights Act dramatically changed political participation in the United States. Within three years, all southern states experienced such substantial increases in black voter registration that not a single one needed the 1965 law's prescribed federal examiners. The legislation changed the nature of politics even more profoundly. White politicians could no longer afford to ignore their black constituents, and blacks could now run for, and win, elected positions. By the end of the decade, thousands of black officeholders, mainly on the local level, had been elected.[49]

Expanding the Great Society

In his State of the Union address of 1966, President Johnson called for yet another civil rights bill, one that would insure fair treatment in jury selection, crime enforcement, and housing access. The fair housing proposal would constitute yet another facet of the Great Society's War on Poverty in that it would help eliminate ghettoization of urban blacks that resulted from unequal opportunity and unfair zoning laws. It would become the center point of debate on the Civil Rights Bill of 1966.[50]

As was their custom, southern senators, including Russell Long, filibustered against the bill. On September 12, Long laid out what he said would be four problematic results of the bill's passage. The first problem related to what he considered inherent rights of property ownership and of association. "The right of a person to own and dispose of his property at his own discretion—and to associate with others as he pleases," Long asserted, "is a fundamental right, and it strikes close to the heart of the liberty and freedom to which all men are entitled." Second, Long emphasized that, without instilling within the black population ideas of self-help and independence, the bill would have very little effect at all, for "the real need of the Negro in this area is for him to improve his own lot, both socially and economically. Most Negroes cannot afford the housing which this bill would seek to make available, so open housing laws would be largely useless, and would serve as only more needless Government regulation and red tape." Third, he regarded the fair housing provisions as ripe for corruption and abuse, because "doubtless, the administrators of this program would include a high percentage of overzealous bureaucrats who want to exercise a reckless disregard of practical problems in their pursuit of total integration." And fourth, he contended that the provision, "even on a purely practical basis," was unfair in that it placed upon the home owner the burden of proof against allegations of discrimination and the cost of defending against such allegations. He was convinced that "troublemakers and militant extremists could cause preliminary injunctions to be issued against housing sales and rentals, without even any testimony or defense."[51]

Long noted in the same speech that "the effort to impart our white culture, economic independence and personal responsibility to the Negroes has been a policy pursued in the South for many years." The words belied a deep conviction held by Long and his southern colleagues in the Senate. At the heart of Long's arguments against the fair housing provisions of the 1966 bill, and against previous civil rights proposals, lay a fundamental belief about the differences between blacks and whites and how those differences could best be reconciled. Long believed, simply enough and like many other southern whites, that the divide could be bridged if, and only if, blacks became more like whites. If they behaved like whites, respected the same institutions as whites, attained the same educational levels as whites, earned the same jobs as whites, then they could be considered equal to whites. Equality meant, for Long, assimilation of blacks into white society.

President Johnson had known from the outset that getting yet another civil rights bill through Congress so soon after the landmarks of 1964 and 1965 would be difficult. He also understood that no amount of legislation would completely end racial discrimination in the United States, and he knew, as did even the most pro–civil rights members of Congress, that other political issues demanded attention. Faced with entrenched opposition on both sides of the Senate aisle and with an ongoing southern filibuster grinding work on other much-needed legislation to a halt, President Johnson abandoned his 1966 civil rights bill.[52]

The next major civil rights battle for southern senators like Long came in 1968, when a House-passed bill, H.R. 2516, specifying punishments for violent acts against civil rights workers, came up for debate in the Senate. Long returned to his well-worn cache of anti–civil rights arguments. He questioned the fairness of the legislation, and because it singled out people engaged in violent activities against civil rights workers only, he argued that it provisions violated the Fourteenth Amendment's equal protection clause. Furthermore, Long contended that the House bill's stipulation that the acts of violence had to take place across the color line dealt with "only one small segment of the problem. Most white men are killed by white men. Most black men are killed by black men." Long tried to turn the tables on civil rights advocates by stating that "if we are going to do it equitably, we should do it for everybody and to everybody. We should not do it for some and to some. Everyone should be treated the same."

He concluded, "I am making the argument against discrimination in this case."[53]

Long found the bill's protections of civil rights workers even more galling because, by early 1968, the dynamics of the black freedom movement had shifted. Martin Luther King's leadership had in many ways been supplanted by younger, more forceful, and at times more violent members of the burgeoning black power movement. Long saw these newer activists as even less deserving of federal protection. Singling out two of the more well-known leaders of the black power movement, Long referred to H.R. 2516 as "a bill to aid and abet H. Rap Brown and Stokely Carmichael," and he warned that the majority of the citizens of the United States would prefer to punish, rather than protect, such people. Why shield those who "stir up hatred and ill will among people of their race and put cities to the torch, as has been known to happen in the past with men of this type of attitude?"[54]

To "protect the public from irresponsible rabble rousers," Long offered his own amendments to the bill. The most significant, for both symbolic and political purposes, proposed to "strike at the very thing which really concerns the people of this country: the rights and the safety of 200 million Americans whose property and whose very lives have been seriously endangered." Long titled his amendment the Civil Disobedience Act of 1968. It prescribed federal penalties for the mere intention of inciting a riot that would interfere with interstate commerce in any way, for traveling across state borders to teach civil disobedience or violent protest, for transporting across state borders various weapons for use in riots, for "sniping" at persons during a riot, for interfering with law enforcement officials during the course of civil disorder, for looting during riots of stores whose inventories included items shipped in across state lines, and for sniping at vehicles on any part of the Interstate Highway System. Long's provisions, most of which were rejected in floor debate, reflected more than just his personal convictions. They also reflected the sensibilities of an increasing number of Americans, particularly in the South, where a growing political theme of "law-and-order" surged.[55]

On February 6, 1968, Senator Walter Mondale called up his own amendment to H.R. 2516. The Minnesota Democrat proposed a federal open housing law that reflected President Johnson's provisions of two years earlier. In opposition, Long used many of the same arguments against the 1968 provisions as he had two years earlier. Notably, Long charged that "those who would argue for such legislation do so on the predication that such a law would enable the Negro to leave the ghetto. This is hollow reasoning, for it fails to consider the economic realities surrounding the Negro in the ghetto." He added that "there is indeed a danger that a fair-housing law not only will fail to improve the lot of the Negro; I worry, frankly, that it will further damage this country's already precarious race relations by being nothing more than an empty, frustrating promise to the Negro." While Long's rhetoric reflected a political stalling tactic, his statement also pointed to a very real political phenomenon: expectations, when raised but not fulfilled, led to frustration, which eventually exploded.[56]

The arguments and delaying tactics of Long and other opponents of the 1968 civil rights bill could not stop its passage; by the late 1960s, southern senators were finding themselves alienated in their own party as a new, more liberal wing of the Democratic Party was coming to prominence. The Senate approved H.R. 2516, with revisions, on March 11; the House agreed to the Senate version on April 10. President Johnson signed it into law the very next day, April 11, 1968, a mere week after Martin Luther King's assassination in Memphis, Tennessee.[57]

Vietnam

If Long fiercely opposed most of Lyndon Johnson's civil rights proposal, he just as strongly endorsed the president's early policies toward Vietnam. American involvement in that Asian nation dated from the Eisenhower administration; Kennedy had inherited and expanded it. After his death, it became a problem for Johnson, and it was magnified in early August 1964, when North Vietnamese boats reportedly fired upon American naval vessels in the Gulf of Tonkin.

Later that month, Russell Long, along with every other member of Congress except two, voted "yea" on the Gulf of Tonkin resolution, which allowed Johnson to "take all necessary measures" to protect American interests and to prevent further aggression in Southeast Asia. In essence, the resolution was no different than the Eisenhower Doctrine of 1957, which Long had opposed. The reason for his shift in voting philosophy probably had more to do with partisan politics than anything else. Eisenhower in 1957 was a Republican who had earned Long's ire by not expanding social welfare spending; Johnson was a Democrat and longtime friend who had assisted in Long's elevation to some of the highest levels of the Democratic Party in Washington. Too, Long's Cold War views had hardened following the Cuban crises of the early 1960s.

In February 1965, Johnson ordered the first bombings of North Vietnam; in March he sent in the first U.S. combat troops; five months later, he sent fifty thousand additional troops to the Southeast Asian nation. Further escalation—by the end of 1965, two hundred thousand American troops were in Vietnam—led to Senate Foreign Relations Committee hearings in January 1966, at which a number of senators and witnesses publicly criticized Johnson's Vietnam policy. The years 1967 and 1968 brought even more escalation; by the latter year, more than half a million American troops were in Vietnam.[58]

Befitting a hard-line Cold Warrior, Russell Long took an aggressive stance on Vietnam. If his stances "make those who disagree describe me as a hawk instead of a dove," he said in 1966, "I shall not quarrel with the term." He explained "I believe that there is much hard fighting ahead before the dove of peace can find a place to roost in Saigon, and it is the hawks, not the doves, who will have to do the fighting if freedom is to exist anywhere in southeast Asia."[59]

Long's arguments for a strong posture in Vietnam reflected his beliefs in the central tenets of military containment and his basic understandings about the Cold War itself. At the root of his support for the Johnson administration's Vietnam policies lay Long's firm conviction that the American systems of democracy and capitalism faced an ongoing, to-the-death, battle royale with the forces of international communism. These beliefs formed the bedrock of his Cold War postures, and they were brought into sharper focus in the mid- and late 1960s. "Communist doctrine"—whether in the Soviet Union, China, or Vietnam—"is to take over the whole world," Long said in March 1965. A month later, he stressed that Americans would have "to accept the fact that it is better to accept the burden of fighting every attack on freedom" than to allow communism to spread from the boundaries within which it was contained.[60]

Long doubted that anything could be gained from backing down or negotiating. "We have found out that the world is round, and that we are on the same planet together," he said in April 1965. "Those who want to back away from Vietnam will find that we will have to stop them somewhere. We must confront them in Vietnam and all over the world; and it is going to be that way in our lifetime." The only other potential outcome "would be to be under the domination of Communist China or Communist Russia." No middle ground existed. Either halt communist expansion through force of arms or allow it to trample the entire globe, including the United States. For proof, Long maintained that one only had to observe recent history. Vietnam was but another example of an extended pattern of "Communist aggression—and subversion—and sabotage and terrorism that could be seen around the world over the previous two decades or so" and "today, in Vietnam, we are seeing the latest efforts by the Communists to seize new lands and to capture a people who want to be independent."[61]

By 1966, Long's statements had coalesced around classic justifications for both an American presence in Vietnam and for escalation. The United States could not afford to take a weak-kneed, appeasement-type of approach to the matter, he argued, because "to permit any of these areas to fall to ruthless aggressions would be merely to whet the appetite of the aggressors." Backing down would only "set the stage for a larger and more fateful showdown somewhere else." Long added that "there is no doubt that the Communist aggressors are going to probe and test our courage. They are going to test our will." Force of arms might stop them, but "if they can defeat us by intimidating or scaring us, that, of course, will be the method they will use." The communists' goal, in Long's understanding, "is no less than the elimination of freedom—first from the territories on their present borders, and then from the territories adjacent to these expanded borders, and on beyond these horizons." If the United States backed down and allowed Vietnam to fall, Long asked, "does anyone think that India is going to stand against Communist China? Does anyone think that Pakistan or Indonesia is going to stand against Communist China? Who is going to stand against Communist China when they see they cannot count on the United States to stand by with fortitude."[62]

Long's stances on Vietnam—and on Johnson's prosecution of the war—reflected those of most of his southern colleagues. Although some southern senators were not particularly vocal one way or the other, many, including Long's Louisiana colleague Allen Ellender, John Stennis and James Eastland of Mississippi, Strom Thurmond of South Carolina, and George Smathers of Florida, consistently voiced their support for American involvement in the war and voted for supplemental appropriations bills to pay for it. They also tended to oppose any negotiations or compromise with the North Vietnamese and, as such, reflected the opinions of southerners in general. Like their elder statesman, Georgia's Richard Russell, most of the southern senators, including Long, assumed that simply because American troops were on the ground, congressional and popular support for their activities should be resolute and unwavering. Although they tended to disfavor any sort of public criticism of the administration's war strategy, they did at times criticize Johnson for fighting under the constraints of limited warfare. If the war was to be won, the southerners believed, it should be fought with an all-out effort, regardless of costs—or casualties.[63]

But a distinct minority of Long's southern colleagues, and a much more substantial group of his fellow Democrats nationally, came to oppose the president's Vietnam policies. As a result of increasing American combat deaths, revelations that the administration's reports on the immediate causes of hostilities might not have been truthful, and widespread bombing of North Vietnam, southerners such as Albert Gore of Tennessee and, most important, J. William Fulbright of Arkansas, began calling for a negotiated settlement. In February 1966 Fulbright, chair of the Senate Foreign Relations Committee, held a series of televised hearings into the administration's conduct of the war; the hearings displayed to the American public the very real strategic and intellectual divergences between the administration and its critics.[64]

Russell Long considered these Senate critics of the Johnson administration a small, if vocal, minority and insinuated that their criticism gave "aid and comfort to the enemy." He also contended that the criticism skewed perceptions about the resolve of the American people and their government for winning the war. Above all, Long maintained that condemnation of the president and his policies undermined Johnson's ability to effectively wage war as commander in chief. Johnson "is the one who has to bear the brunt of the responsibility. He has to decide what we will do. He must take the final step. He must make the final plan for victory or for the success our forces may achieve while fighting on any battlefield." Long's frustrations with the stances of colleagues on Foreign Relations led him to resign his committee seat in the spring of 1966.[65]

Long and Louisiana in the 1960s

Although some observers had suggested Russell Long would take over the Long political machine following his Uncle Earl's death, by the mid-1960s he had clearly become a national politician, and his interest in his home state's internal politics waned. Yet his influence on Louisiana and its citizens remained powerful. Within the space of a few weeks in March and April 1961, for instance, Long proposed an amendment to the Federal Water Protection Control Act to allow the federal government "to see to it that future reservoirs are constructed not only to furnish relief against impending floodwaters, but also to give due consideration to the collection and proper distribution of much-needed water of good quality" along the Red River, and he introduced legislation to protect the state's shrimping industry by means of a tariff on imported shrimp. As he had throughout his career, he took an active role in debates over the Sugar Act, which directly affected thousands of south Louisiana farmers and seasonal workers. And in 1965, he played a crucial role in garnering a professional football franchise—the Saints—for New Orleans, thanks to a deal struck with National Football League commissioner Pete Rozelle. Long and his fellow Louisianian, Congressman Hale Boggs, shepherded through Congress antitrust legislation that allowed the NFL and its rival, the American Football League, to merge. In exchange, Rozelle oversaw the awarding of an expansion team to the Crescent City.[66]

Also in 1965, Long reacted swiftly following the devastating September 9 landfall of Hurricane Betsy. The storm left most of New Orleans without power, inundated many of the city's neighborhoods, and left sixty-five dead. The next day, Long telephoned President Johnson to ask him to visit Louisiana and let him know "we have really had it down there, and we need your help." He also emphasized the help a visit could provide for Johnson, politically. "You lost that state last year," he reminded Johnson. "You could pick it up just like looking at it right now by going down there as the President just to see what happened." When Johnson seemed noncommittal about the visit and said he might send his "best man" in his place, Long countered "we are not the least bit interested in your best man." Three hours later, Long and the president boarded a helicopter on the White House grounds, flew to Andrews Air Force Base, and boarded Air Force One for a flight to New Orleans. That evening the president said, "I am here because I want to see with my own eyes what the unhappy alliance of wind and water have done to this land and to its good people. And when I leave today to go back to Washington you can be sure that the federal government's total resources, with the help of the fine Louisiana Delegation, will be turned toward helping this state and its citizens find its way back from this tragedy." Johnson promised to send in teams from the Office of Emergency Management and the Corps of Engineers to help with the recovery effort and said, "The Small Business Administration has already declared this area a disaster area and will be prepared to make long-term loans to rehabilitate both business establishments and all the homes that we saw, their roofs under water a few moments ago."[67]

A month later, Long joined with his colleagues from Louisiana, Mississippi, and Florida in seeing though to passage a bill "to provide assistance to sufferers from disasters caused by Hurricane Betsy." According to Long, the bill provided for forgiveness of Small Business Administration loans made to those too poor to repay them or who did not have insurance against tidal surges caused by hurricanes, and it proposed that the government study the feasibility of creating a "Federal program to insure people against the devastating effects of hurricanes." Long explained that

> the bill does not provide any sort of Federal grant for any situation in which people were able to insure themselves against this disaster. Unfortunately, insurance companies, for a number of reasons which they have explained logically, will not insure people

> against the effects of tidal waves. Sometimes hurricanes have a way of pushing ahead of them huge amounts of water. The tidal wave pushed ahead of Hurricane Betsy was from 9 to 20 feet high when it hit the flat coast of Louisiana. In a number of areas all homes and buildings were completely wiped out by the tidal wave.

To highlight the importance of the legislation, Long contrasted his own situation following the hurricane with those who had either no insurance or the wrong type of insurance. A tree had been uprooted and fallen into his house, causing thousands of dollars worth of damage. Although insurance covered his damages, he noted that "very little could be done for these poor people who were wiped out and lost everything they had as a result of the tidal wave which accompanied the hurricane. It was the worst disaster as far as property damage is concerned that has ever hit the United States."[68]

Long used his personal relationship with President Johnson for more than simply prodding the Texan to act following Hurricane Betsy. In late 1964, he called the president and pleaded with him not to close Fort Polk, an army training base in central Louisiana. The base had been closed once before, following the end of the Korean War, and Long had influenced President John Kennedy's decision to reopen it in 1961. By November 1964, however, the base was rumored to be on a list of dozens of military installations to be shuttered. Long reminded Johnson that he had fought on Johnson's side during the Medicare debates that year, and he hoped the favor would be returned by the president through a call to Secretary of Defense Robert McNamara to at least find out if the base was on the list. "As much as I've done for you," Long said, "you could at least make a telephone call to see if I'm dead or not." Johnson promised to do it "as soon as I hang up here." The president called Long later to tell him Fort Polk would remain open.[69]

Long also made certain the oil industry, which drove Louisiana's economy during the 1960s, received as much legislative help as he could muster. From his perch in the Senate Finance Committee, he kept a watchful eye on import quotas and tariffs on oil, and he consistently defended the oil depletion allowance that allowed oil companies to shelter a portion of their gross income from federal income taxes. Long maintained that the depletion allowance was a necessary mechanism for companies involved in hit-and-miss operations like exploring for new pockets of oil under dry land and increasingly offshore. Of course, Long contended that what was good for the oil companies was good for Louisiana, and to an extent he was correct. The state's severance tax, levied on nonrenewable resources taken out of the ground—oil and natural gas, for the most part, in Louisiana—provided an enormous source of revenue and funded many of Louisiana's governmental programs. The depletion allowance, in Long's estimation, led to more oil production in his home state, which meant more money for things like state-sponsored education, public works, and medical care in Louisiana.[70]

What was good for Louisiana was also good for Long himself. His father had left thirty-one shares of the Win or Lose Oil Company's stock to the family at the time of his death. Win or Lose had been founded by Huey in 1934 with three partners, who used their insiders' knowledge of state landholdings and oil exploration to sell mineral leasing rights on state-owned properties. In 1935, the company paid out its first dividends: Huey received $2,000 for each of his thirty-one shares, for a total of $62,000. Over the ensuing decades, the company was reorganized and renamed Independent Oil and Gas, and its stock came to be worth millions for the Long family.[71]

Owning shares of oil companies—and profiting from them—did little to undermine Long's voting support in Louisiana. Nor did his support of most of Johnson's Great Society diminish his popularity back home. And his strong support of the president's escalation policies placed him squarely within the majority of Louisiana's voters, as did his stances on civil rights initiatives. He handily won the election of 1962, trouncing his Republican opponent, Shreveport attorney Taylor O'Hearn. Even after the passage of the Voting Rights Act of 1965 and its resultant massive increase in black voter turnout, Long commanded a substantial amount of admiration and political cachet in the Bayou State, so much so that he won 87 percent of the vote in the 1968 Democratic primary.[72]

1968

Long's popularity in 1968 contrasted sharply with Lyndon Johnson's. Despite the liberal legislative triumphs of the Great Society, certain policies of the Johnson administration had come under increasing assault. At the center of these attacks lay a widespread critique of the administration's prosecution of the war in Vietnam and the still contentious debates over American race relations. The antiwar movement, fueled by a growing youth counterculture but also fostered by political, social, and religious leaders, grew rapidly during 1966 and 1967. At the same time, black Americans continued to express their discontent with the slow pace of civil rights advances; their frustration increasingly boiled over into violence during the mid-1960s.

In early 1968, the North Vietnamese leadership and the National Liberation Front launched the Tet Offensive, which, although an eventual American victory, seriously undermined American public confidence that the war was being won. Democratic "peace" candidates, including Long's Senate colleagues Eugene McCarthy and Robert Kennedy, emerged as challengers to a Johnson presidential reelection bid. That bid never came, however. On March 31, 1968, the president announced that he would not seek reelection. Four days after the president's announcement, an assassin's bullet took the life of Martin Luther King Jr., leaving the nation stunned; Robert Kennedy's assassination, a scant two months later, further battered a weary public. Vice President Hubert H. Humphrey assumed the mantle of administration candidate. Humphrey promised, for the most part, to carry on Johnson's policies. When the Democratic Party gathered in Chicago for its nominating convention, the political battles between Humphrey's backers and McCarthy's antiwar supporters in the convention hall were overshadowed only by the violent confrontations between police and protesters in the streets.[73]

Conservatives capitalized on the growing public discontent with the Democratic Party. Former Alabama governor George Wallace, running on an anti–big government, anti–civil rights platform, waged one of the most vigorous and successful third party campaigns in American history. Wallace won a plurality in Long's home state of Louisiana and carried four other Deep South states. Republican candidate Richard M. Nixon promised "peace with honor" in Vietnam and a return of law and order on American streets. He also wooed both southern voters and southern politicians in an attempt to capitalize on white southern disaffection with the politics of the national Democratic Party. When election day rolled around in November, Nixon narrowly defeated Humphrey in the popular vote while scoring a decisive victory in the electoral college. Only four years after Johnson's massive landslide election, the tide of American politics had turned.[74]

Between 1960 and 1968, Russell Long achieved heights of political influence rivaled by few of his contemporaries. As Democratic whip and chair of the Senate Finance Committee, he oversaw the creation of some of the greatest liberal programs of the post–World War II era, yet as he had since arriving in the Senate in the late 1940s, during the 1960s Long consistently opposed all federal legislation to guarantee more equitable civil and political rights to black Americans. Especially after the Bay of Pigs failure, he strengthened his commitment to aggressive diplomatic and military prosecution of the Cold War. In Louisiana, Long increasingly took a hands-off policy to the state's internal politics, even while using his influence in Washington to directly benefit the state and its citizens.

As the 1960s gave way to the 1970s, Long would maintain his pragmatic political philosophy. He also continued to work across political boundaries, often supporting the initiatives of the Republican presidents Richard Nixon and Gerald Ford as much, if not more so, than he subsequently did those of Democrat Jimmy Carter. Yet American politics were changing around Long, and his political style was falling out of favor as both parties became more rigid in their stances as the 1970s progressed.

CHAPTER FIVE

Power Broker, 1969–1980

NOT LONG BEFORE the 1968 elections, Russell Long received a letter from historian T. Harry Williams. "At 12:15 noon today I finished the book!" wrote Williams. "I feel as though a great load has been lifted." After thirteen years of working on a biography of Long's father, Huey, Williams was ready to ship the manuscript off to his publisher. "It's been worth it. I think this is a great book," Williams unabashedly stated, "and although there may be some things in it you won't like, it will give him his deserved place in history." Before sending the book in, however, the professor asked Long to read over it. "I hope you give it a fairly quick reading so that I will have ample time to consider your suggestions," Williams added. If Long had any suggestions, and if Williams took them, is unknown. Long must have been pleased, however, to see that Williams had written an assessment of his father that was largely, although not uniformly, positive. The book showed a Huey Long driven by good intentions and concern for the underprivileged, and it portrayed him as a racial moderate.[1]

For Russell Long, Williams's portrayal of his father in *Huey Long* (1969) provided a crucial turning point in two aspects of his life. From a personal point of view, Long likely learned more about his father from Williams's book than he knew from his own life. For most of the sixteen years that Russell and Huey Long had both been alive, and especially after Huey became governor when Russell was nine years old, their lives had intersected very little. Huey typically was campaigning or politicking across Louisiana or in Washington D.C.; when in Baton Rouge or New

Orleans, he spent most of his time away from the family residence. From a political standpoint, the revisionist portrayal of Huey Long that Williams presented to the world stood in stark contrast to almost all of the earlier works on the subject, and this fact had an important political effect. Williams's argument that Huey had actually been trying to do good for the people of Louisiana, and for the nation, justified Russell Long's use of the memory of his father as a political tool and bolstered his stance as a champion of the little people. Even after he had become established as a successful politician in his own right, Long continued to call forth the image of his father. Long had used the memory of his father and his father's political stances to win elections and to justify votes on particular issues. Now he had the judgment of an esteemed historian to defend his use of those memories.[2]

Russell Long's ability to use the historical Huey provided him with a ready arsenal of political justifications, stories, and anecdotes. But, as would become evident in the late 1960s and 1970s, he could not use the historical Huey as a political precedent for all matters, even those that, had he still been alive, would have been close to Huey's political heart. In part, this reality reflected the fact that Long had become more ensconced in the Washington, D.C., political arena than ever before—and he had determined that the best way to help Louisiana was to stay out of internal state politics and take care of business in Washington—and the Huey stories resonated much more strongly with Louisianians than with national politicians. Russell grappled during these years with proposals—either his own or others'—that in effect sought to fulfill his father's economic principles as laid out in Share Our Wealth, albeit by different means. In the early 1970s, Long led the opposition to a proposal that came nearest to what his father had called for, the Nixon administration's Family Assistance Plan (FAP), but at mid-decade he offered up his own program, Employment Stock Ownership Plans (ESOPs), that purportedly would achieve Share Our Wealth's goals. His opposition to FAP and support of ESOPs came to define Long's politics in the 1970s.

Those years also brought with them shifts in the national party system that redefined the political foundations of both the Democrats and the Republicans. As the consensus on American liberalism fractured, thanks largely to the Johnson administration's perceived failure in Vietnam and the perception of big government run rampant, both parties reacted by slowly shifting toward extremes of the political spectrum, the Democrats to the left and the Republicans to the right. Long, however, maintained his allegiance to the Democratic Party and his commitment to the practical political stances he had held throughout his career. As the parties shifted around him, Long remained relatively constant, and as a result, appeared to be increasingly conservative when, in actuality, it was his context, the Democratic Party, that was becoming more liberal. Long's consistency most often meant ignoring the political boundaries that were becoming more rigid during the 1970s, as in his support for many—but certainly not all—of Republican president Nixon's programs, while later opposing many of Democrat Jimmy Carter's.

Shifting Political Winds in the Senate

Long's political influence, which had grown steadily during the first two decades of his career, took a hit in January 1969 when Massachusetts senator Edward Kennedy challenged him for the majority whip position. The contest stoked Long's competitive fires, but he had not set himself up well for victory. Long had challenged Majority Leader Mike Mansfield's authority on numerous occasions and had exhibited a penchant for taking odd political stances. In 1966, for instance, he had defended embattled Connecticut senator Thomas Dodd, who had been charged with using campaign funds for personal expenses and was eventually censured by a vote of 92 to 5. Mansfield also thought that Long neglected his whip's duties while focusing too much on his Senate Finance chairmanship. He felt that Long might soon be out of step with the majority of the Democratic Party, which was becoming more youthful and more liberal with the rise of such politicians as Kennedy and Edmund Muskie. Long was part of the old structure of the party, one which had been dominated, in the Senate at least, by southerners. That structure was changing. Ultimately, the Democrats were reshaping their party into a much more exclusively liberal party at the same moment that the Republicans veered toward conservatism. Russell Long, whose pragmatic political style and philosophy could not be labeled exclusively conservative or liberal, did not fit into the Democratic leadership's plans. Finally, Mansfield had grown anxious about Long's tendency to consume alcohol excessively.[3]

Long's battle with the bottle had been festering since the end of World War II. His arrival in the Senate had not helped matters. "Alcoholism permeated the institution," Louis Gould has written, and the problem ran particularly rampant at mid-century, when Long was establishing himself as a new senator. The list of alcohol-dependent senators of the day reads like a who's who of well-known and influential politicos. Richard Russell, Joseph McCarthy, Estes Kefauver, John McClellan, and Everett Dirksen were among the most prominent. The American public knew very little about the upper house's culture of overindulgence; senators, their staff members, and the press corps all downplayed, if they did not downright ignore, indiscretions and drunkenness, even when they took place on the Senate floor. For Russell Long, the problem was compounded by the fact that, in 1957, his wife, Katherine, and children had moved back to Baton Rouge, and from then until 1969, Long lived the life of a bachelor. During those twelve years, the still relatively young man was elevated to positions of extraordinary stress, which he handled by turning to the bottle. It was not until after he and Katherine divorced, in early 1969, and his marriage to Carolyn Basson in December of that year, that Long began to cut back on his drinking.[4]

Two years later, Long's senior colleague from Louisiana, Allen Ellender, died of a heart attack during his 1972 reelection campaign. At the time of his death, Ellender chaired the Senate Appropriations Committee and served as the Senate's president pro tem. Although personality and age differences had kept Long and Ellender from becoming close friends during their twenty-three years together in the Senate, Ellender had been a near-constant presence in Long's political life. Ellender had supported Huey Long as a member of the Louisiana House of Representatives in the mid-1930s and had been rewarded with the speaker's position. Following Huey's death and Rose Long's brief Senate career, he had been elected to fill the empty Senate seat in 1936. Twelve years later, Russell and Earl Long plotted their strategy for getting Russell elected to the Senate following John Overton's death in 1948. Ellender provided crucial advice, encouraging Earl to offset any political damage that might have occurred as a result of Russell's youthfulness by appointing a temporary seat warmer until a special election could be held after Russell's thirtieth birthday.[5]

Long and Ellender shared a political philosophy based on practical considerations and reflecting their mid-twentieth-century southern political context. Ellender's biographer, Thomas Becnel, has called him a "coalition builder" and "consensus politician," terms that might just as easily be applied to Long for most of his career. Both Ellender and Long tempered their conservatism in certain realms, race relations and civil rights in particular, with stances in support of those facets of New Deal liberalism that most directly benefited or reflected the opinions of their constituents, notably aggressive Cold War posturing along with support for public works and certain types of social welfare legislation. Ellender and Long were both willing to cross party lines at times, and they both understood the necessity of compromise in order to gain political results. In short, although Ellender may have been slightly more conservative than Long, they both plainly understood the dangers of being rigidly defined by their politics.[6]

When Ellender died, his opponent for the 1972 Democratic nomination, J. Bennett Johnston, immediately became the front-runner and won election to the Senate shortly in November. Johnston was a graduate of West Point and a lawyer, and he had grown up in Russell Long's boyhood hometown of Shreveport. His father had been a loyal supporter of Earl Long who worked as an attorney to assist the inheritance tax collector for Louisiana. Johnston was elected to the Louisiana House of Representatives in 1962 and to the state Senate in 1968. In those offices, he made a name for himself as a fiscally conservative Democrat and a good government reformer. In 1971, Johnston ran against Edwin Edwards for the Democratic gubernatorial nomination; the race turned out to be the closest ever in the state. Edwards received 50.2 percent of the vote, Johnston 49.8. Following that defeat, Johnston had focused his energies on winning Ellender's seat.[7]

Once he reached the Senate, Johnston and Long quickly formed a formidable working relationship. By 1977, they were considered as "the most effective, taking-care-of-its-own-interests delegation in the Senate." In particular, both took pains to protect what they considered to be Louisiana's most vital interest: the oil industry. Until the mid-1980s, Long from his position in the Senate Finance Committee and Johnston from his seat (and later chairmanship) of the Appropriations Committee's Subcommittee on Energy and Water Development, kept watchful eyes on any legislation that could threaten the foundation of Louisiana's economy.[8]

Long and Nixon

Long lost his whip position to Kennedy on January 3, 1969. That year he also watched his former Senate colleague, Richard Nixon, be sworn in as president. Nixon had won the presidential election the previous year by championing "backlash politics." Denouncing Johnson's failures in Vietnam and the protestors who challenged American involvement, Nixon promised "peace with honor," and he championed a return to law and order in the United States. In the South, he courted conservative white voters who for decades had been members of the Democratic Party, and he tried to convince conservative southern politicians to jump to the Republican camp.

The plan to pull southern Democratic politicians into the Republican fold was largely unsuccessful, although the GOP made, and would continue to make, significant inroads into the southern white electorate. Nixon and his advisors understood that claiming the conservative mantle for the Republican Party broadened the party's appeal to many southerners. Yet many of the Nixon administration's actual legislative initiatives reflected a continuation of the politics of the New Deal liberal coalition rather than the burgeoning New Right. For southerners and their political leaders, therefore, support for Nixon's proposals did not always mean support for a conservative agenda. Thus, although Long did support the Republican president on a significant number of legislative proposals, that support did not necessarily reflect a shift to more conservative stances. Rather, Long continued to show a willingness to transcend political boundaries that had always defined his political philosophy.[9]

Long's support for Nixon came early. In 1969 and 1970, he joined almost every other southern senator in voting for Nixon's conservative Supreme Court nominees, Clement Haynesworth and Harold Carswell. Besides being an attempt to shift the Court away from the judicial activism that had annoyed conservatives since the 1950s, Nixon's nominations reflected yet another appeal by Nixon for southern support. Both of the judges were southerners themselves, and both were strict constructionists. Haynesworth, however, had engaged in unethical practices, and unions and civil rights groups opposed him with a well-organized campaign. Carswell had rendered blatantly racist decisions while on the bench in Florida and had done nothing to distinguish himself in jurisprudence. After both nominations failed, Nixon put forth Harry Blackmun, a northerner with few red flags on his record. Long supported Blackmun's nomination.[10]

As chair of the Senate Finance Committee, which oversaw matters of fiscal policy, Long supported many of Nixon's taxation policies. He backed the president's 1969 proposal to extend a 10 percent surtax to cover the costs of the Vietnam War, and he repeatedly endorsed the administration's requests for increases in the federal debt ceiling. Long also provided crucial support for the Revenue Act of 1969, which implemented many of the administration's tax reform policies. In order to more equitably distribute the burden of taxation across all classes, the Finance Committee version of the bill cut down on the overall number of tax preferences and created minimum income levels—below which a citizen could escape taxation—for those that remained. Long said that the bill would "reduce the scope of the tax preferences that enable some individuals and corporations to escape their fair share of the tax burden." As floor manager of the bill, Long called the committee's version "the best approach to our tax problems that I have seen in my career as a Senator," and he challenged his colleagues not to add "too many costly additional tax relief provisions" or to whittle "away on the tax reform provisions in the bill." To Long's way of thinking, if the current tax system placed too much of a burden on one segment of the population while leaving too many unburdened, then it needed reform. And if members of Congress used the bill to gain passage of their own pet projects, then the legislators doing so did not really care about reform. Long noted that during Finance Committee deliberations, he had compromised by not challenging the majority's decision to reduce depletion allowances for oil and gas industries. Such a reduction would adversely affect Louisiana's oil economy. Despite that, Long emphasized that he was "wholeheartedly in favor of adoption of the bill because it represents the most fundamental and far-reaching reform measure since the adoption of the income tax."[11]

Long's stance led to a showdown with Finance Committee

member Albert Gore of Tennessee, who offered an amendment to raise the personal income tax exemption from six hundred to one thousand dollars. Long contended that Gore's amendment, if approved, would lead to significant revenue losses and a more complicated tax process. Both of these factors, but particularly the potential loss of revenue, could lead to a presidential veto if the Gore amendment made it into the bill. The full Senate ultimately compromised on the matter by raising the personal exemption to eight hundred dollars. The Senate voted to pass the tax legislation on December 11, 1969; despite his opposition to the Gore amendment, Long voted "yea." President Nixon signed the measure into law on December 30.[12]

Long's support of many of Nixon's proposals continued in 1970, when he voted in favor of the administration's Air Quality Act amendments, which set five-year deadlines for creating low-pollution vehicles, and its Occupational Safety and Health Act, which created safety standards for Americans in the workplace. The following year, he again served as point man for a Nixon tax reform package. As amended by Long's Finance Committee, the package increased both the personal income tax exemption and the minimum standard deduction. It authorized new deductions for child care expenses and removed excise taxes on automobiles and trucks. In hopes that it would spur the economy while at the same time reducing unemployment, the reform bill instituted tax credits for investments in business; granted deductions of up to 20 percent of wages for workers recently removed from the welfare rolls; and included various changes to depreciation, export, and import taxes. As he had in 1969, Long urged his colleagues to "exercise restraint in offering additional floor amendments to the pending bill," but over the next week and a half, senators added so many amendments that one opponent, John Tower of Texas, said, "We have treated it on this floor as a Christmas tree and have hung all manner of ornamentation on it." Nevertheless, a majority of the Senate, including Long, approved the legislation and sent it to conference committee, where many of the Senate amendments were stripped off. Long endorsed the conference committee version of the bill that was later signed into law by Nixon, although his old populist proclivities reared their heads when he admitted that he had lingering misgivings that "permanent new tax relief of tremendous magnitude is being provided for the business community" while "unfortunately, so far as individual taxpayers are concerned the bill adds little new relief to the tax cuts" Congress had approved in 1969.[13]

Long and Nixon both publicly opposed the Supreme Court's *Swann v. Mecklenburg* decision of 1971, which mandated busing public school students if necessary to achieve true desegregation. As he had earlier in his career, Long argued that such forced integration of the races actually undermined rather than guaranteed rights. Busing, he said, revoked from parents one "of their most precious rights, at least one right that once existed, which should certainly be the right of all parents, under the usual circumstances, to send their children to the school nearest their homes."[14]

Long approved of most of Nixon's policies toward Vietnam, too. When Nixon campaigned for the presidency in 1968, he had promised "peace with honor" in Vietnam. That peace was not quick in coming. Although the American troop presence in the Big Muddy gradually declined through a process Nixon referred to as Vietnamization, the Nixon administration geographically expanded the war by first bombing and then invading Cambodia in 1970. According to a United Press International poll, Long and only two other Democrats, his fellow southerners Richard Russell and John Stennis, approved of Nixon's decision to expand the war into Cambodia. On April 10, 1970, Long further showed his commitment to both Nixon's Vietnam policies and, more broadly, to his belief in presidential authority in matters of war when he voted against the repeal of the Gulf of Tonkin Resolution. That same year, he opposed an amendment sponsored by

Frank Church of Idaho and John Sherman Cooper of Kentucky that proposed cutting off funds for American forces fighting in Cambodia if they were not withdrawn by June 30, 1970.[15]

Long's commitment to Nixon's Vietnam policies had limits, however, and in 1973, he joined a substantial majority of senators in voting to pass the War Powers Resolution, which stated that if a president sent troops into overseas combat without first gaining congressional backing, he would have two days to inform Congress and sixty days to receive congressional approval of the actions; without the approval, the troops would have to be brought back home. A deliberate swipe at the sort of actions that Lyndon Johnson had used to escalate American involvement in Vietnam, the War Power Resolution was vetoed by Nixon, but Congress overrode the veto in November 1973. Long's support of the resolution probably reflected a disillusionment that Nixon, like Johnson before him, was fighting a limited war in a situation that Long felt required a stronger commitment. Too, the Louisiana senator may have reflected more deeply on the nature of the Senate-executive relationship, and as he had during debates over the Eisenhower Doctrine in 1957, determined that the upper house had to protect its role in diplomatic affairs.[16]

However, Long was not always so anxious to extend the Constitution's protections and privileges for certain segments of the American population. In 1970, he voted against extending the provisions of the Voting Rights Act of 1965 for another five years, and he opposed efforts to lower the federal voting age to eighteen. Two years later, however, Long voted to expand the constitutional standing of women by joining a large majority of his colleagues in approving the Equal Rights Amendment. He did so despite concerns that the amendment, if passed by the states, would do away with "a myriad of laws passed to protect women, for their advantage as the weaker sex." He was particularly worried that women might be required to register for the draft and make alimony payments to men.[17]

Welfare Reform

Although Long used his considerable influence over tax policy to support many of the Nixon administration's fiscal programs, at times he could be a formidable foe of the president. This was especially true on matters of welfare reform. From the chair's seat on the Senate Finance Committee, Long wielded an enormous amount of influence over social welfare legislation. All changes to Social Security, welfare programs, Medicare, and Medicaid had to make their way through Finance. Beginning in 1969, Long's power on the committee, and his bitter opposition to a Nixon welfare reform scheme, resulted in a showdown with the administration that lasted for nearly three years.

The origins of the clash lay in the backlash politics of 1968 that had energized Nixon's candidacy. Swelling rolls of the Aid to Families with Dependent Children program (AFDC), particularly in northern cities like New York and Detroit, made welfare a hot political topic that year. In 1960, AFDC had constituted the largest single federal welfare program, and its rolls more than tripled over the next ten years. By the middle of the 1960s, many American voters had developed a perception that AFDC recipients had become dependent on welfare, resulting in what Long, among many others, called the "welfare mess." Welfare dependency allegedly contributed to the disintegration of the traditional American family—particularly the traditional American *black* family—by rewarding, through AFDC payments, families headed by single women. The subsequent breakdown of black family life led to the destructive violence racking American cities, while the welfare payments undermined any incentive to work, according to critics. Nixon had capitalized on the growing unrest during the 1968 presidential campaign, yet it was Nixon who, within a year of his election, proposed a plan to significantly expand the welfare rolls.[18]

On August 8, 1969, President Nixon delivered a televised speech outlining his welfare reform program. Echoing the contentions of most welfare critics, he termed the contemporary system "a colossal failure," unfair in its benefits and destructive to families. People who did not want to work disrupted a system designed to aid those would could not work, Nixon argued, and gainfully employed Americans paid the bill. The president declared that, therefore, "we will abolish the present welfare system." In its place he proposed "a new family assistance system." This new system, known more properly as the Family Assistance Plan, initially would be more expensive than the old AFDC, but the cost would be more than offset by future benefits. FAP would aid the "working poor," in addition to the unemployed, by creating "a foundation under the income of every American family with dependent children that cannot care for itself." To discourage people from giving up work to go on the dole, Nixon promised "a family head already employed at low wages could get a family assistance supplement; those who work would no longer be discriminated against." President Nixon expected that most Americans would be willing to work, but he also thought that a certain segment of the population would prefer not to. Therefore, "under this proposal, everyone who accepts benefits must also accept work or training, provided suitable jobs are available either locally or at some distance if transportation is provided." He emphasized that there were exceptions to this final stipulation, including "those unable to work and mothers of preschool children."[19]

The Family Assistance Plan, Nixon assured his audience, was not a guaranteed income, under which "everyone would be assured a minimum income, regardless of how much he was capable of earning, regardless of what his need was, regardless of whether or not he was willing to work." Guaranteed incomes encouraged laziness and irresponsibility, Nixon asserted, and therefore were contrary to American ideals. "Family assistance," on the other hand, "recognizes a need and establishes a responsibility. It provides help to those in need and, in turn, requires that those who receive help work to the extent of their capabilities."[20]

Nixon's rhetoric struck a chord with Russell Long. In February 1970, before the legislation creating FAP made its way to the Finance Committee, Long wrote that "there is much to be said in favor of any approach which will both strengthen family life and aid families to become economically independent." But what FAP sounded like when Nixon discussed it, and what its provisions actually would have created, were two dramatically different things, as Long soon discovered.[21]

The Family Assistance Plan had been in formulation for months before Nixon announced it. Its provisions called for a guaranteed income of $500 for each adult and $300 for each child in a family with no income, a $720 work disregard in the form of food stamps, and a taxation rate designed to make work attractive. The plan's benefits would be available only to families with one or more dependent children. Total benefits for a family of four could reach a maximum of $2,320. Although this level would be only about two-thirds of the poverty level, the Nixon administration maintained that it would provide a foundation upon which future income could be built. The plan included work incentives, designed so that they would not interfere too much with the plan's provisions for a guaranteed income, a phrase Nixon's aides tried not to use when making their proposals. Instead, they most often referred to a "negative income tax," which paid individuals or families if their income fell below a certain threshold.[22]

According to the Nixon administration, FAP signaled a new emphasis on providing direct cash benefits as opposed to government services, and unlike Lyndon Johnson's Great Society, focused on equality of results rather than opportunity. Providing direct payments to the people who needed it most would then allow them to decide, rather than have the government decide for them, what they would use that money for. Such emphasis on individual responsibility meshed well with conservative arguments that the federal government should minimize its involvement in the day-to-day lives of the citizens. FAP would also provide greater benefits for states that had not received equal shares of the welfare pie; indeed, it would have its greatest effect in places like Russell Long's Louisiana, where AFDC benefits barely dented poverty. And, although Nixon left it unstated in his August 8 speech, the Family Assistance Plan, by expanding the nation's welfare rolls with some 13 million new recipients, would function as a means of redistributing national wealth. If the program was going to guarantee an income for all Americans through the means of a reverse income tax, then FAP would cost an enormous amount of money. Those funds would have to come from Americans well above the "break-even" level. Although not exactly taking from the rich and giving to the poor, FAP marked the first serious call for massive redistributionist economics since the Great Depression, when Russell Long's father Huey had championed just such a cause.[23]

Nixon's Family Assistance Plan showed remarkable similarities to Share Our Wealth. As Daniel Patrick Moynihan, one of Nixon's top welfare advisors and the chief architect of FAP, later wrote, "Had this been the 1930s, and had Roosevelt included Family Assistance in the Social Security Act . . . Senator Huey Long of Louisiana, had he differed with the president on this issue, would almost certainly have done so by outbidding him." Given the fact that Huey's eldest son, Russell, chaired the Senate Finance Committee, which would have to recommend FAP to the entire Senate if it were to be approved, and given Long's penchant for stating allegiance to his father's ideals, the Nixon administration must have felt comfortable that Chairman Long would endorse FAP and, if necessary, force the Finance Committee's approval.[24]

Russell Long, however, passionately opposed the Family Assistance Plan. Although he was not the plan's only opponent—FAP proved unpalatable to both liberals and conservatives—Long certainly became its most formidable.[25]

The Senate Finance Committee began hearings on FAP in April 1970. Chairman Long and ranking Republican John L. Williams of Delaware quickly complained that the executive branch had misconstrued the overall cost estimates for FAP. The program would actually be extraordinarily expensive, they charged, and would require additional forms of revenue in order to pay for it. Long and Williams also stated flatly that the Nixon administration had overstated FAP's work incentives, and they demanded that more exact details be provided. More liberal members of the Finance Committee, such as Abraham Ribicoff of Connecticut and Fred R. Harris of Oklahoma, on the other hand, "argued that the program did not provide enough money for the poor people it would help and did not help enough people in the first place." On May 1, the committee sent the FAP proposal back to the White House to be reworked.[26]

The executive branch returned the revised bill on June 10, and the Finance Committee resumed hearings on July 21. Long, and most of the other members of the Finance Committee, greeted the bill unenthusiastically. The committee rejected the plan by a 14 to 1 test vote on October 8, 1970, and instead approved "a period of testing of different welfare reform approaches, with further Congressional action required upon completion of the testing before any new plan would be implemented on a nationwide basis." Scrapping the old AFDC system that, even with its problems, did manage to help some of the millions of people who used it, without even testing to see if FAP would really work, was a potentially dangerous step, the committee asserted.[27]

On December 11, Long argued for a test program in a meeting with the president. Nixon "insisted upon the Administration proposal," according to a memorandum prepared by George Schultz, Nixon's director of the Office of Management and Budget. The president's intransigence led Long to push the bill through the Finance Committee, with the understanding that the program would probably not be approved by the full Senate, particularly as it was attached to a complicated and divisive set of other legislation. The bill included controversial trade reform legislation plus substantial changes to Social Security, Medicare, and Medicaid. Floor debate continued through the Christmas recess. On December 28, 1970, in an effort to salvage at least the Social Security amendments, the Senate approved a motion by Long to recommit the bill to the Finance Committee with instructions to delete the FAP and trade sections of the bill. The revised bill passed the Senate the next day. The House, however, did not have time to vote on it before the Ninety-First Congress came to a close. Neither the Family Assistance Plan, nor trade reform, nor the Social Security amendments became law in 1970.[28]

On December 30, Long met with President Nixon and reiterated that he would not support FAP as the administration had proposed it. The next day, he took the floor of the Senate to explain his stance on the Family Assistance Plan and to lament the lack of substantial social legislation from the Ninety-First Congress. He was particularly upset that the Social Security, Medicare, and Medicaid amendments had not passed. "The fact of the matter," he said, "is that this Congress has failed to enact the social legislation which the Nation had a right to expect because the administration—with good intentions but poor advice—was determined to enact a fantastically complex and unworkable monstrosity, referred to as a family assistance plan." FAP, he said, would have vastly expanded the public welfare rosters without eliminating any of the problems of AFDC. And FAP would have undermined the ability of employers to hire workers for low-paying jobs, in Long's estimation, because the negative income tax/guaranteed income would be too much of a disincentive. Long held out hope for future welfare reform, however, particularly for wage subsidies "to employers in order that those employers can pay a living wage to their workers." He concluded that "I have always favored whatever might be necessary to bring about this result"—higher wages—but guaranteed incomes and wealth redistribution were not the answers, in his estimation.[29]

In his 1971 State of the Union address, Nixon proclaimed that the time had come to scrap AFDC, which "penalizes work, breaks up homes, robs recipients of dignity," and adopt "in its place the program of income support, job training, and work incentives which I recommended to the Congress last year." The House of Representatives passed the reintroduced FAP on June 22. The bill then made its way to the Senate, where it was referred to the Finance Committee. The committee began hearings on July 27, and soon after, Long expressed consternation that "the so-called welfare reforms . . . would start by doubling the welfare rolls and set an irresistible foundation to redouble, and then to double again, the list of recipients." Nothing had changed, in Long's estimation, and the more pressing issue of the tax reform package of 1971, plus a request from Nixon for a one-year delay, caused the Finance Committee to postpone hearings.[30]

By the time of the FAP postponement, Long had formulated a concrete set of arguments against the administration's welfare reform package. He disliked the projected costs of FAP, but he absolutely abhorred the expected massive expansion of the welfare rolls. Because the Nixon administration was concerned that some welfare recipients would actually receive less money under FAP than they had under AFDC, the newer system would not have actually done away with the AFDC program at all. Instead, the administration expected to maintain AFDC while trying to gradually replace it with FAP. Long could not see how this solved the welfare problem, and he was certain that the American people would "be shocked to find that practically no one would be removed from the rolls" if the Family Assistance Plan passed. Long further believed that FAP created work disincentives that would push the working poor into unemployment. A guaranteed income would be too tempting to a worker barely scraping by on low wages, he surmised, and "once we start paying large numbers of people a living wage for not working, we will find it very difficult to ever make workers out of drones."[31]

Nothing in the program created an incentive to work, Long

noted, and that was a fundamental necessity. If the president and his administration would not create work incentives to get people off the welfare rolls, then Long had two options. He could simply oppose the welfare reform scheme at all costs, or he could try to get the Finance Committee to address the idea of a work incentive itself. Long chose the latter, and before giving up all hope for welfare reform, he gave his committee a shot at fixing the work incentive problem.[32]

In 1972, Long pushed the Finance Committee to create its own reform proposal in the form of a "workfare" project. That January, Long released a statement defining his objectives for welfare reform: "It must discourage family breakup and foster family unity," he said, while it also "must prevent cheating and dishonesty," or at least be able to "detect it and deal firmly with it." Long hoped that whatever the Finance Committee came up with would "reward efforts at self-help rather than rewarding idleness among the employable." Finally, he stated that a reformed welfare program "must provide adequate child care services for children of low-income working mothers and mothers on welfare." Over the next five months, Long and his allies on the Finance Committee produced a rival plan to FAP that purported to attain these goals.[33]

At the root of the workfare plan that Long and his colleagues produced was a requirement that over a million current beneficiaries of the AFDC program be taken off the rolls and placed in guaranteed jobs. Whether those jobs came from the private sector, as Long suggested much of them might, or whether the government had to step in and create "make-work" jobs, Long believed that making people work for the money they received was inherently better than simply handing over the cash. He hoped that such a requirement would "truly begin to end the 'welfare generation'" by inculcating a work ethic into former welfare recipients. Workfare critics often argued that the economy would never support the creation of so many new jobs, but Long and other supporters argued that many jobs already existed. He told the *Chicago Daily News* that "There are million of jobs, plenty enough to absorb the entire welfare caseload of those who are interested in working which are, today, staying vacant or not being filled." They are unfilled "because they are not sufficiently attractive to the welfare people who are drawing those payments."[34]

A significant addition to the welfare reform package that the Senate Finance Committee devised sprang from Long's desire to see the family unit of father/mother/children reconstituted. Opponents of AFDC often stated that the welfare benefit system provided incentives for fathers to abandon the home. Long agreed, and said so in a July 1972 speech: "Today, a father knows that he can desert his family or not marry the mother of his children and they [will] be adequately cared for on welfare with no trouble to himself." Any reform of the welfare system, therefore, "should convince him that he has nothing to gain by deserting." Long said that absentee fathers should be tracked down and put on trial "for criminal nonsupport." Once found and charged, the government could "either make him contribute to the support of his family or put him in jail." The workfare program that the Senate Finance Committee proposed thus included a requirement that single mothers cooperate with the government to identify and locate their children's fathers. The plan also provided funding for states to determine paternity cases and to force absentee fathers to provide child support.[35]

The Finance Committee reported the revised bill to the full Senate on September 26, 1972, more than three years after President Nixon had first proposed the Family Assistance Plan. Debate began the following day. The bill included three welfare reform proposals—the Nixon administration's original FAP, the Finance Committee's workfare program, and an amendment by Ribicoff that would have provided higher benefits in a format similar to FAP. After days of deadlock, the Senate decided on October 6 that it could not settle on any one of the welfare proposals and voted instead for a test period for all three. Following passage in the Senate, the bill went to a House-Senate conference committee, which could not reconcile the differences between the House and Senate welfare reform proposals. On October 17, the conference committee reported the bill without the welfare reform proposals. Both the Senate and House of Representatives approved the conference bill the same day. After more than three years, the debate over Nixon's welfare reform came to an end.[36]

Long later told a reporter that helping kill the Family Assistance Plan had been "the most rewarding victory of his thirty-eight Senate years." Yet the Family Assistance Plan bore such a resemblance to Huey Long's Share Our Wealth that it is reasonable to ask how the son who for decades had brought to mind his father's image as a champion of the "little guy," as an advocate of social welfare programs, and as a political precedent could oppose FAP. The fact of the matter is that Russell Long simply did not agree with his father on the issues that brought Huey Long the greatest national renown—guaranteed national income and large-scale redistribution of wealth—and he was unwilling to back a plan that might have brought Huey's goals at least partly to fruition. Long was a different type of politician from his father. Huey had seen the Senate and Share Our Wealth as means to an end: they allowed him to garner more notoriety on his path to the White House. Russell Long, however, had become a Senate insider and power broker by the early 1970s. Indeed, he had attained real political power on a national scale his father only dreamed of, and he was comfortable enough in his position to discard his political inheritance when necessary, as in the case of FAP. To the relatively few interviewers or correspondents who brought his father up during the welfare reform debate, Long made it clear that "I am not Huey Long; I am Russell Long. I have to do what I think I should do, as the good Lord gives me the light to see it, and I assume that is what he did."[37]

Long did recognize the same problem of wealth distribution that his father had. In a 1972 television interview, he noted:

> My father had a "share the wealth" program which I heard him discuss as a boy. That program had a lot of appeal to me for reasons of loyalty if not for reasons of logic. I tend to think he was right about what he had in mind. I may look upon it as right but for different reasons today, the idea being that the concentration of economic wealth in just a few hands is not necessarily a good thing for democracy. It gives too much power to too few people. It might be that a democracy ought to have power more diffused among more people. Also, you know, there tends to be an oligarchy in the country when a few people have great power and they have it generation to generation without ever having to give it up. Maybe it ought to be passed around more.[38]

Long may have agreed with his father on the matter, but he was also more cautious than his father. By the early 1970s, he had become an incrementalist in most matters of social welfare, and he simply could not bring himself to advocate the drastic steps proposed by the Family Assistance Plan. He thus rarely brought up his father in the debate over the Family Assistance Plan. On this issue, Russell simply cut his ties with his political legacy. That he did so can be attributed to any number of reasons. The Family Assistance Plan was a national issue—it transcended the Louisiana political realms where his father's memory held the most political currency, and he could therefore disregard Huey's stance without too many political ramifications. Long also probably understood that Share Our Wealth had had very little chance of becoming a reality, and the program's harmful aspects would not have been enacted. The Family Assistance Plan, however, very possibly could have been enacted and therefore deserved the outright opposition of one who disagreed with both plans' guaranteed income and wealth redistribution concepts.

Yet Russell Long found it hard to give up completely his father's memory as a political tool. In the face of criticism that he had betrayed the ideals of Share Our Wealth, he stated, "Some of you have criticized me saying that my father turns over in his grave after seeing the position I have taken. . . . I have great sympathy with everything my father wanted to do with that program. I never felt that it could be done immediately. I have thought that the kinds of things he hoped to bring about would have to be done step-by-step."[39]

Watergate

Long faced no opposition to his reelection bid in 1972. In that year's presidential campaign, Richard Nixon handily defeated Democratic senator George S. McGovern. But the president's fortunes soon changed. Not long after his 1972 reelection, Nixon's political fate became ensnared in the twin traps of economic stagflation and political cover-up. Inflation and recession combined with an impending energy crisis and new international economic competition to stagnate the economy. Try as it might, the Nixon administration had very little success in alleviating the situation. Even more politically problematic for the president were the hearings that followed the arrest of a group of men caught breaking into the Democratic National Campaign Headquarters at Washington's Watergate Hotel. The hearings brought to light the active involvement of high-level administration officials in the scandal and spotlighted the darker side of Nixon's own personality. As evidence of a cover-up mounted, and as the House of Representatives debated impeachment resolutions, Nixon's political future dimmed.[40]

In late 1973, Long voted yea on Senate Resolution 60, which established a Senate Select Committee to investigate the 1972 presidential campaigns. The Select Committee uncovered evidence of cover-ups, bribes, and other illegal activities on the part of the Committee to Re-elect the President. Compelled by that evidence, the House Judiciary Committee began deliberations that eventually led to a vote of impeachment against the president. Long played an active role in uncovering Nixon's misdeeds. Along with House Ways and Means chairman Wilbur Mills, Long co-chaired a special Joint Congressional Committee on Internal Taxation which determined that President Nixon owed almost half-a-million dollars in back taxes in April 1974.[41]

On August 8, 1974, Richard Nixon became the first president of the United States to resign from office. Gerald Ford, who had risen to the vice presidency following Vice President Spiro Agnew's October 1973 resignation, became president. Ford's administration had little more success than Nixon's administration in coping with the major issues of the day, particularly stagflation and the energy crisis, and the lingering Watergate controversy tarnished Ford's presidency, particularly after he granted Nixon a full pardon.

The Ford Presidency

Almost as soon as Ford took his seat in the Oval Office, he and Long engaged in an economic showdown over the Energy Transportation Security Bill. Since before Nixon's resignation, Long had served as Senate floor leader for the Energy Transportation Security Act, which required that one-fifth of all oil imported into the United States be transported on "privately owned U.S.-flag vessels to the extent such vessels are available at fair and reasonable rates." The legislation allowed for federal environmental regulation of the oil vessels, an increasingly salient concern in the 1970s. Other nations, including many American trading partners, already had such rules in effect, and it seemed only fair to Long for the United States to do the same. According to the legislation's rules, the percentage would rise to nearly one-third of all oil imports by 1977. Long believed that the use of American ships would improve national security by reducing American reliance on other, sometimes unfriendly, nations and save consumers money by lowering import fees. Long also contended that using American ships would profit their American owners and have a positive effect on both the balance of payments and unemployment. Long's enthusiasm for the bill, however, was not shared by Ford. The president expected that the bill would cause a spike in the cost of oil and gas for American consumers, a jolt that would only increase the problems of stagflation. Higher prices for oil and gas would then lead to higher prices for other items—groceries, hardware, durable goods—that relied on such energy for their transport. Thus, when the bill reached Ford's desk, he simply ignored it. The presidential pocket veto killed the legislation.[42]

Despite their differing opinions on the Energy Transportation Security measure, more often than not Long worked toward ends agreeable to Ford. In late 1974, he supported the administration's push to extend the life of the Export-Import Bank through June 1978. The bank provided credit to businesses that exported their products overseas, particularly to developing areas that traditional lenders considered high risk, and thus helped level the nation's balance of trade. That same year, Long supported the administration's Emergency Unemployment Compensation program, which recognized "the pressing problem of rapidly rising unemployment" and provided for an extra thirteen weeks of payments for Americans who could not find jobs. The unemployment rate had reached 7.2 percent in 1974, its highest level since the recession of the late 1950s.[43]

Ford supported the Trade Reform Bill of 1974, which Long had been shepherding through the Senate since before Nixon's resignation. The bill granted "a large and significant delegation of trade authorities to the President," because in the Finance Committee's view,

> The United States can no longer stand by and expose its markets, while other nations shelter their economies—often in violation of international agreements—with variable levies, export subsidies, import equalization fees, border taxes, cartels, discriminatory government procurement practices, dumping, import quotas, and a host of other practices which effectively discriminate against U.S. trade and production.

On December 13, 1974, the Senate voted 77 to 4 to adopt the Finance Committee's version of the legislation, and Ford signed the bill into law on January 3, 1975. Ford later called it "the most significant trade legislation" of the preceding forty years.[44]

Also in 1975, the Ford administration proposed an enormous tax cut that it hoped would jump-start the economy by increasing consumer spending. Originally planned as a one-time, one-year, $16 billion cut, Long got the Finance Committee to increase the cut to $29 billion and to reinstitute the oil and gas depletion allowance. The depletion allowance, which granted oil companies the privilege to write off nearly a quarter of their profits earned from drilling operations, was particularly popular in Long's home state of Louisiana. The House had repealed it during its deliberation of the administration's bill. The legislation that resulted provided $21 billion in tax cuts to individuals and $8 billion in breaks to businesses, plus an earned income credit for the working poor. Long had been espousing the latter since the early 1970s, and he considered it one of his career's crowning achievements. The bill passed the Senate by a 60 to 29 vote on March 21, 1975. In conference committee deliberations, some of the Finance Committee's amendments were removed, but the one closest to Long's heart, the earned income credit, was allowed to remain. The Senate agreed to the conference report on March 26, and President Ford signed the Tax Reduction Act of 1975 three days later.[45]

Employee Stock Ownership Plans

Long had other reasons for supporting the tax reduction bill of 1975. Chief among those was its provisions for Employee Stock Ownership Plans (ESOPs). Long argued that ESOPs created a new, more responsible way of achieving his father's goal of redistributing national wealth. Despite the fact that he had helped destroy the Family Assistance Plan, which had come remarkably close to instituting Huey's redistributionist goals, Long still maintained that there existed in the United States a fundamental maldistribution of wealth that had to be addressed. Huey's goals, however, could not be achieved by the same means as Huey had proposed during the Great Depression. Long therefore put forth his own answer, ESOPs.[46]

The ESOP concept was part of a much grander rethinking of the whole idea of capitalism developed by San Francisco–based lawyer and economist Louis O. Kelso. Since the 1950s, Kelso had called for a greater role for American workers in the capitalist system. For centuries, labor had been the key portion of the wealth-producing equation, Kelso noted: wealth could not be created without labor. But Kelso argued that thanks to the technological and financing advances of the nineteenth and twentieth centuries, capital—"inanimate things [that] produce wealth"—had displaced labor as the main source of wealth production. This led to a fundamental problem: the ownership of capital, unlike that of labor, lay in the hands of only a small portion of the population, and because of that limited control, most Americans could not benefit from capital's wealth production. Kelso maintained that the capital used to produce wealth, not wealth itself, needed to be redistributed. With capital thus redistributed, more Americans—particularly American workers—would then be able to accumulate more wealth. Kelso referred to his idea variously as "universal capitalism," "democratized capitalism," or simply upper-case "Capitalism." By spreading wealth-producing capital around, Kelso said, an economic democracy would be created in the United States to go along with its political democracy. In order to achieve the goals of universal capitalism, new mechanisms for distributing capital ownership would be needed. Kelso proposed eight devices for creating "new capitalists," but only one, the ESOP idea, ever really got off the ground.[47]

ESOPs provided a means for employees to gain a portion of the corporation they worked for in the form of stocks, and the plans encouraged corporations to disburse stock to its employees through tax deductions—already part of the IRS code—that corporations received for contributions to employee benefit plans. The deductions could reach up to 25 percent of a corporation's total payroll. The ESOP plans were especially useful for companies needing cash for expansion, debt repayment, or buyouts. The corporation would determine how much cash it needed and would issue stock in that amount. A trust set up for the benefit of all of the corporation's employees would then borrow cash from a lender and purchase the newly issued stock, with the corporation guaranteeing the loan. At this point the trust held the stock and the corporation held the cash. To pay the loan off, the corporation would make payments into the trust in the amount of the tax deduction granted to the corporation. This payment would be made in pre-tax dollars, thus lowering the total cost of the loan. The trust would then make its payment to the lender. Thus, the corporation received its cash and paid off the loan with funds that otherwise would have been paid as taxes. The workers would receive a percentage of the trust's stock in proportion to their wages, salaries, or seniority. Upon retirement, or departing the corporation for any reason, the employee would receive his/her share of the stock. Before then, dividends from the stock could be used to buy more stock or to diversify the employee's ownership portfolio. In the end, the company would receive the money it needed, the lender would get its return, and the employees would all own shares of the corporation. Thus hundreds, perhaps thousands, of new capitalists would have been created, all at no expense.[48]

Russell Long met Kelso on November 27, 1973. Over dinner, the two men discussed Kelso's ideas. Long became an immediate and avid advocate of ESOPs. If Kelso was looking for an ally in creating "universal capitalism," he could not have picked one in a better position than the chair of the Senate Committee on Finance. Convinced that "ESOPs embody an idea whose time has come in our society, and I expect to see its widespread acceptance in the near future," Long turned his attention to getting ESOP provisions added to major economic legislation.[49]

Long's first target was the Regional Rail Reorganization Act of 1973. An amendment he offered allowed Consolidated Rail Corporation to use an ESOP to fund its takeover of financially troubled northeastern railroads.[50] Long explained to Warren Magnuson, chair of the Senate Commerce Committee, that an ESOP "is *the* solution to our present rail crisis." He said it would benefit all involved and "would hurt no one," including the railroads' existing creditors, who would be paid off in short order; also, the "employees of the new rail corporation, through this highly effective financing innovation, would gain stock ownership without any cash outlay or loss of other present benefits." Long concluded that "to the relief of our taxpayers and railroad users, the ESOP is the only logical alternative to nationalizing our railroads. And to rail union officials, the ESOP opens a wholesome new era of broader bargaining potential in behalf of their members. No one stands to lose anything." Long's amendment passed, and the first ESOP was created.[51]

Getting ESOP provisions added to the rail reorganization legislation was just a beginning for Long. He sponsored an amendment to the Foreign Trade Act of 1974 that provided ESOP preferences for companies being harmed by international competition. That same year, he pushed through an amendment to pension legislation that made ESOPs the only employee-benefit mechanism corporations could use to borrow money. In 1975, Long attached to the Tax Reduction Act an amendment that raised the amount of tax credit a corporation using ESOPs could take; it also allowed for an additional one percent tax credit if the savings from the credit were contributed to the ESOP. In 1976, he pushed to double that special tax credit. In 1981, Long sponsored amendments to the Economic Recovery Tax Act that encouraged labor-intensive corporations to set up ESOPs.[52]

For Long, ESOPs provided a way of enacting some of the goals his father had proclaimed during the 1920s and 1930s without wielding the redistributionist means Huey had espoused. At the height of the Great Depression, Huey's Robin Hood–like calls for taking excess wealth from the very rich and using it to provide "basic necessities of life" to all American families struck deep chords within a population sludging through an economic morass. Russell Long, on the other hand, felt that similar ends could be met without the confiscatory taxation of Huey's plan through the means of ESOPs.

Long reasoned that ESOPs provided an ideal method for dealing with the twin menaces of high unemployment and high inflation battering the nation in the 1970s, and beyond that, he felt that the ESOP concept offered a means of transforming the very basis of the American economy.[53] He argued not only that "this extraordinary, versatile financing tool can be used to provide low cost capital for practically any corporate need,"[54] but also that those corporate needs would be balanced by the personal needs of the American people. Creating a stake for workers in the continued success of capitalism would also help protect the nation from the communist menace. "If we don't have enough capitalists in this country, who are interested in defending Democratic capitalism, then our system will have lost its appeal," Long stated in a 1976 press release. "Unless capitalism offers something for the average man, his interest in defending it will surely wane."[55] What's more, Long believed that the democratization of capitalism through ESOPs would cure the social and economics ills that had led to swelling welfare rolls. "Rather than creating a constituency for capitalism," Long contended, "we have been steadily adding people to our welfare rolls. And to our make-work rolls. And to the countless other transfer programs designed to disguise the onus of welfare."[56] Employee Stock Ownership Plans, conversely, would fix the so-called welfare mess by tying workers to the success of their labors and providing them with the wealth-producing mechanism of capital. And those new capitalists would have an incentive to work hard: maximizing productivity would maximize wealth.

Long's chief goal for ESOPs during the stagflation era was to bring the American economy back into a position of world leadership, from which "we will see America move back in front of Japan and West Germany as the most productive economy in the world." Ultimately, he said, "this is a movement that can SAVE AMERICA and keep it at the top. Yes, and this is a movement that can provide the answer to the hopes and needs of people around the world."[57]

Besides working on ESOPs, Long filled his days as chair of the Senate Finance Committee in the mid-1970s waging war on stagflation. In 1976, for instance, he supported yet another extension and broadening of the Unemployment Compensation program. But such programs treated only a symptom of the nation's economic illness. Nothing, it seemed, cured the disease. In 1976, therefore, the Ford administration called for major revisions to the tax code, changes that Long escorted first through the Finance Committee and then through the full Senate. Put into effect as the Tax Reform Act of 1976, the legislation achieved "four principal goals," according to Long. It contained "a series of tax revisions designed to increase the equity of the tax system and improve the performance of the economy." It then installed "several provisions that effect an important simplification of the tax system." Continuing what had been begun the year before, the bill extended "the 1975 tax cuts for an additional year" and made "about half of the cuts permanent." And finally, the bill revised the way tax laws were administered, "particularly in terms of strengthening taxpayers' rights." Although the four goals Long pointed out sounded attainable enough, the Tax Reform Act did little to resuscitate the American economy. Stagflation continued.[58]

The Carter Presidency

While the nation descended even further into economic doldrums, Ford readied for a run at a full presidential term. The odds were against him. Aside from his pardoning of Nixon and the lingering political distrust of the Republican Party thanks to the Watergate washout, stagflation, which neither Ford nor

Nixon had been able to whip, burdened his campaign. When November's presidential election rolled around, Democratic nominee Jimmy Carter took the prize. Carter, the former governor of Georgia, ran as a political outsider and portrayed himself as being beyond the reach of the rank, corrupt politics of Washington, D.C. His victory reflected a general revulsion at the state of American politics in the mid-seventies. Carter truly was a political outsider, but this was no real blessing, for he managed to alienate many Washington insiders, whom he needed to get things done, by being hardheaded and doctrinaire.[59]

The Carter administration proved adept at dealing with diplomatic difficulties. Against staunch Republican opposition, Carter managed in 1978 to garner Senate approval of treaties to turn the Panama Canal over to the government of Panama. It was no easy task, though. Portrayed as a deal that would leave American interests in the Central American nation ripe for the picking, the canal treaties were initially unpopular in the Senate, but Carter, in a show of political craftsmanship that was all too lacking for most of his presidency, managed to convert influential senators who then worked the floor on his behalf. Notably, Russell Long took the president's side and was instrumental in sealing the deal for a number of his hesitant colleagues. His stance was unpopular back home in Louisiana, but as he told his Senate colleagues, "My best judgment is that the new treaties do serve the present and long-run strategic interests of the United States." His vote had political ramifications, and his Republican opponent in the 1980 election cycle would use it for political leverage. Many of Carter's major diplomatic achievements came the following year, 1979. Among these were the brokering of an Egypt-Israeli peace treaty, the finalizing of the Strategic Arms Limitation Treaty II with the Soviet Union, and the formalizing of diplomatic relations with China. But 1979 also brought renewed international crises, most notably the taking of fifty-three American hostages in Iran and the Soviet invasion of Afghanistan.[60]

Carter's domestic leadership foundered on the rocks of stagflation. During his 1976 presidential campaign, Carter had referred to what he called the "misery index." This index combined the percentages of inflation and unemployment—the two aspects of stagflation. In 1977, when Carter entered office, the misery index stood at fourteen: six percent inflation and eight percent unemployment. The problem for Carter, though, was that the misery index, which had been a wonderfully handy campaigning tool, became an easy way for his opponents to point out that his administration was no more successful than his predecessors at dealing with stagflation. Inflation continued, and in fact worsened, as did unemployment, and the energy crisis continued unabated.[61]

President Carter and Senator Long's political relationship presented a great irony. Long proved less supportive of Carter's domestic politics than he had been of Nixon's and Ford's, despite sharing with Carter a region of birth, the South, and a political allegiance, the Democratic Party. Their distinctiveness had more to do with generational differences than with anything else. Long had entered southern Democratic politics at the middle of the twentieth century, and he still practiced, even in the late 1970s, a mid-twentieth-century southern Democratic political style. Carter, however, had come of political age as a southern Democrat in the mid-1960s, and although he had evoked a certain amount of the older style of southern politics in which Long had been immersed, he tended to be a different type of politician. Thus, although both Long and Carter were southerners and Democrats, deep political differences separated them.

Moreover, Long, like most of his Senate colleagues, viewed the new president with misgiving. Carter's political personality combined inexperience, self-righteousness, and inflexibility. What was worse, he apparently expected Congress to submit to the executive branch's leadership without asking questions. In short, Long saw Carter as a political novice who frequently asked for too much while doing too little to get it, and he was often stunned by the president's unwillingness to compromise. A notable case in point came with Carter's energy bill in 1977.

In April 1977, Carter told the American people in a televised address that "the energy crisis has not yet overwhelmed us, but it will if we do not act quickly." A week later, he sent an energy bill to Congress. Its provisions included new taxes on automobiles with poor fuel economy, higher federal gasoline taxes, and more taxes on the oil and gas industry. The House of Representatives passed Carter's legislation largely unchanged, but Long and his Senate Finance Committee completely overhauled it. By the time the committee presented the bill to the full Senate, only a four-cent tax on gas and a series of tax cuts designed to foster conservation of resources remained. At the root of the differing versions of the energy bill lay a fundamental difference of opinion between Long and Carter on how fiscal policy could be used to deal with the nation's energy shortage. Carter maintained that taxes should be used to punish waste and inefficiency among American energy producers and consumers. Conversely, Long held that tax incentives should be created to spur production, a logical stance for a senator from an energy-producing state and a person who made his living from oil leases. Long also felt that Carter had snubbed his committee and himself by not consulting with Finance before presenting the bill. When the energy bill went to conference committee for consideration, the House committee members and their Senate counterparts could not agree on a compromise, and the administration's 1977 energy proposals never saw the light of day.[62]

Long's resistance to Carter's domestic initiatives, particularly in matters of energy and fiscal policy, continued for the rest of the Georgian's term. In late 1977, Long supported the Natural Gas Policy Act of 1978 partly because Carter opposed it. The legislation provided for the gradual deregulation of the natural gas industry in the United States. In a case of political tit for tat, Long's stance on natural gas deregulation reflected his annoyance at the administration's ill-fated attempt to reduce "pork barrel" politics by canceling or cutting funding that had already been appropriated by Congress for waterway projects. Five major Louisiana projects would have lost funding, and Long and his fellow Louisianian, Senator J. Bennett Johnston, led the charge against the cuts, amending the gas policy bill to force the administration to spend the money for the projects as appropriated.[63]

In 1978, Long again butted heads with Carter over an administration energy bill. This time, Long bottled up the proposed legislation in the Finance Committee because it included a crude oil equalization tax that would have artificially inflated domestic oil's price to a level equal with world prices. Carter argued that the equalization tax actually would benefit consumers, who would receive tax rebates as a result of the bill's provisions, but Long preferred to give rebates to producers, whom he felt certain would pass their savings along to the consumers. That same year, during Finance Committee deliberations over the Revenue Act of 1978, Long proposed cutting capital gains taxes in order to spur spending and investment. Carter and his administration countered that the decrease would cut government revenue, but Long carried the day. And in 1979, Long opposed Carter's proposal for a Windfalls Profit Tax, designed by the administration to raise revenues and to keep energy companies from gouging customers during the energy crisis. Long argued that the plan would be a disincentive to production at a time when the nation's energy supplies were already low, and he persuaded his Finance Committee colleagues to weaken the tax significantly.[64]

Long's interest in protecting energy producers and providing them incentives for production transcended purely political or economic considerations and ventured into personal territory. Writing in 1976, Jack Bass and Walter DeVries noted that Long's wealth, much of it derived from his father's old Win or Lose oil investments, was "estimated in excess of $100 million." Because of his chairmanship of the Finance Committee and his sway over policies regarding oil—particularly the depletion allowance—Long was often accused of conflict of interest. To those charges,

Long responded, "I come from an oil-producing state, and if I was not cooperating with oil against those people who are out after it, I really don't think I'd be representing my state."[65]

Long's opposition to Carter could be vigorous, but it was not all-encompassing, and he occasionally supported the president's domestic policies. Notably, in 1977, the Louisiana senator backed the administration's program for countercyclical aid, which shifted federal funding to the nation's most depressed areas, and he backed Carter's economic stimulus tax cuts, which were designed to spur spending and investment. That same year, Long voted in favor of the creation of a separate Department of Energy within the federal government, a cornerstone of Carter's efforts at dealing with the nation's energy crisis. In 1979, Long supported an administration proposal to provide a series of loan guarantees to help save the Chrysler Corporation from bankruptcy. The Chrysler bill was one of the few administration victories of late 1979, and Long paid particular attention to it because of its provisions for the creation of a $175 million Employee Stock Ownership Plan for Chrysler's workers.

ESOPS As a Way to "Share Our Wealth"

Long's advocacy of ESOPs continued during the late 1970s, and he came to believe that, if given the chance, they could have far-reaching results. Besides helping domestic corporations, such as Chrysler, and their workers, Long maintained that ESOPs could tilt the balance in European nations that were flirting with socialism. In late 1978, he wrote President Carter regarding attempts to create ESOP legislation in France. "Clearly, the United States is in the vanguard of the broadened stock ownership movement," he noted, "and I think we should extend every effort to assist France in implementing its program, as an alternative to the radical program which the Communists and Socialists are offering the working people there." The following year, Long wrote British prime minister Margaret Thatcher about ESOPs. Her reply indicated curiosity, if not an outright commendation of Long's pet program. "I certainly agree that there are very real benefits to be derived from encouraging wider stock ownership," Thatcher wrote,

> and I think that this applies not only to owning shares in the company in which people work but also to investing in company shares more generally. Like you, I am convinced that by increasing the commitment of employees to the financial wellbeing [sic] of their company, and perhaps by making them more aware of the problems and requirements of other aspects of the operation of the company, employee share ownership schemes can make a significant contribution to improving productivity and consequently profitability.

She concluded that "this can only be to the advantage of those associated with the company, including the existing shareholders, and clearly if these improvements were to be reflected across the whole of industry the impact on the economy would, I am sure, be substantial."[66]

Because Long claimed that ESOPs would drastically rearrange the way wealth was distributed in the United States, and because he happily connected the plan with historical antecedents, comparisons with Huey Long's Share Our Wealth inevitably occurred. Some comparisons were valid. Both ESOPs and Share Our Wealth proposed cures for a basic flaw of the laissez-faire system of capitalism—the maldistribution of either wealth or the capital that produced wealth. And both Huey Long and his son Russell occasionally framed the arguments for their respective proposals in a rhetoric of failure: the current system was not working as a way of producing wealth for all segments of the population, and that failure presented perhaps the single most important challenge to American government. Their proposals, Share Our Wealth and ESOPs, formulated solutions to that failure, and they were solutions that had to be considered. Otherwise, only two options existed: continue down the path of an increasingly inequitable distribution of wealth, or go in the opposite direction toward more drastic programs, whether the European fascism of Huey's era or the communism of Russell's.

In supporting ESOPs, Long found it useful to remind his listeners and correspondents of his father's stances while acting in a manner that partly contradicted those stances. The differences between ESOPs and Share Our Wealth were substantial. The major dissimilarity was in coverage. Share Our Wealth, at least in Huey Long's rhetoric, would have been universal; all American families—except those of millionaires—would have been beneficiaries of the redistribution. On the other hand, the ESOPs provided benefits only for employees of corporations. Huey Long also proposed giving a guaranteed income—direct cash benefits—to the poor, and he wanted to do it at the expense of the owners of corporations. Russell Long, on the other hand, wanted to provide stock ownership for the advantage of both the workers *and* the corporations.

Russell Long's ESOP advocacy also revealed a basic assumption that differed greatly from what his father proclaimed: in effect, the younger Long made the case for what was not a redistribution of current wealth but rather a more equitable distribution of future wealth. He believed that "it would be shortsighted to redistribute current wealth. That wealth already has owners. And regardless of how they may have accumulated that wealth, we cannot assure ourselves of a strong private property system tomorrow by taking anyone's private property today."[67] His incrementalism reflected his concern with creating a proposal that would be palatable to his fellow politicians, the public, and those who already possessed a great deal of wealth. "As far as I am concerned, those who are rich can stay rich and make more," he said. "I would simply like to assure those who are not rich an opportunity to create and achieve something for themselves."[68]

This very un-Huey-like statement typified Russell Long's

stance on wealth distribution in America. From 1973 through his retirement in 1986, Long championed ESOPs as a means of reshaping the American economic landscape. The Louisiana senator perceived that the stock ownership plans provided a means of fulfilling a populistic political goal he had inherited from his father—a wider distribution of the nation's wealth—by using much more practical methods.

As Louis Kelso pointed out, "Russell Long liked the idea of populism that he more or less inherited from his father . . . but he didn't like the means, the tools. He abhorred the idea of taking from the rich or the middle class to give to the poor. When he found that he could make haves out of the have-nots without taking away from someone else, he felt he had discovered what his father was searching for."[69]

In the end, Russell Long thought he had found the way to achieve his father's purpose without undermining his own practical political nature. In reality, however, ESOPs were only available to a very limited number of American workers. Worse still, many corporations would soon begin using ESOPs for leveraged buyouts of competitors, thus lessening the competition that both Russell Long and his father had trumpeted in their respective careers.[70]

By the end of the 1970s, Long was a Washington force to be reckoned with. On January 2, 1980, the *New York Times* said he "is often described as the most powerful member of the Senate." From his perch as chair of the Senate Finance Committee, he held significant sway over legislation related to taxation, welfare, and energy policy, and he had shown that his influence extended beyond the walls of the Capitol. Presidents Nixon, Ford, and Carter had all run afoul of Long and each had the political losses to show for it, but Long had also worked with them to implement many of the important programs and policies they called for. His unwillingness to allow previous disputes—whether over welfare programs, energy policies, or any number of other matters—to put up roadblocks to future negotiations reflected his practical political proclivities.[71]

At the same time, Long had established such a strong reputation for protecting Louisiana's interests, which increasingly meant protecting the state's flourishing oil-based economy, that he had reached, according to one observer, "a position of political invulnerability." As a result, Long felt little compunction to involve himself in state affairs. He had no regular offices in the state, and because of his popularity he rarely, if ever, needed to engage in campaign fund-raising. At times, in fact, he even returned contributions to donors because he simply did not need them to dispatch what often was token opposition.[72]

All of that was about to change, however. Long's focus on Senate politics would soon be construed by an opponent in the 1980 election cycle as absenteeism and lack of interest in matters that directly affected the people of Louisiana. And his ability to engage in the practical politics that had been a hallmark of his career would be severely tested by the coming of the so-called Reagan Revolution, which ushered in a political style predicated on ideology rather pragmatism.

CONCLUSION

In Descent, 1981–2003

THE NATIONAL ELECTIONS of 1980 saw the coalescence of political, economic, and religious conservatism behind the candidacy of the Republican presidential nominee, Ronald Reagan. The former actor and California governor championed individual freedom and private enterprise in his showdown with Jimmy Carter. Reagan blamed the government itself for the difficulties the United States had faced in the late 1970s, particularly the nation's economic stagnation. "The people have not created this disaster in our economy; the federal government has," he said in his announcement for the presidential candidacy. "It has overspent, overestimated, and over regulated. It has failed to deliver services within the revenues it should be allowed to raise from taxes." In the same speech, he laid out his basic economic ideology: "The key to restoring the health of the economy lies in cutting taxes. At the same time, we need to get the waste out of federal spending." Political and economic ideology aside, Reagan seemed to be everything his predecessor was not: charismatic, vigorous, and reassuring. The election marked a sea change in American politics, despite the fact that neither of the candidates seemed to inspire much enthusiasm among the voting public, and voter turnout that year was among the lowest in American history.[1]

The election brought a great deal of change to Russell Long's political life. Since the 1950s, Long, as a Democrat, had been a member of the Senate's majority party. But Reagan's coattails brought with him a Republican Senate majority. Long would have to give up his chairmanship of the Finance Committee, which he had held since 1965, and would be relegated instead to the position of ranking minority member. However, Long's experience, and his knowledge of the tax code, kept him at the forefront of fiscal policy making.

The Reagan presidency culminated a series of developments that had been occurring since the 1960s. Taken as a whole, they comprised the rise of an American New Right. Three main elements—initially separate and distinct from one another—coalesced in the late 1970s into a powerful movement that shifted American politics in a way that nothing had since the construction of the Depression-era New Deal liberal coalition. Those developments that formed the foundation for the New Right were the rise of the religious right, the expansion of political conservatism, and a tax revolt.

Although there had always been a portion of religious Americans who defined themselves as politically conservative, it was not until the 1970s that they coalesced to exert widespread pressure on politics. New political issues had propelled the change. In particular, the Supreme Court's *Roe v. Wade* decision of 1973, which legalized abortion in the United States, electrified the religious right. So, too, did the Court's decisions outlawing prayer and Bible reading in public schools. Using electronic media, particularly television, to reach millions of evangelicals, leaders such as Pat Robertson and Jerry Falwell attacked "secular humanism" and called for change at the highest levels of American government. Falwell, in particular, bridged the gap between religion and politics when he created the Moral Majority, an organization that used modern communications methods to sway voters on issues such as the Equal Rights Amendment and the "right to life." During the 1980 campaign season, the Moral Majority mailed out a billion pieces of campaign literature, all aimed at getting conservative politicians elected.

Like religious conservatives, political conservatives had been a constant in American history, but unlike their religious counterparts, they had, at times, dominated the political landscape.

That was not the case following World War II. Although conservative politics had greater appeal in certain areas of the nation—notably the South—than in others, conservatives did not command a majority of either of the two main political parties for the thirty-five years between 1945 and 1980, and they did not have the support of a majority of the American people. That changed in 1980, but the shift had been brewing for some time.

The resurgence of political conservatism on a national scale can be traced back to 1964, when Russell Long's colleague, Arizona senator Barry Goldwater, ran as the Republican presidential candidate. Goldwater's platform called for a dramatic escalation of American involvement in Vietnam, including the wholesale bombing of the North. He promised to dismantle much of the liberal state that had been created during and after the New Deal, and he pledged to repeal current civil rights laws while killing future ones. In short, Goldwater promised to reduce the role of federal government in the day-to-day lives of the people and roll back social changes that had occurred over the previous decades, all the while maintaining an aggressively combative Cold War posture. The American people at the time were not ready for that brand of political conservatism, however, and Lyndon Johnson trounced Goldwater at the polls.

Four years later, cracks were beginning to show in the New Deal liberal coalition. Johnson's prosecution of the Vietnam War undermined the liberal consensus, as did the explosive growth of the federal government. Richard Nixon, hoping to maintain the allegiance of the Republican conservatives to whom Goldwater had appealed, cultivated relationships with southern conservatives and brought on as his running mate Spiro Agnew, the former governor of Maryland, whom the Nixon team unleashed to spew vicious rhetoric against all things liberal. But the true conservative innovations in 1968 came from a third-party candidate, former Alabama governor George Wallace, who more than any of his conservative contemporaries, understood that political conservatism would have to broaden its base if it were to be successful. Wallace appealed to white working-class members, both inside his native South and out of it, by denouncing Vietnam protestors, urban rioters, the welfare system, and the growth of a federal government that seemed to many to be more committed to the rights of minorities than those of the majority. Wallace used populist appeals to capture these voters' support, but Nixon was smart enough to co-opt the Alabama governor's approach.

But for Watergate, Nixon might have fashioned a New Right during the 1970s. His successor, Gerald Ford, was much too moderate for Republican political conservatives, and Ford's vice president, Nelson Rockefeller, had long been a fixture in the party's liberal camp. The Ford presidency marked a turning point: conservative Republicans were determined to take control of their party, as they had in 1964. This time, their task would be made easier by the growth of the religious right and the fruition of the New Right's third element, the tax revolt.

The tax revolt first emerged in California, where in 1978 conservative activists managed to push through to passage a proposition forcing the state to roll back property taxes by 30 percent. Conservatives elsewhere picked up the model, and soon calls for lowering taxes of all sorts were being heard around the nation. The fact that citizens do not appreciate giving up a portion of their money to the government deserves some credit for the success of the tax revolt, but there was more to it than that. Since the New Deal era, conservatives had challenged the near-constant growth of the federal government, and they had become even more disconcerted as, in the 1960s, the nation developed the apparatuses of a full-fledged welfare state. The conservatives would have liked to dismantle the overgrown government, but they faced a problem. Programs such as Social Security and Medicare were enormously popular. Challenging them was not politically feasible; they had millions of beneficiaries and therefore an enormous amount of support. The conservatives thus needed a way of attacking the massive federal programs indirectly. A movement to lower—or, even better, eliminate—taxes fit perfectly. Tax cuts reduced funding for programs, but simply by lowering voters' tax bills, they turned out to be very nearly as popular as the programs they undermined.

By the late 1970s, Ronald Reagan was primed to rise to the top of this rapidly developing New Right. Engaging, self-assured, smooth, and eloquent, he had been involved in conservative politics since the mid-1960s and had served as California's governor between 1967 and 1975. He had first gained national prominence in the 1976 presidential campaign, when he launched a strong challenge against Gerald Ford for the Republican nomination. Following that election, Reagan and his advisors had diligently cultivated all three sectors of the New Right. In the 1980 campaign, Reagan focused on Americans' disillusionment with their leaders and their government, and he denounced criminality, drug addiction, and immorality while championing patriotism, religion, family life, "traditional" values, stronger national defense, lower taxes, and a balanced budget.

The Reagan administration bet its economic house on what it called supply-side economics, and it was in the economic realm that Russell Long, though no longer chair of the Senate Finance Committee, would have the greatest influence on the United States during the Reagan era. Supply-side economics called for massive tax cuts that, according to Reagan, would stimulate investment as a cure for the nation's economic doldrums. The new president promised that he would reduce expenditures enough to make up for the lost revenue from lower taxation. Ultimately, his administration calculated that the increased investment would lead to more productivity, higher incomes, and greater profits, which would then allow the government to increase its revenues without raising old taxes or creating new ones. The plan reminded some of the economic programs of the pre-Depression Republican presidents Warren Harding, Calvin Coolidge, and Herbert Hoover.

Russell Long and "Reaganomics"

Russell Long had his doubts about supply-side economics. He had advocated tax breaks for investors in the past, but nothing ever so large as what Reagan called for. His misgivings did not stop him from voting to approve Reagan's economic policies as embodied in the Budget Reconciliation Act and the Economic Recovery Tax Act, both of which passed in 1981. The Budget Reconciliation Act reduced government spending by $39 billion, mainly by transferring certain regulatory and welfare programs to the individual states and providing the states with less money to run them. The budget act also proposed a cap on Medicare expenses, shifted the nature and scope of Aid to Families with Dependent Children, and reduced expenditures for other welfare programs. All told, the legislation reduced spending on social welfare programs by $25 billion, although Medicare and Social Security, still politically sacrosanct, remained untouched. The Economic Recovery Tax Act lowered individual taxes by one-quarter over three years; after a half decade, the cut would total $750 billion. Besides lowering individual income taxes, the legislation also lowered business, capital gains, gift, and inheritance taxes. Because the individual cuts were across-the-board, the wealthy received a disproportionate reduction in their tax burden; it was expected by the administration that they would turn around and invest their windfall into the economy.[2]

Long joined other southern Democrats, some of whom were much more fiscally conservative than he was, and who were called the boll weevils by Reagan, in supporting the plans. Part of Long's thinking reflected exasperation that nothing the Nixon, Ford, or Carter administrations had tried to solve the stagflation crisis had worked. Perhaps Reagan's formula was the sort of desperate measure that the desperate times called for, he thought. Too, the tax act included amendments that encouraged labor-intensive corporations to set up Employee Stock Ownership Plans. And although he thought "Reaganomics" oversimplified the enormously complicated relationship between fiscal policy and economic growth, and despite his grave fears that the unprecedented tax cuts would lead to budget deficits, in the end, Long acknowledged with his vote that he understood just how popular the tax cuts were to the people of the United States. He had gained some understanding of that, and of just how prevalent the New Right was becoming in Louisiana, during his 1980 campaign for reelection.[3]

That year, Long had faced his first serious competition in three decades when Democratic state Representative Louis "Woody" Jenkins launched an energetic campaign against him. Jenkins's challenge to Long rested on the simple argument that, although Long wielded an enormous amount of influence in Washington, "Senator Long has forgotten who sent him to Washington." Long no longer understood what his home state constituents thought important, Jenkins said, and all the power that Long had garnered provided but few tangible benefits for Louisiana. In particular, Jenkins harped on the Panama Canal Treaty, which most Louisianians opposed and Long supported. Long's vote, according to Jenkins, "was cast in the full knowledge it went against the overwhelming public opinion in this state and was a deliberate slap in the face of Louisiana citizens." Jenkins, a purveyor of New Right rhetoric if not a member of the Republican Party just yet, caricatured Long as a remnant of the past, out of step with the rising tide of conservatism that was spreading across the South and into Louisiana. Jenkins proposed tax cuts, a balanced budget, and increases in defense spending—the basic formula espoused, if not necessarily fulfilled, by Reagan—as cures for the nation's economic ills, and his spirited campaign brought him more success on election day than anybody had had against Long since 1950. But it still was not enough. Long received 58 percent of the vote as compared to Jenkins's 38 percent. He would return to Washington for another term.[4]

Supply-side economics did not immediately have the effect the Reagan administration predicted. Scarcely a year following the budget and tax reductions of 1981, the United States faced a serious recession. By 1983, however, the economy had picked up steam, and it would continue to grow through the end of Reagan's terms. This economic resurgence resulted partly from the Federal Reserve Board's decision to keep interest rates high and partly from the supply-side tax cuts, which did indeed spur investment and spending on the part of businesses and individuals. Just as important, the economy found footing on the government's rapidly increasing spending; over five years, the administration spent $1.2 trillion on defense alone. Long had warned that the Reagan economic plan might lead to budget deficits, and as usual in matters of finance, he was on the money. The Reagan administration's increase in spending, which pumped money into the economy and created jobs in a way that New Deal liberals would have found both familiar and likeable, led to budget deficits three times larger at the end of Reagan's term than at the beginning.[5]

The huge increases in defense spending reflected Reagan's tough talk against what he termed the "evil empire" of the Soviet Union. Russell Long, for decades an avid Cold Warrior, found the military buildup easy to support. He voted for Reagan's defense appropriations requests, and he supported the development of new weaponry such as the MX missile. The money allocated to defense needs went to increasing the size and quality of both the nation's conventional fighting forces and nuclear weaponry, but it also resulted in funding what some considered pointless research projects. Probably the most well-known of those projects, the Strategic Defense Initiative, or "Star Wars" to its detractors, studied the feasibility of using lasers and satellites to provide a shield for the United States against nuclear missiles. Reagan's spending spree had an important consequence: it forced the Soviets into an arms race that they could not win. Ultimately, the Soviets determined that they simply could not keep up. They could not outspend Ronald Reagan, and they were therefore forced to rethink their relationship with the United

States, and even to reconsider their form of government and system of economics.[6]

Following his smashing defeat of Walter Mondale in the 1984 presidential election, Ronald Reagan turned his attentions once more to fiscal policy. By early 1985, his administration sent to Congress the Tax Reform Act. Long initially harbored serious doubts about the measure, and he played a role in having it returned to the White House for revision. The Reagan administration had promised that the reform package would simplify the nation's tax structure, but in Long's opinion, the administration's zeal for simplicity had led it to do away with important provisions of the tax code. The bill called for the elimination of loopholes and business deductions in exchange for a flat business rate, and it reduced individual tax brackets from fifteen to three. When the revised reform proposal, known by then as Treasury II, came back to the Senate in May 1986, Long found it more palatable, and he provided strong support in the Finance Committee, on the Senate floor, and in conference committee for weeks before its passage on September 18. His newfound enthusiasm for the bill reflected the administration's inclusion of ESOP incentives and deductions for the oil and gas industry, yet Long still voiced concerns that by eliminating certain deductions, the oversimplified tax structure had eliminated important inducements that influenced Americans' decisions to buy homes, contribute to charities, or make investments.[7]

By the time the Senate had begun deliberations on the initial Reagan Tax Reform Act, Russell Long had already announced the pending conclusion of his nearly four-decade career as a United States Senator. At a February 25, 1985, news conference, Long stated that "every senator should decide for himself at what point he thinks he should retire from the Senate if he has the good fortune to live his term out. After 36 years here I've made that decision. It's that simple." Long continued on in the Senate until the end of his term on January 3, 1987. At the time, he was ranked second in Senate seniority behind only his fellow southerner, John Stennis of Mississippi, and he had served longer than all but three other senators in history. He had also attained heights of political power rarely, if ever, reached by previous Louisianians, including his father.[8]

Long in Retirement

In his retirement years, Long remained active in national politics as a lobbyist for various interest groups. His most notable successes came in the early 1990s, when he garnered congressional funding of $20 million to support Connecticut biotechnology firm MicroGeneSys for work on an AIDS vaccine. From a seat on the board of directors of the American Council of Capital Formation, Long continued his advocacy of using fiscal policy to spur economic growth. Representing the Council, Long lobbied Congress to lower capital gains and corporate dividend taxes, and he continued to promote his Employee Stock Ownership pet projects. He also served on the board of the New York Stock Exchange.[9]

When not working, Long divided his time between his ranch atop Rattlesnake Mountain in Virginia's Blue Ridge Mountains, an apartment in Washington, D.C., and a farm outside of Baton Rouge. On the evening of May 9, 2003, he and his wife, Carolyn, attended a movie in Washington. That evening, the retired senator collapsed in his apartment. Rushed to George Washington University Medical Center, Russell Long was pronounced dead of heart failure.[10]

Russell Long's thirty-eight-year political career is but one example of the type of practical politics that was common among almost all national politicians during the mid-twentieth century. Before the hardening of ideology within the two main parties—first, conservatism among the Republicans, then liberalism among the Democrats—shifting ground between policy postures was not just common, it was expected. Viewed through the prism of mid-twentieth-century American politics, at times

Long voted in a way that might be defined as "liberal," at others, "conservative." Particularly during the first two decades of his Senate tenure, those stances were quite evident, and he only occasionally deviated from them: Long was conservative on matters of race relations, liberal on almost everything else. Even in Louisiana politics, Long attempted to transcend the political boundaries early in his career by asserting that the Longite/Anti-Longite divide could be straddled.

Long's liberal stances on social welfare issues such as Social Security and Medicare may have been expected, given his family and political background. What's more, Long came of political age in an era dominated by the New Deal–inspired liberal consensus. The notions that the government can do good for the people of the nation, that economic growth—rather than forced redistribution—can resolve the dilemma of poverty, that the United States should actively export its political and governmental philosophies around the world and counter opposing forces, all of these things Long not only was comfortable with but also championed. And, for the most part, he did not deviate from those stances, even later in his career.

Long's conservatism is more curious. It is tempting to situate Long's politics as being in the vanguard of some positions of the New Right that emerged in the 1970s, but that would be wrong. He certainly took a strong stance on national defense and was an avid Cold Warrior—that much cannot be denied—but these stances differed very little from that of some of the chief liberals of mid-century, including Democratic presidents Harry Truman, John Kennedy, and Lyndon Johnson. Strong defense postures did not a conservative make. Too, the Louisiana senator never pandered to the religious right, a key component of the New Right's political coalition, even after the rise of groups like the Moral Majority. Indeed, Long said very little publicly on matters such as school prayer and abortion.

Long supported and, in some instances, led the charge during Senate consideration of every major tax cut between 1964 and

1986. Certainly, such stances might place him at the forefront of the tax revolt. Yet Long's position on tax cuts reflected a belief in Keynesian fiscal policy—temporary tax cuts were designed to spur spending by returning money to the middle and lower classes and were to be coupled with government spending. Long's stance fundamentally differed from the supply-side economics of the New Right, which extolled cutting taxes permanently for the upper classes in order to spur investment, increase productivity, and create demand while at the same time decreasing governmental spending. Despite his support for the Reagan administration's 1981 and 1986 tax reforms, Long expressed serious reservations about supply-side economics, and he might not have been as supportive of the Republicans' tax packages had they not included benefits for his personal pet projects like Employee Stock Ownership Plans.

Long, like the proponents of New Right supply-side economics, also espoused restraint in government spending, and especially later in his career, he supported tax incentives for big businesses, particular big oil and gas. Yet he never coupled these stances with the other aspects of supply-side economics, and he certainly never espoused the anti-government philosophy that the New Right held so dear. If he learned anything from his father and his Uncle Earl, it was that big government, if functioning properly, could be used to help the most needy in society. Although his perspective shifted somewhat in the late 1960s as a result of the so-called welfare mess, his only major dispute with national social welfare policy had less to do with the goal of a program like the AFDC and more to do with the means to that end. After all, in the debates over the Family Assistance Plan, Long had fought not to destroy the government program but to destroy the program that most proposed to take the government out of the welfare arena.

Long's true conservatism had much more to do with his state and regional context than the national. During the first two decades of his career, Long's obstructionist attacks on civil rights legislation, and his outspoken criticism of the civil rights movement itself, placed him firmly within the conservative camp. He reflected the social milieu in which he grew up and lived, and he responded to the political realities of the day. As such, his stances reflected much the same sentiment as those of his Deep South compatriots in the Senate.

Long's conservative stance on race relations further reflected the influence of those southern senators he shared the upper house with in the 1940s, 1950s, and 1960s—senators such as Allen Ellender, Richard Russell, Walter George, Olin Johnston, Strom Thurmond, John Stennis, and James Eastland. The main difference, in fact, between Long and all of those senators but Stennis and Thurmond, is sheer longevity. He was, as Jack Bass and Walter DeVries wrote in 1975, "the youngest of the old breed of southern power brokers in Congress," and he simply stayed in office longer than most of his contemporaries.

Although Long outlasted virtually all of the older southern Democrats who were in office when he first entered the Senate, his political stances—stances he shared with most of his early southern contemporaries—on matter like defense policy, social welfare programs, government intervention in the economy, and civil rights remained largely unchanged. Long remained in the Senate, and he carried on an older tradition that, by the mid-1970s, was fading rapidly. His enduring practical politics, combining liberal and conservative stances, when juxtaposed with the shifting political sands around him, made him *seem* different, as if he had changed his place on the political spectrum. But in reality it was the American political parties that had shifted, not Long. The New Right came to dominate the Republican Party, and the Democrats, in a reflexive rather than an active approach to politics, more firmly situated themselves on the Left. The distinctions between Left and Right, liberal and conservative, became hardened, and the older, more pragmatic method of the politics of transcendence became outmoded and passé.

But Russell Long was still around, and he had a good many

years left in his Senate career. Looking at Long's party voting pattern in the 1970s, it would appear that, as he grew older and more entrenched in the Senate, he became more conservative. Indeed, it might be tempting to say that Long was caught up in the rising tide of the Goldwater to Wallace to Agnew to Reagan development of the New Right. Certainly, other southern politicians were. Yet this was not the case with Long.

The perception of Long's increasing conservatism can be attributed to the leftward movement of the Democratic Party itself. Long outlasted virtually all of the southern Democrats that he had worked with for decades, and the endurance of his *conservative* stances reflected his coming of age, so to speak, among that particular cohort. Lewis L. Gould reminds us in his recent history of the modern Senate that those southern senators dominated the upper house from the New Deal through the mid-1960s and were motivated by "fears about civil rights, government regulation, and social change." While this more conservative portion of Long's political philosophy remained, the Democratic context in which it functioned changed in the last two decades of his career. Indeed, the leftward movement of his Democratic Party under the leadership of younger politicians like Edmund Muskie and Edward Kennedy made him *seem* more conservative than earlier in his career. But his liberal stances remained unchanged, as well. The party itself shifted to the left. Long stayed where he was. Relative to the party's shift, it appeared as if Long had moved to the right, but it was the party, not the senator, which had done the moving. Because of the party's change, he became viewed as a conservative within his own party.

In 1980, Charles Bartlett wrote in the New Orleans *Times-Picayune* that Long "has been compiling a political record that defies ideological classification ever since he began his Senate life in 1948. And there is no shred of evidence in the entire record that he ever had a political ideology."[11] The defiance of ideology, indeed the lack of ideology, is the defining characteristic of Long's practical politics.

In the political climate of the early twenty-first century, Russell Long would probably be identified as weak, wishy-washy, and unsure. None of these terms, however, properly define him. His willingness to engage in work across party and ideological lines was a sign of strength and increased his power within the Senate. "Russell had the rare talent of being able to understand people, and I don't ever recall him having any acrimony over his politics," recalled former state Senator Edgar J. "Sonny" Mouton. "He could understand an opponent and still respect him. A lot of people in politics, if you're not for them, they think it's a personal thing, and hate comes from that and that shouldn't be. Personality should not take place in politics, unless family's involved. But Russell had . . . the perfect temperament to be in politics, he really did." He certainly was not an ideologue; he was not married to a doctrine of beliefs that tied him solely to either the conservative or the liberal camp. He ridiculed such affiliations a half decade after his retirement when he likened senators voting according to a party or ideological line as "cattle going to a dipping pad." Russell Long instead had all the marks of a practical politician—he understood that conservative and liberal stances were not mutually exclusive and that they could be mixed when needed.[12]

NOTES

Introduction

1. *Times-Picayune* (New Orleans), January 8, 1980.

2. Huey's indirect effect might have been more important, particularly his role in pushing the Second New Deal further to the left than planned.

3. Robert Mann, *Legacy to Power: Senator Russell Long of Louisiana* (New York: Paragon House, 1992), 316.

4. Julian E. Zelizer, "Introduction to Roundtable: The U.S. Congress in the Twentieth Century," *Social Science History* 24 (2000), 310.

5. Ibid., 311.

Chapter 1

1. George Douth, *Leaders in Profile: The United States Senate, The Ninety-Second Congress* (New York: Sperr and Douth, 1972), 161; *Biographical Directory of the American Congress, 1774–1949* (Washington, DC: U.S. Government Printing Office, 1950), 1474; Information Sheet, "Russell B. Long," March 7, 1961, John F. Kennedy Presidential Papers, White House Staff Files, Lawrence O'Brien Files: Long, Russell, Louisiana, D, Folder 2, John F. Kennedy Presidential Library, Boston; Robert Mann, *Legacy to Power: Senator Russell Long of Louisiana* (New York: Paragon House, 1992), 33; Stan Opotowsky, *The Longs of Louisiana* (New York: Dutton, 1964), 194.

2. Mann, 33; Richard White, *Kingfish: The Reign of Huey P. Long* (New York: Random House, 2006), 38.

3. The following discussion of Huey Long's life and career is drawn from the best of the available biographies, notably T. Harry Williams, *Huey Long* (New York: Knopf, 1970); William Ivy Hair, *The Kingfish and His Realm: The Life and Times of Huey P. Long* (Baton Rouge: Louisiana State University Press, 1991); Glen Jeansonne, *Messiah of the Masses: Huey P. Long and the Great Depression* (New York: Longman, 1993); and Richard White, *Kingfish: The Reign of Huey P. Long* (New York: Random House, 2006). Other important works on Huey and his politics include the relevant chapters in V. O. Key, *Southern Politics in State and Nation* (New York: Knopf, 1949), 156–182; Walter Bass and Jack DeVries, *The Transformation of Southern Politics: Social Change and Political Consequence since 1945* (New York: Basic Books, 1976), 158-185; and Anthony J. Badger, *New Deal/New South: An Anthony J. Badger Reader* (Fayetteville: University of Arkansas Press, 2007), 1–30, 144–167.

4. Hair, 26; Mann, 33–36; Opotowsky, 195; Thomas Martin, *Dynasty: The Longs of Louisiana* (New York: G. P. Putnam's Sons, 1960), 190.

5. Mann, 36–37; Martin, 190; Richard White, 46–47.

6. Mann, 38, 40–41; Opotowsky, 195; Martin, 190.

7. For detailed analyses of the events surrounding Long's assassination, see David Zinman, *The Day Huey Long Was Shot, September 8, 1935* (New York: Ivan Obolensky, 1963); Hermann Deutsch, *The Huey Long Murder Case* (Garden City, NY: Doubleday, 1963); and Ed Reed, *Requiem for a Kingfish: The Strange and Unexplained Death of Huey P. Long* (Baton Rouge, LA: Award Publications/E. Reed Organization, 1986).

8. Mann, xi–xiii; Zinman, 140–141.

9. For the long-term effects Huey had on Louisiana, see "Introduction: Longism and Louisiana Politics," in *Earl K. Long: The Saga of Uncle Earl and Louisiana Politics*, by Michael L. Kurtz and Morgan D. Peoples (Baton Rouge: Louisiana State University Press, 1990), 1–14; Wayne Parent, *Inside the Carnival: Unmasking Louisiana Politics* (Baton Rouge: Louisiana State University Press, 2004); Anthony Badger, "'When I Took the Oath of Office, I Took No Vow of Poverty': Race, Corruption, and Democracy in Louisiana, 1928–2000," in *New Deal/New South: An Anthony J. Badger Reader* (Fayetteville: University of Arkansas Press, 2007): 144–167.

10. Opotowsky, 195; Mann, 39.

11. Mann, 37–41.

12. Ibid., 43–44; R. White, 223–224.

13. *Biographical Dictionary of the American Congress*, 1474.

14. Mann, 45, 47–49, 52; Opotowsky, 195–196; Martin, 188.

15. Mann, 47–48, 53; Opotowsky, 195–197; Martin, 190.

16. Betty M. Field, "The Louisiana Scandals," in *The Age of the Longs, 1928–1960*, ed. Edward F. Haas, vol. 8, The Louisiana Purchase Bicentennial Series in Louisiana History (Lafayette: Center for Louisiana Studies, 2001), 277, 278.

17. Michael L. Kurtz and Morgan D. Peoples, *Earl K. Long: The Saga of Uncle Earl and Louisiana Politics*, Southern Biography Series (Baton Rouge: Louisiana State University Press, 1990), 95–103.

18. Ibid., 54–56; Douth, 161; Opotowsky, 197; Martin, 190; *Biographical Dictionary of the American Congress*, 1474.

19. Kurtz and Peoples, 58–63; Opotowsky, 197; Martin, 190.

20. Kurtz and Peoples, 65–66.

21. On the Anti-Longs, see Mark T. Carleton, "Four Anti-Longites: A Tentative Assessment," *Louisiana History* 30 (Summer 1989): 249–262

22. Ibid., 71–72.

23. Ibid., 69, 71–73; Opotowsky, 197.

24. "Why I Am For Earl Long, A Statewide Radio Broadcast," by Russell Long (1948), Russell B. Long Collection, Louisiana and Lower Mississippi Valley Collections, LSU Libraries, Louisiana State University, Baton Rouge, Box 5, folder 5 (hereafter RBL Collection 5:5).

25. Mann, 73–74; Kurtz and Peoples, 123–124, 128; Perry H. Howard, *Political Tendencies in Louisiana*, rev. and expanded ed. (Baton Rouge: Louisiana State University Press, 1971), 132; Opotowsky, 197.

26. Mann, 79.

27. Ibid., 78, 80–82.

28. Kurtz and Peoples, 140–142.

29. Mann, 79–80; Opotowsky, 197–198; Martin, 184.

30. Announcement, July 2, 1948, RBL Collection 5:8; Kurtz and Peoples, 145.

31. Doris Dorcas Carter, *Robert Floyd Kennon: Reform Governor* (Lafayette: Center for Louisiana Studies, 1998), 51, 53, 75–78; Kurtz and Peoples, 145; Mann, 83, 87–89.

32. Allan P. Sindler, *Huey Long's Louisiana: State Politics, 1920–1952* (Baltimore: The Johns Hopkins University Press, 1959), 214.

33. Mann, 84–86.

34. Carter, 76; Sindler, 214–215.

35. William C. Havard, Rudolf Heberle, and Perry H. Howard, *The Louisiana Elections of 1960*, Louisiana State University Studies, Social Science Series, no. 9 (Baton Rouge: Louisiana State University Press, 1963), 30; Howard, 129, 131, 133, 139, 177–178; Martin, 186; Sindler, 249, 254–256, 258.

36. Mann, 92, 96; Opotowsky, 199.

Chapter 2

1. Robert Mann, *Legacy to Power: Senator Russell Long of Louisiana* (New York: Paragon House, 1992), 92, 96; Stan Opotowsky, *The Longs of Louisiana* (New York: Dutton, 1960), 199.

2. William E. Leuchtenburg, *Franklin D. Roosevelt and the New Deal, 1932–1940* (New York: Harper and Row, 1963), 327; Anthony J. Badger, *The New Deal: The Depression Years, 1933–1940* (Chicago: Ivan R. Dee, 1989), 299–312.

3. Leuchtenburg, *Franklin D. Roosevelt and the New Deal*, 335, 340; Alonzo Hamby, *Liberalism and Its Challengers, from F.D.R. to Bush* (New York: Oxford University Press, 1992), vii, 3; Alan Lawson, *A Commonwealth of Hope: The New Deal Response to Crisis* (Baltimore: The Johns Hopkins University Press, 2006), 6, 244.

4. Thomas A. Becnel, "Allen J. Ellender, Consensus Politician," *Louisiana History* 32 (Summer 1992): 232, 234.

5. James Patterson, *Grand Expectations: The United States, 1945–1974* (New York: Oxford University Press, 1996), 165–166; Merl E. Reed, *Seedtime for the Modern Civil Rights Movement: The President's Committee on Fair Employment Practice, 1941–1946* (Baton Rouge: Louisiana State University Press, 1991), 1, 15.

6. Alonzo Hamby, *Beyond the New Deal: Harry S. Truman and American Liberalism* (New York: Columbia University Press, 1973), 293; Earl Black and Merle Black, *The Rise of Southern Republicans* (Cambridge, MA: Belknap Press of Harvard University Press, 2002), 54; Robert E. Lang and Rebecca R. Sohmer, "Editor's Introduction: Legacy of the Housing Act of 1949: The Past, Present, and Future of Federal Housing and Urban Policy," *Housing Policy Debate* 11:2 (2000), 291–298; Diary entry, November 30, 1950, in *Off the Record: The Private Papers of Harry S. Truman*, ed. Robert H. Ferrell (New York: Harper and Row, 1980), 201.

7. *Congressional Record—Senate* (hereafter *CR*): August 31, 1949, 12567, 12572; April 29, 1949, 5323.

8. *CR*: April 29, 1949, 5326; May 3, 1949, 5471; May 5, 1949, 5687; Richard E. Neustadt, "Congress and the Fair Deal: A Legislative Balance Sheet," in *Harry S. Truman and the Fair Deal*, ed. Alonzo Hamby (Lexington, MA: D.C. Heath and Company, 1974), 29. Long's stance in support of federal aid to education is remarkable also for the fact that Louisiana's large Catholic population would have opposed the legislation because it only aided public schools.

9. *CR*: October 3, 1951, 12524.

10. Fritz Machlup, *The Basing-point System: An Economic Analysis of a Controversial Pricing Practice* (Philadelphia: Blakiston, 1949), 1; *CR*: July 8, 1949, 9124; August 10, 1949, 11166.

11. *CR*: June 2, 1950, 7974; March 31, 1950, 4481.

12. *CR*: August 1, 1951, 9295; January 23, 1967, 1284; *New York Times* (hereafter *NYT*), April 14, 1952.

13. Hamby, *Beyond the New Deal*, 61–62, 214, 313.

14. William E. Leuchtenburg, *The White House Looks South: Franklin D. Roosevelt, Harry S. Truman, Lyndon B. Johnson* (Baton Rouge: Louisiana State University Press, 2005), 214; *Addresses on the History of the United States Senate*, vol. 2 (Washington, DC: U.S. Government Printing Office, 1991), 127.

15. *CR*: March 2, 1949, 1719.

16. Byrd, vol. 2, 127–128; Hamby, *Beyond the New Deal*, 345.

17. *CR*: May 12, 1950, 6993, 6994.

18. Ellender is quoted in Leuchtenburg, *The White House Looks South*, 217.

19. Joseph A. Fry, *Dixie Looks Abroad: The South and U.S. Foreign Relations, 1789–1973* (Baton Rouge: Louisiana State University Press, 2002), 223, 227.

20. Randall B. Woods and Howard Jones, *Dawning of the Cold War: The United States' Quest for Order* (Athens: University of Georgia Press, 1991), 145.

21. *NYT*, September 26, 1949; September 11, 1950.

22. Woods and Jones, 235; Fry, 230; *CR*: April 3, 1951, 3167; June 14, 1960, 12548.

23. Cecil V. Crabb and Pat M. Holt, *Invitation to Struggle: Congress, the President, and Foreign Policy*, 4th ed. (Washington, DC: CQ Press, 1992), 134, 137; Mann, 112–116; *NYT*, May 6, 1951.

24. Woods and Jones, 171–173.

25. Fry, 229–230, 251–252; *New York Times Magazine*, March 3, 1957; *Congressional Quarterly Almanac*, 1971, vol. 27 (Washington, DC: Congressional Quarterly News Features, 1972), 401; *NYT*, June 14, 1957.

26. Thomas C. Reeves, "Introduction," in *McCarthyism*, ed. Thomas C. Reeves (Huntington, NY: Robert E. Krieger Publishing, 1978), 3, 4; Richard Rovere, "McCarthyism as a Bipartisan Doctrine," in ibid., 94.

27. Rovere, "McCarthyism as a Bipartisan Doctrine," 94. Long was not alone in his silence. Among his quiet Democratic counterparts in the Senate were Paul Douglas, never known for not speaking his mind, and future president John Kennedy, who was writing *Profiles in Courage*, published in 1955.

28. Ellen Schrecker, *Many Are the Crimes: McCarthyism in America* (Boston: Little, Brown, 1998), 263; *CR*: May 10, 1954, 6260.

29. Reeves, "Introduction," 4; Schrecker, 265; "Censure," *United States Senate Virtual Reference Desk*, available at www.senate.gov/reference/reference_index_subjects/Censure_vrd.htm (retrieved May 1, 2007); Byrd, vol. 1, 579, 580.

30. *CR*: December 1, 1954, 16290.

31. *CR*: December 1, 1954, 16291; Ibid.: December 2, 1954, 16392; Byrd, vol. 1, 581.

32. Michael L. Kurtz and Morgan D. Peoples, *Earl K. Long: The Saga of Uncle Earl and Louisiana Politics*, Southern Biography Series (Baton Rouge: Louisiana State University Press, 1990), 156; Mann, 110, 111.

33. Portions of the discussion of the election of 1952 were previously published in Michael S. Martin, "'High Time We Put Behind Us the Blind Prejudice of the Past': Russell Long and Louisiana Politics, 1948–1952," *Louisiana History* 46 (Spring 2005): 133–153; Thomas Martin, *Dynasty: The Longs of Louisiana* (New York: G. P. Putnam's Sons, 1960), 192; Glen

Jeansonne, *Leander Perez: Boss of the Delta* (Baton Rouge: Louisiana State University Press, 1977), 150–151.

34. Michael L. Kurtz, "Government by the Civics Books," in *The Age of the Longs, 1928–1960*, ed. Edward F. Haas, vol. 8, The Louisiana Purchase Bicentennial Series in Louisiana History (Lafayette, LA: Center for Louisiana Studies, 2001), 401; Jeansonne, *Leander Perez*, 150.

35. Allan P. Sindler, *Huey Long's Louisiana: State Politics, 1920–1952* (Baltimore: The Johns Hopkins University Press, 1959), 234–235.

36. Thomas H. Ferrell and Judith Haydel, "Hale and Lindy Boggs: Louisiana's National Democrats," *Louisiana History* 35 (Fall 1994): 390–391; Scott E. Balius, "The Courage of His Convictions: Hale Boggs and Civil Rights" (PhD diss., Tulane University, 1993), 9, 22; Memorandum, Larry F. O'Brien to Robert Kennedy, November 13, 1959, Presidential Papers of John F. Kennedy, Box 941, Louisiana, Organization, "10/29/59–6/24/60" (folder).

37. Farrell and Haydel, 390–391; T. Martin, *Dynasty*, 193; Lindy Boggs, with Katherine Hatch, *Washington through a Purple Veil: Memoirs of a Southern Woman* (New York: Harcourt Brace, 1994), 127; Perry H. Howard, *The Louisiana Elections of 1960*, Louisiana State University Studies, Social Science Series, no. 9 (Baton Rouge: Louisiana State University Press, 1963), 164; Opotowsky, 199.

38. Edward F. Haas, *DeLesseps S. Morrison and the Image of Reform: New Orleans Politics, 1946–1961* (Baton Rouge: Louisiana State University Press, 1974), 39–40; Mark T. Carleton, "Four Anti-Longites: A Tentative Assessment," *Louisiana History* 30 (Summer 1989): 259.

39. Farrell and Haydel, 390; Edward F. Haas, "De Lesseps S. Morrison and the Governorship: A Reassessment," in *The Age of the Longs: Louisiana, 1928–1960*, ed. Edward F. Haas, vol. 8, The Louisiana Purchase Bicentennial Series in Louisiana History (Lafayette: Center for Louisiana Studies, 2010), 421; Kurtz, "Government by the Civics Book," 401–402.

40. Haas, *DeLesseps S. Morrison*, 150; Kurtz and Peoples, 139; Haas, "DeLesseps S. Morrison and the Governorship," 421–422.

41. Haas, "DeLesseps S. Morrison and the Governorship," 421, 422; *Times-Picayune* (New Orleans), June 17, 1951, June 29, 1951; *Morning Advocate* (Baton Rouge), June 17, 1951; Sindler, 235; Kurtz and Peoples, 160.

42. Haas, "DeLesseps S. Morrison and the Governorship," 422–423, 424; Haas, *DeLesseps S. Morrison*, 151–152; *Times-Picayune*, September 9, 1951; *Morning Advocate*, September 9, 1951.

43. RBL to Boggs, September 10, 1951, RBL 720:31; Address of Mayor Chep Morrison, Statewide Radio, September 10, 1951, RBL 720:29.

44. Address of Mayor Chep Morrison, Statewide Radio, September 10, 1951, RBL 720:29.

45. Sindler, 234–235, 238; Haas, "DeLesseps S. Morrison and the Governorship," 420; Kurtz and Peoples, 158.

46. Sindler, 234, 238; Haas, "DeLesseps S. Morrison and the Governorship," 420; Kurtz and Peoples, 158, 192; Carleton, "Four Anti-Longites," 254; Michael L. Kurtz, "Robert F. Kennon," in *Louisiana Governors: From Iberville to Edwards*, ed. Joseph G. Dawson III (Baton Rouge: Louisiana State University Press, 1990), 263–267; Jeansonne, *Leander Perez*, 151, 156; Kurtz, "Government by the Civics Book," 401. It is possible that McLemore entered the race at Earl Long's urging. Long and McLemore were friends and occasional business partners, and many contemporary observers, including Russell Long, accused Cadillac Mac of being a Long machine "stalking horse" who had entered the race to steal conservative votes from other anti-Long candidates.

47. Sindler, 236–237; Perry H. Howard, *The Louisiana Elections of 1960*, Louisiana State University Studies, Social Science Series, no. 9 (Baton Rouge: Louisiana State University Press, 1963), 163–165.

48. For the most complete account of the Grace-Perez accusations and their subsequent fallout, see Garry Boulard's *The Big Lie: Hale Boggs, Lucille May Grace, and Leander Perez in 1951* (Gretna, LA: Pelican, 2001). Boggs and Hatch, 128–129; Allan P. Sindler, *Huey Long's Louisiana: State Politics, 1920–1952* (Baltimore: The Johns Hopkins University Press, 1956), 237; Haas, "DeLesseps S. Morrison and the Governorship," 424–425; Jeansonne, *Leander Perez*, 152; Kurtz and Peoples, 161.

49. Jeansonne, *Leander Perez*, 154–155; Sindler, *Huey Long's Louisiana*, 237; Boggs and Hatch, 130; *Times-Picayune*, October 16, October 18–21, November 1–2, 1951; *Morning Advocate*, October 16, October 19–20, October 29–November 4, 1951.

50. Boggs and Hatch, 130, 132; Jeansonne, *Leander Perez*, 158; Kurtz and Peoples, 160; Haas, "DeLesseps S. Morrison and the Governorship," 425.

51. Transcript of statewide radio broadcast by Hale Boggs, October 1, 1951, RBL 720:29; RBL, handwritten speech, n.d., RBL 720:5.

52. RBL to T. J. Bernard, July 10, 1951, RBL 720:34; RBL to S. D. Duplissey, August 24, 1951, RBL 720:30.

53. RBL to Ovey H. Hernandes, July 10, 1951, RBL 720:34; RBL to Rev. F. L. Shows, August 9, 1951, RBL 720:32.

54. RBL to T. J. Bernard, July 10, 1951, RBL 720:34.

55. RBL to Mrs. P. K. Forrest, July 12, 1951, RBL 720:33; RBL to J. F. Wallace, August 6, 1951, RBL 720:32.

56. Transcript of speech by George S. Long, n.d., RBL 720:31.

57. Boggs and Hatch, 132–133; Haas, "DeLesseps S. Morrison and the Governorship," 425.

58. L. Vaughan Howard and David R. Deener, *Presidential Politics in Louisiana, 1952*, vol. 1, Tulane Studies in Political Science (New Orleans: Tulane University Press, 1954), 66–67; Bennett H. Wall et al., *Louisiana: A History*, 2nd ed. (Arlington Heights, IL: Forum Press, 1990), 314; Kurtz, "Robert F. Kennon," 264; Sindler, *Huey Long's Louisiana*, 239; T. Martin, *Dynasty*, 194; *Times-Picayune*, January 17, 1952.

Chapter 3

1. RBL, interview by Hugh Cates, April 23, 1971, transcription, Oral History #61, Richard B. Russell Oral History collection, Richard B. Russell Library for Political Research and Studies, The University of Georgia Libraries, Athens, Georgia; *New York Times* (hereafter *NYT*), April 1, 1952; Robert Mann, *Legacy to Power: Senator Russell Long of Louisiana* (New York: Paragon House, 1992), 139–146.

2. *NYT*, July 26, 1950.

3. James Patterson, *Grand Expectations: The United States, 1945–1974* (New York: Oxford University Press, 1996), 274; Alonzo Hamby, *Liberalism and Its Challengers, from F.D.R. to Bush*, 2nd ed. (New York: Oxford University Press, 1992), 118, 123.

4. Among Eisenhower's conservative causes was cutting dividend taxes. Ironically, Long, who would later in his career champion such cuts, denounced the president's proposal as benefiting the wealthy at the expense of the poor. Mann, 164–168.

5. *NYT*, May 18, 1956; Ibid., July 2, August 19, 1957; *Congressional Quarterly Almanac* (hereafter CQA), (Washington, DC: Congressional Quarterly News Features, 1958), 230, 422.

6. *CQA* (1958), 458, 435; *NYT*, August 28, 30, 1960; *Congressional Record* (hereafter CR): August 23, 1960, 17226, 17235.

7. Gregory Blaine Miller, "Louisiana's Tidelands Controversy: *The United States of America v. State of Louisiana Maritime Boundary Cases*," *Louisiana History* 38 (Spring 1997), 204, 206, 207, 208; Ernest R. Bartley, *The Tidelands Oil Controversy: A Legal and Historical Analysis* (Austin: University of Texas Press, 1953), 196, 197, 202.

8. Bartley, 216–217; 224.

9. *CR—Senate*: March 6, 1952, 1908, 1915, 1920.

10. Ibid., 1915, 1924, 1927, 1928.

11. Bartley, 226–227.

12. *CR*: May 5, 1953, 4458; Miller, 209–210.

13. Aaron L. Shalowitz, "Boundary Problems Raised by the Submerged Lands Act," *Columbia Law Review* 54 (November 1954), 1021; Miller, 211, 213–214. For fifteen years following the Supreme Court's so-called Loui-

siana II decision, a detailed and oft-disputed survey was conducted to determine the exact geographical boundary from which to draw the three-nautical-mile line.

14. "Record of the 83rd Congress (Second Session)," in *Editorial Research Reports 1954*, vol. 2 (Washington, DC: CQ Press, 1954), from CQ Electronic Library, CQ Researcher Online, available at 54082100 (retrieved June 5, 2007); *CR*: January 20, 1954, 489; *NYT*, January 19, January 21, January 25, 1954.

15. "Record of the 84th Congress (Second Session)," in *Editorial Research Reports 1956*, vol. 2 (Washington, DC: CQ Press, 1956), from CQ Electronic Library, CQ Researcher Online, available at http://library.cqpress.com/cqresearcher/cqresrre1956073000 (retrieved June 5, 2007).

16. *CR*: June 26, 1956, 10969; *NYT*, June 27, 1956; *CQA*, vol. 15 (1959), 290, 442.

17. *NYT*, February 6, February 15, 1953; *CR*: February 16, 1953, 1103, 1105.

18. Thomas J. McCormick, *America's Half-Century: United States Foreign Policy in the Cold War and After*, 2nd ed. (Baltimore: The Johns Hopkins University Press, 1995), 105; Warren I. Cohen, *America in the Age of Soviet Power*, vol. 4 of *The Cambridge History of American Foreign Relations* (Cambridge: Cambridge University Press, 1993), 87.

19. Randall B. Woods, *Quest for Identity: America since 1945* (Fort Worth, TX: Harcourt College Publishers, 2001), 103; Donald W. White, *The American Century: The Rise and Decline of the United States as a World Power* (New Haven, CT: Yale University Press, 1996), 289.

20. *NYT*, January 27, 1955; *CR*: January 28, 1995, 994.

21. James Patterson, "*Brown v. Board of Education*: A Civil Rights Milestone and Its Troubled Legacy," in *Pivotal Moments in American History*, ed. David Hackett Fischer and James M. McPherson (New York: Oxford University Press, 2001), 65–67.

22. *CR*: May 18, 1954, 6750.

23. Helen B. Shaffer, "School Desegregation," in *Editorial Research Reports 1955*, vol. 1 (Washington, DC: CQ Press, 1955), from CQ Electronic Library, CQ Researcher Online, available at http://library.cqpress.com/cqresearcher/cqresrre1955011200 (retrieved June 5, 2007).

24. *CR*: May 18, 1954, 6750; Ibid.: May 9, 1956, 7746.

25. Ibid.: May 9, 1956, 7746.

26. David R. Goldfield, *Black, White, and Southern: Race Relations and Southern Culture, 1940 to the Present* (Baton Rouge: Louisiana State University Press, 1990), 94, 95, 97–102; J. Mills Thornton III, "First Among Equals: The Montgomery Bus Boycott," in *The Walking City: The Montgom-*

ery Bus Boycott, 1955, ed. David J. Garrow (Brooklyn, NY: Carlson Publishing, 1989), xix, xx.

27. Thornton, xvii; Russell Long Speech on H.R. 2516 (1968), Russell B. Long Collection, Louisiana and Lower Mississippi Valley Collections, LSU Libraries, Louisiana State University, Baton Rouge: Box 557, folder 23 (hereafter RBL collection 557:23).

28. The quotes are from Steven Lawson and Charles Payne, *Debating the Civil Rights Movement, 1945–1968* (Lanham, MD: Rowman & Littlefield, 1998), 54–59.

29. Mann, 172–173; Michael L. Kurtz and Morgan D. Peoples, *Earl K. Long: The Saga of Uncle Earl and Louisiana Politics*, Southern Biography Series, ed. William J. Cooper (Baton Rouge: Louisiana State University Press, 1990), 182, 183.

30. William E. Leuchtenburg, *The White House Looks South: Franklin Roosevelt, Harry S. Truman, Lyndon Johnson* (Baton Rouge: Louisiana State University Press, 2005), 257–260; Helen B. Shaffer, "Racial Issues in National Politics," in *Editorial Research Reports 1956*, vol. 1 (Washington: CQ Press, 1956), from CQ Electronic Library, CQ Researcher Online, available at http://library.cqpress.com/cqresearcher/cqresrre1956041800 (retrieved June 6, 2007).

31. George Reedy, "The True Dawn of Civil Rights," *Washington Monthly* 14 (1982): 49; Robert Caro, *The Years of Lyndon Johnson: Master of the Senate* (New York: Knopf, 2002), 870; Steven F. Lawson, *Black Ballots: Voting Rights in the South, 1944–1969* (New York: Columbia University Press, 1976), 153; Lawson and Payne, 14–16.

32. Lawson, *Black Ballots*, 169–170, 176–177, 181.

33. Ibid., 176; Caro, 915, 944; Robert Dallek, *Lone Star Rising: Lyndon Johnson and His Times, 1908–1960* (New York: Oxford University Press, 1991), 521.

34. Caro, 853, 861, 892, 945; Dallek, *Lone Star Rising*, 521.

35. Lawson, *Black Ballots*, 178–179; Dallek, *Lone Star Rising*, 522, 524; Caro, 935–938.

36. *CR*: July 22, 1957, 12310.

37. Ibid. Black voter registration in Louisiana increased from 7,000 to 161,000 between 1946 and 1956. Twenty-five thousand of these voters called New Orleans home, but blacks were also registered in fifty-nine of the state's other sixty-three parishes. Adam Fairclough, *Race and Democracy: The Civil Rights Struggle in Louisiana, 1915–1972* (Athens: University of Georgia Press, 1995), 106, 183.

38. Lawson, *Black Ballots*, 182; Dallek, *Lone Star Rising*, 521, 524.

39. Caro, 891; Lawson, *Black Ballots*, 173, 182; Dallek, *Lone Star Rising*, 524.

40. Fairclough, 198–199, 206–207, 220–221.

41. *CR*: July 25, 1957, 12695–12696, 12893.

42. Lawson, *Black Ballots*, 185, 189; Caro, 945–946, 950–951; Dallek, *Lone Star Rising*, 525.

43. *CR*: July 29, 1957, 12892.

44. Ibid.: 12921; Ibid.: July 31, 1957, 13124.

45. Caro, 987; Lawson, *Black Ballots*, 193, 195; Dallek, *Lone Star Rising*, 526.

46. *CR*: August 30, 1957, 16662; Dallek, *Lone Star Rising*, 526.

47. *CR*: August 28, 1957, 16214.

48. Ibid.; Ibid.: August 29, 1957, 16475–16476.

49. Woods, *Quest for Identity*, 110–112.

50. *Executive Sessions of the Senate Foreign Relations Committee Together With Joint Sessions With the Senate Armed Services Committee* (Historical Series), vol. 9, 58th Cong., 1st sess. (Washington, DC: U.S. Government Printing Office, 1979), 5; Cohen, 114; McCormick, 139; John Lewis Gaddis, *We Now Know: Rethinking Cold War History* (New York: Oxford University Press, 1997), 174.

51. Mann, 172–173.

52. *NYT*, February 12, 1957.

53. Ibid.; *CR*: February 11, 1957, 1864; Ibid.: February 25, 1957, 2533, 2534; Ibid.: March 5, 1957, 3129.

54. Kurtz and Peoples, 185.

55. Fairclough, 170, 191–195; Kurtz and Peoples, 203.

56. Fairclough, 228; Kurtz and Peoples, 206–207.

57. Kurtz and Peoples, 216–217; Michael Martin, "Insiders and Outsiders: Earl K. Long and the Media, May–July 1959," *Louisiana History* 40 (Spring 1999): 197, 203; Fairclough, 228.

58. A. J. Liebling, *The Earl of Louisiana* (Baton Rouge: Louisiana State University Press, 1970), 32; Kurtz and Peoples, 217–218.

59. RBL, handwritten notes on program of Loyola University commencement exercises, n.d., RBL collection 5:18.

60. Kurtz and Peoples, 217–218; Thomas Martin, *Dynasty: The Longs of Louisiana* (New York: G. P. Putnam's Sons, 1960), 216–217.

61. T. Martin, *Dynasty*, 219; RBL, speech manuscript (undelivered), n.d., RBL Collection, 5:17.

62. Kurtz and Peoples 218–219; T. Martin, *Dynasty*, 223–224.

63. Kurtz and Peoples, 218–219, 230–231; *Newsweek*, June 15, 1959, 33;

NYT, June 1, 1959; Stan Opotowsky, *The Longs of Louisiana* (New York: Dutton, 1960), 201–202.

64. RBL, copy of speech, RBL Collection 5:16.

65. *NYT,* June 16, 1959, 23; T. Martin, *Dynasty,* 236–237; *NYT,* June 17, June 18, 1959.

66. Kurtz and Peoples, 219–221.

67. Press release, June 25, 1959, RBL Collection 595:28; Mann, 195.

68. Opotowsky, 201.

69. T. Martin, *Dynasty,* 231; WDSU editorial, "Senator Long's Speech," July 1, 1959, RBL Collection 5:14.

70. Kurtz and Peoples, 221–223.

71. Ibid., 231–242; M. Martin, "Insiders and Outsiders," 206–208.

72. Kurtz and Peoples, 244–256; Jim Chubbuck, interview by Jack Bass and Walter DeVries, January 7, 1974, transcription, Interview 84, Southern Oral History Programs #4007, Southern Historical Collection, Wilson Library, University of North Carolina at Chapel Hill.

73. Lawson, *Black Ballots,* 222, 227.

74. *CR*: September 14, 1952, 19531; Lawson, *Black Ballots,* 230.

75. Lawson, *Black Ballots,* 237, 238; Dallek, *Lone Star Rising,* 562–563; Thomas A. Becnel, *Senator Allen Ellender of Louisiana: A Biography* (Baton Rouge: Louisiana State University Press, 1995), 212.

76. Fairclough, 232; Edward F. Haas, *DeLesseps S. Morrison and the Image of Reform: New Orleans Politics, 1946–1961* (1974; paperback ed., Baton Rouge: Louisiana State University Press, 1986), 247–248; Perry Howard, "Louisiana: Resistance and Change," in *The Changing Politics of the South,* ed. William C. Havard (Baton Rouge: Louisiana State University Press, 1972), 556.

77. Howard E. Shuman, interviewed by Donald E. Ritchie, August 13, 1987, transcription, Interview #3, United States Senate Historical Office—Oral History Project, available at http://www.senate.gov/artandhistory/history/resources/pdf/Shuman_interview_3.pdf, 146-147, 154.

78. *CR*: March 2, 1960, 4165; Ibid.: February 24, 1960, 3393.

79. Ibid.: February 26, 1960, 3614; Ibid.: March 2, 1960, 3186.

80. Ibid.: March 2, 1960, 4205; Ibid.: February 26, 1960, 3602.

81. Ibid.: March 2, 1960, 4184, 4196.

82. Ibid.: March 2, 1960, 4186, 4189.

83. Ibid.: March 8, 1960, 4856.

84. Ibid.: February 26, 1960, 3614; Ibid.: March 2, 1960, 4163.

85. Ibid.: March 5, 1960, 4613.

86. Ibid.: February 26, 1960, 3613, 3614; Ibid.: March 2, 1960, 4182.

87. *CQA* (1960), 185, 190; Lawson, *Black Ballots,* 243, 244; Nicole L.

Gueron, "An Idea Whose Time Has Come: A Comparative Procedural History of the Civil Rights Acts of 1960, 1964, and 1991," *Yale Law Journal* 104 (March 1995): 1215.

88. *CQA* (1960), 488; *CR*: April 8, 1960, 7810.

89. On Huey's and Earl's racism, see Glen Jeansonne, "Huey Long and Racism," *Louisiana History* 33 (Summer 1992), 265–282, and Kurtz and Peoples, 194–210. George A. Smathers, interviewed by Donald A. Ritchie, transcript, August 29 and October 24, 1989, Interview #3, United States Senate Historical Office, Oral History Project, available at http://www.senate.gov/artandhistory/history/resources/pdf/Smathers_interview_3.pdf), 71.

90. Jesse R. Nichols, interviewed by Donald A. Ritchie, transcript, April 12, 1994, Interview #4, United States Senate Historical Office, Oral History Project, available at http://www.senate.gov/artandhistory/history/resources/pdf/Nichols_interview_4.pdf, 81; Nichols, interviewed by Ritchie, transcript, March 26, 1994, United States Senate Historical Office, Oral History Project, available at http://www.senate.gov/artandhistory/history/resources/pdf/Nichols_interview_1.pdf, 14.

Chapter 4

1. Robert Mann, *Legacy to Power: Senator Russell Long of Louisiana* (New York: Paragon House, 1992), 204–205; Camille Gravel, interview by John Stewart, May 23, 1967, transcription, John F. Kennedy Presidential Library, John F. Kennedy Presidential Oral History Collection, Part II: The Congress, the Judiciary, Public Figures, and Private Individuals, Boston, Massachusetts.

2. Robert Dallek, *An Unfinished Life: John F. Kennedy, 1917–1963* (Boston: Little, Brown, 2003), 274–276.

3. Ibid., 334–335; James E. Anderson, "Poverty, Unemployment, and Economic Development: The Search for a National Anti-Poverty Policy," *Journal of Politics* 29 (February 1967): 77–78; James N. Giglio, *The Presidency of John F. Kennedy* (Lawrence: University of Kansas Press, 1991), 97; James N. Giglio, "John F. Kennedy and the Nation," in *Debating the Kennedy Presidency*, ed. James N. Giglio and Stephen G. Rabe (Lanham, MD: Rowan & Littlefield, 2003), 101–102; *Congressional Record—Senate* (hereafter *CR*): April 20, 1961, 6372; Ibid.: March 15, 1961, 4040; Ibid.: June 2, 1961, 10008.

4. Dallek, *Unfinished Life*, 379; Giglio, "John F. Kennedy and the Nation," 102.

5. *CR*: May 25, 1961, 9054.

6. Dallek, *Unfinished Life*, 379; Pearl Bierman, "The Special Problems of Low-Income Groups and the Aged: Meeting the Health Needs of Low-

Income Families," *Annals of the American Academy of Political and Social Science* 37 (September 1961), 110–111; *Congressional Quarterly Almanac* (1963), 671 (hereafter *CQA*).

7. *CQA* (1962), 500; *CR*: September 6, 1962, 18742.

8. Dallek, *Unfinished Life*, 583, 584; Lizabeth Cohen, *A Consumer's Republic: The Politics of Consumption in Postwar America* (New York: Knopf, 2003), 351; William H. Chafe, *The Unfinished Journey: America since World War II*, 6th ed. (New York: Oxford University Press, 2007), 185, 186; Mann, 210–211.

9. *CR*: March 18, 1960, 5966.

10. Joseph A. Fry, *Dixie Looks Abroad: The South and U.S. Foreign Relations, 1789–1973* (Baton Rouge: Louisiana State University Press, 2002), 234; *CR*: June 29, 1960: 14889.

11. John Lewis Gaddis, *We Now Know: Rethinking Cold War History* (Oxford: Oxford University Press, 1997), 179–182; Dallek, *Unfinished Life*, 356–360, 361, 364–366.

12. Fry, *Dixie Looks Abroad*, 234–235; *CR*: May 29, 1961, 9185.

13. *CR*: May 19, 1961, 9186.

14. Ibid., September 12, 1962: 19191; *CQA* (1962), 689.

15. Warren I. Cohen, *America in the Age of Soviet Power*, vol. 1, *The Cambridge History of American Foreign Relations* (Cambridge: Cambridge University Press, 1993), 139–144; Fry, *Dixie Looks Abroad*, 235; Dallek, *Unfinished Life*, 535–575.

16. Dallek, *Unfinished Life*, 693–694; *CR*: December 11, 1963, 24197.

17. Paul Conkin, *Big Daddy from the Pedernales: Lyndon Baines Johnson* (Boston: Twayne, 1986), 209.

18. Mann, 277, 278, 279.

19. Transcript, Lawrence F. O'Brien Oral History Interview X, June 25, 1986, by Michael L. Gillette, Lyndon Baines Johnson Presidential Library (hereafter LBJ Library), Austin, Texas, 11; Transcript, Lawrence F. O'Brien Oral History Interview XI, July 24, 1986, 11.

20. Transcript, Lawrence F. O'Brien Oral History Interview XVII, December 17, 1986, by Michael L. Gillette, LBJ Library, 1.

21. *CR*: February 7, 1964, 2393; Ibid.: February 26, 1964, 3692; *CQA* (1964), 518.

22. Robert Dallek, *Flawed Giant: Lyndon Johnson and His Times, 1961–1973* (New York: Oxford University Press, 1998), 79; *CR*: July 23, 1964, 16787; *CQA* (1964), 704.

23. *CQA* (1965), 24, 1025, 1067; *CR*: January 28, 1965, 1545; Ibid.: April 9, 1966, 7718; Ibid.: September 22, 1965, 24783; Randall Bennett Woods, *Quest for Identity: America since 1945* (Fort Worth, TX: Harcourt, 2001), 195,

200; James T. Patterson, *Grand Expectations: The United States, 1945–1974* (New York: Oxford University Press, 1996), 577; Roger Daniels, *Guarding the Golden Door: American Immigration Policy and Immigrants since 1882* (New York: Hill and Wang, 2004), 133–136.

24. *CR*: July 9, 1965, 16157; Ibid.: July 16, 1964, 13664–13666.

25. Transcript, Wilbur Mills Oral History Interview II, March 25, 1987, 3/25/87, by Michael L. Gillette, Internet Copy, LBJ Library, 7; *CR*: July 6, 1965, 15601–15602; July 8, 1965, 15925.

26. Adam Fairclough, *Race and Democracy: The Civil Rights Struggle in Louisiana, 1915–1972* (Athens: University of Georgia Press, 1995), 234–264.

27. Kenneth M. Holland, "J. Skelly Wright," in *Great American Judges*, vol. 2, *L–Z*, ed. John Vile (Santa Barbara: ABC-CLIO, 2003), 824–825.

28. "WDSU TV SHOW," transcript, April 9, 1962 [1960], RBL Collection 556:41; RBL, written communication, April 10, 1962 [1960], ibid.

29. On the New Orleans school integration crisis, see Fairclough, *Race and Democracy*, 234–264, and Liva Baker, *The Second Battle of New Orleans: The Hundred-Year Struggle to Integrate the Schools* (New York: HarperCollins, 1996), 293–311, 325–436.

30. Baker, *Second Battle of New Orleans*, 395, 414–415, 416, 419, 457–461; Edward F. Haas, *DeLesseps S. Morrison and the Image of Reform: New Orleans Politics, 1946–1961* (Baton Rouge: Louisiana State University Press, 1974), 269–274.

31. *CQA* (1964), 344, 345–348. Excellent overviews of the Second Reconstruction include Hugh Davis Graham, *The Civil Rights Era: Origins and Development of National Policy, 1960–1972* (New York: Oxford University Press, 1990); Steven Lawson, *Black Ballots: Voting Rights in the South, 1944–1969* (New York: Columbia University Press, 1976); and Carl Brauer, *John F. Kennedy and the Second Reconstruction* (New York: Columbia University Press, 1977).

32. Graham, 144; *CR*: March 13, 1964, 5220; Ibid.: March 24, 1964, 6078; Ibid.: May 11, 1964, 10572.

33. *CR*: March 24, 1964, 6071, 6078.

34. Ibid., 6073.

35. Ibid., 6072.

36. Chafe, 298; *CR*: March 24, 1964, 6090–6091.

37. Graham, 145; Thomas A. Becnel, *Senator Allen Ellender of Louisiana: A Biography* (Baton Rouge: Louisiana State University Press, 1995), 212.

38. *CR*: April 14, 1964, 7904, 7905, 7910.

39. Ibid.: April 27, 1964, 9170, 9177, 9174; Ibid.: May 11, 1964, 10565.

40. Ibid.: April 24, 1964, 9180; Ibid.: May 11, 1964, 10563.

41. Louis Gould, *The Most Exclusive Club: A History of the Modern United States Senate* (New York: Basic Books, 2005), 243; *CR*: March 13, 1964, 5242; Ibid.: April 27, 1964, 9169; Graham, 151–152; Dallek, *Flawed Giant,* 120.

42. Michael R. Beschloss, *Taking Charge: The Johnson White House Tapes, 1963–1964* (New York: Touchstone, 1997), 458–459.

43. Roman J. Heleniak, "Lyndon Johnson in New Orleans," in *Louisiana since the Longs, 1960 to Century's End,* ed. Michael L. Kurtz, vol. 9, Louisiana Purchase Bicentennial Series in Louisiana History, (Lafayette, LA: Center for Louisiana Studies, 1998), 353, 358, 360; William E. Leuchtenburg, *The White House Looks South: Franklin D. Roosevelt, Harry S. Truman, Lyndon B. Johnson* (Baton Rouge: Louisiana State University Press, 2005), 320.

44. Dallek, *Flawed Giant,* 218–219; Leuchtenburg, 327–330; Keith Finley, *Delaying the Dream: Southern Senators and the Fight against Civil Rights, 1938–1965* (Baton Rouge: Louisiana State University Press, 2008), 293.

45. *CQA* (1965), 533–534. The six Dixie states were Alabama, Georgia, Louisiana, Mississippi, South Carolina, and Virginia.

46. *CR*: March 18, 1965, 5398; Ibid.: April 22, 1965, 8305; Ibid.: May 25, 1965, 11479, 11481; Ibid.: July 24, 1975, 24768; Finley, 286, 296–297.

47. Finley, 295, 296.

48. Ibid., 284; *CQA* (1965), 533.

49. Dallek, *Flawed Giant,* 220–221.

50. Ibid., 325, 326; Graham, 260.

51. Dallek, *Flawed Giant,* 326; *CR*: September 12, 1966, 22307.

52. Dallek, *Flawed Giant,* 326–327.

53. Ibid., 517; Graham, 270; *CR*: January 29, 1968, 1292, 1293; Ibid.: January 19, 1968, 391.

54. *CR*: January 18, 1968, 332; Ibid.: January 29, 1968, 1290, 1294.

55. Ibid.: January 29, 1968, 1295, 1297; Ibid.: March 6, 1968, 5532–5545; Dan T. Carter, *The Politics of Rage: George Wallace, the Origins of the New Conservatism, and the Transformation of American Politics* (Baton Rouge: Louisiana State University Press, 1995), 348.

56. Graham, 270; *CR*: February 19, 1968, 3361. See Patterson's "Preface" in *Grand Expectations* on the matter of rising expectations.

57. Graham, 271–272.

58. For the best overview of the Vietnam conflict, see George C. Herring, *America's Longest War: The United States and Vietnam, 1950–1975* (Boston: McGraw-Hill, 2002).

59. *CR*: January 27, 1966, 1313.

60. Ibid.: March 1, 1965, 3780; Ibid.: April 29, 1965, 8983.

61. Ibid.: April 29, 1965, 8983; Ibid.: March 4, 1965, 4201–4202.

62. Cohen, *America in the Age of Soviet Power*, 95; Ibid., January 27, 1966: 1313, 1314; Ibid., January 31, 1966: 1582; Ibid., February 16, 1966: 3161.

63. Fry, *Dixie Looks Abroad*, 268–269, 273, 283–286; Joseph A. Fry, *Debating Vietnam: Fulbright, Stennis, and Their Senate Hearings* (Lanham, MD: Rowman & Littlefield, 2006), 12.

64. Gould, 245, 246–247; Fry, *Dixie Looks Abroad*, 275–276, 277.

65. Mann, 245; *CR*: February 26, 1966, 2803; Ibid.: January 31, 1966, 1583.

66. *CR*: March 29, 1961, 5109; Ibid.: April 13, 1961, 5719. On the Sugar Act, see, for instance, ibid.: March 29, 1961, 5173–5177, July 2, 1962, 12455–12467, September 20, 1965, 25520–25521, October 19, 1965, 27396–27405, and October 20, 1965, 27517–27528. On the creation of the New Orleans Saints, see Michael S. Martin "New Orleans Becomes a Big-League City: The NFL-AFL Merger and the Creation of the New Orleans Saints," in *Horsehide, Pigskin, Oval Tracks, and Apple Pie: Essays on Sports and American Culture*, ed. Jim Vlasich (Jefferson, NC: McFarland, 2006): 119–131.

67. On Hurricane Betsy, see Edward F. Haas, "'Don't Believe Any False Rumors . . . ': Mayor Victor H. Schiro, Hurricane Betsy, and Urban Myths," *Louisiana History* 45 (2004): 463–468; Kent Germany, "LBJ and the Response to Hurricane Betsy," White House Tapes, Presidential Recordings Program, #8858, WH6509.03, LBJ Library, available at http://www.whitehousetapes.net/exhibit/lbj-and-response-hurricane-betsy (retrieved May 1, 2010); The President's Daily Diary for September 10, 1965, available at ane/19650910.pdf (retrieved May 1, 2010); "Transcript of Audio of President Johnson in New Orleans Following Landfall of Hurricane Betsy, September 10, 1965," LBJ Library, available at http://www.lbjlib.utexas.edu/johnson/AV.hom/Hurricane/audio_transcript.shtm (retrieved May 1, 2010).

68. *CR*: October 21, 1965, 27946, 27950.

69. Mann, 207, 276; Michael Beschloss, *Reaching for Glory: Lyndon Johnson's Secret White House Tapes, 1964–1965* (New York: Touchstone, 2002), 147.

70. *CR*: October 20, 1962, 22953–22954; Ibid.: July 1, 1964, 15712, 15715–15716; Ibid.: June 8, 1967, 15260–15261; Ibid.: August 23, 1967, 2377–23781; Edward Greelegs, *Russell B. Long: Democratic Senator from Louisiana*, Ralph Nader Congress Project, Citizens Look at Congress (New York: Grossman Publishers, 1972), 1, 2, 6.

71. Mann, 43, 66; Greelegs, 6; T. Harry Williams, *Huey Long* (New York: Knopf, 1970), 825, 827; R. White, 223–224.

72. Mann, 209; *CQA* (1968), 958; Greelegs, 4.

73. Patterson, *Grand Expectations*, 678–709; Chafe, 329–364.

74. Numan V. Bartley, *The New South, 1945–1980* (Baton Rouge: Louisiana State University Press, 1995), 397; Carter, *Politics of Rage*, 368.

Chapter 5

1. T. Harry Williams to Russell B. Long (hereafter RBL), August 29, 1968, RBL 2:3.

2. RBL to Lloyd Glaudi, February 16, 1959, RBL Collection, 1:25; RBL, statement, July 2, 1948, RBL Collection, 5:8; "Script Written by Senator Long for Television Program in Behalf of Gillis Long's Candidacy for Governor—Program Presented Week of December 2–7, 1963," RBL Collection, 1:33.

3. Louis L. Gould, *The Most Exclusive Club: A History of the United States Senate* (New York: Basic Books, 2005), 232; Robert Mann, *Legacy to Power: Senator Russell Long of Louisiana* (New York: Paragon House, 1992), 236, 244, 243, 260–266, 294.

4. Mann, 63, 222, 286–289, 290–291; Gould, *Most Exclusive Club*, 97, 128, 188–189.

5. Mann, 79–80, 223, 304. For a biography of Ellender, see Thomas A. Becnel, *Senator Allen Ellender of Louisiana: A Biography* (Baton Rouge: Louisiana State University Press, 1995).

6. Thomas A. Becnel, "Allen J, Ellender: Consensus Politician," *Louisiana History* 32 (Summer 1992): 232.

7. Jack Bass and Walter De Vries, *The Transformation of Southern Politics: Social Change and Political Consequence since 1945* (New York: Basic Books, 1976), 163; John Maginnis, *The Last Hayride* (Baton Rouge: Gris Gris Press, 1984), 19, 20; Wayne Parent, *Inside the Carnival: Unmasking Louisiana Politics* (Baton Rouge: Louisiana State University Press, 2004), 38; "JOHNSTON, John Bennett, Jr., (1932 –)," *Biographical Directory of the United States Congress*, available at http://bioguide.congress.gov/scripts/biodisplay.pl?INDEX=J000189 (retrieved June 17, 2010).

8. Joan McKinney quoted in Mann, 349; Dan Yergin, Senator Bennett Johnston, and John Deutch, "Oil Lessons from the 1970s," *The International Economy* (Fall 2009): 60.

9. Alonzo Hamby, *Liberalism and Its Challengers, from F.D.R. to Bush*, 2nd ed. (New York: Oxford University Press, 1992), 130.

10. *Congressional Record* (hereafter *CR*): November 21, 1969, 35396; *Congressional Quarterly Almanac* (hereafter CQA) (1970), 21-S; Gould, *Most Exclusive Club*, 253–254.

11. *CQA* (1969), 12-S, 171; Ibid. (1970), 32-S; Ibid. (1971), 4-S; Ibid. (1972), 16-S; *CR*: November 24, 1969, 35485, 35488.

12. *CR*: December 2, 1969, 36423, 36425, 36427, 36428; Ibid.: December 11, 1969, 38369; *NYT*, December 23, 1969.

13. *CQA* (1970), 53-S, 61-S; *CR*: November 11, 1971, 40804, 40806; *CQA* (1971), 16, 430, 441, 66-S; *CR*: November 22, 1971, 42685, 42687; Ibid.: December 9, 1971, 45817, 45819.

14. For more detailed analyses of the War on Poverty, see Allen Matusow, *The Unraveling of America: A History of Liberalism in the 1960s* (New York: HarperCollins, 1984); John Schwarz, *America's Hidden Success: A Reassessment of Twenty Years of Public Policy* (New York: Norton, 1983); Charles Murray, *Losing Ground: American Social Policy, 1950–1980* (New York: Basic Books, 1984).

15. The UPI poll is reported in *CQA* (1970), 930; Ibid., 953, 33-S.

16. *CQA* (1973), 50-S; Gould, *Most Exclusive Club*, 262.

17. *CQA* (1970), 17-S, 18-S; *CR*: March 20, 1972, 9088; Ibid.: March 22, 1972, 9598; James Patterson, *Grand Expectations: The United States, 1945–1974* (New York: Oxford University Press, 1996), 714.

18. Daniel Patrick Moynihan's *The Negro Family: The Case for National Action* (Washington, DC: U.S. Government Printing Office, 1965) was the first work to elucidate most of these assumptions; the book would define the welfare debate for the next two decades. James T. Patterson, *America's Struggle against Poverty in the Twentieth Century* (Cambridge, MA: Harvard University Press, 2000, 2001), 65–67, 83, 186; Charles Murray, *Losing Ground: American Social Policy, 1950–1980* (New York: Basic Books, 1984), 45–46. Edward Berkowitz, *America's Welfare State: From Roosevelt to Reagan* (Baltimore: The Johns Hopkins University Press, 1991), 123, 125; Alex Waddan, "A Liberal in Wolf's Clothing: Nixon's Family Assistance Plan in the Light of 1990s Welfare Reform," *Journal of American Studies* 32 (1998): 210, 215; Robert F. McNown, "The Story of the Family Assistance Plan," *Current History* 65 (1973): 57; *CQA* (1972), 900. According to Daniel Moynihan, the number of AFDC recipients increased by one-third in 1969 alone. Moynihan, *The Politics of a Guaranteed Income: The Nixon Administration and the Family Assistance Plan* (New York: Random House, 1973), 425; Jill Quadagno, "Race, Class, and Gender in the U.S. Welfare State: Nixon's Failed Family Assistance Plan," *American Sociological Review* 55 (1990): 16–17, 25; Robert Asen, "Nixon's Welfare Reform: Enacting Historical Contradictions of Poverty Discourses," *Rhetoric and Public Affairs* 4 (2001): 266–268.

19. *Public Papers of the Presidents of the United States: Richard Nixon, Containing the Public Messages, Speeches, and Statements of the President, 1969* (Washington, DC: U.S. Government Printing Office, 1971), 637, 639–640; Patterson, *America's Struggle*, 186; Herbert S. Parmet, *Richard Nixon*

and His America (Boston: Little, Brown, 1990), 554; Berkowitz, 128; Martin Anderson, *Welfare: The Political Economy of Welfare Reform in the United States* (Stanford, CA: Hoover Institution, Stanford University Press, 1978), 82; Moynihan, *Politics of a Guaranteed Income*, 220; Quadagno, 11, 15; Asen, 268–272.

20. *Public Papers of Richard Nixon, 1969*, 640–641, 645; Asen, 272–275.

21. RBL, form letter to correspondents, January 1971, RBL Collection 130:13; RBL to Mrs. J. A. Standridge, February 20, 1970, RBL Collection, 122:23; Transcript of TV Interview, RBL interviewed by Sam Shaffer, May 3, 1972, RBL Collection, 611:34.

22. Stephen E. Ambrose, *Nixon*, vol. 2, *The Triumph of a Politician, 1962–1972* (New York: Simon and Schuster, 1989), 291, 293; Patterson, *America's Struggle*, 186; Berkowitz, 129; Anderson, 77, 81; Edward Berkowitz and Kim McQuaid, *Creating the Welfare State: The Political Economy of Twentieth-Century Reform*, 2nd rev. ed. (New York: Praeger, 1988), 206; Moynihan, *Politics of a Guaranteed Income*, 138–139; Waddan, 204, 213–216; Leslie Lenkowsky, "Welfare Reform and the Liberals," *Commentary* 67 (1979): 57; McNown, 58–59; Otto A. Davis and John E. Jackson, "Senate Defeat of the Family Assistance Plan," *Public Policy* 22 (1974): 247.

23. Berkowitz, 123–124, 128; Anderson, 79; Berkowitz and McQuaid, 206; Patterson, *America's Struggle*, 186–187; Moynihan, *Politics of a Guaranteed Income*, 140–141, 355; Lenkowsky, 57; McNown, 57–59; Ambrose, 291–292; Quadango, 23.

24. Moynihan, *Politics of a Guaranteed Income*, 395

25. Liberal opponents of FAP believed that the guaranteed income level was placed too low, that the plan would only benefit the South, and that the work requirements were repressive; they also tended to oppose the plan simply because of Nixon's advocacy. Conservatives tended to voice opposition to FAP because they thought it would be too expensive, in terms of cost to the taxpayer, and too expansive, in terms of increasing welfare rolls. Patterson, *America's Struggle*, 188–189; Parmet, 554–555, 557; Ambrose, 314–315, 366; Berkowitz, 130; Moynihan, *Politics of a Guaranteed Income*, 327; Waddan, 204; McNown, 59; Asen, 276.

26. Anderson, 84; *CQA* (1970), 1031; McNown, 60; Davis and Jackson, 247; Ambrose, 366; Quadagno, 11; *CR*: April 23, 1970, 12723; *CQA* (1970), 1031, 1034, 1035; *NYT*, April 30, May 2, 1970; Patterson, *America's Struggle*, 190; Parmet, 558–559; Berkowitz, 132; Moynihan, *Politics of a Guaranteed Income*, 291, 425, 428, 430, 437, 453, 456, 480–481, 487, 490, 500, 523.

27. *CR*: April 23, 1970, 12723; RBL to Effie Mae Jaubert, November 2, 1970, RBL Collection, 122:21. Long had been a sponsor of the Work Incentive Program of 1967.

28. George P. Schulz, Memorandum for the President's File, December 11, 1970, Nixon Presidential Materials Project, College Park, MD, President's Office Files, Box 80, "Beginning December 6, 1970"; *CR*: December 28, 1970, 43625, 43627, 43646, 43868.

29. *CQA* (1970), 1031, 1040; *NYT*, October 9, December 29, 1970; McNown, 61; Davis and Jackson, 245; Ambrose, 391; Moynihan, *Politics of a Guaranteed Income*, 533; John D. Ehrlichman, Notes, December 30, 1970, Nixon Presidential Materials Project, College Park, MD, John Ehrlichman Papers, Box 4, "JDE Notes of Meetings with the President 7/1/70–12/31/70 [8 of 8]"; *CR*: December 31, 1970, 44478, 44479.

30. *Public Papers of the Presidents of the United States: Richard Nixon, Containing the Public Messages, Speeches, and Statements of the President, 1970* (Washington, DC: U.S. Government Printing Office, 1971), 10; *CR*: August 6, 1971, 30544; *CQA* (1971), 519; *NYT*, July 28, 1971; Parmet, 556, 559.

31. RBL interview, *Chicago Daily News*, December 14–15, 1971, RBL Collection, 610:6; Moynihan, *Politics of a Guaranteed Income*, 461; McNown, 58, 60, 86; Quadagno, 19–20; RBL form letter to correspondents, August 1970, RBL Collection, 122:24; RBL to James L. Burns, September 28, 1970, RBL Collection, 122:22.

32. RBL, form letter to correspondents, January 1971, RBL Collection, 130:13; Transcript of TV Interview, RBL interviewed by Sam Hanna and Sam Shaffer, May 25, 1972, RBL Collection, 611:49; RBL, interview with *Frontgrounders*, January 26, 1972, RBL Collection, 610:45; Transcript of interview, RBL interviewed by Paul Leventhal, May 11, 1972, RBL Collection, 611:42; Transcript of TV Interview, RBL interviewed by Sam Shaffer, May 3, 1972, RBL Collection, 611:34.

33. Press Release, Opening Statement of Chairman at Hearings on H.R. 1, January 1, 18, 1972, RBL Collection, 610:43.

34. RBL to Alberta Gates, August 19, 1970, RBL Collection, 122:23; *CQA* (1972), 904; RBL to Opry J. Serpas, July 29, 1970, RBL Collection, 122:23; Transcript of interview, RBL interviewed by *Chicago Daily News*, December 14–15, 1971, RBL Collection, 610:6.

35. Speech, RBL to Baton Rouge Rotary Club, July 12, 1972, RBL Collection, 611:75; Transcript of interview, RBL interviewed by *Chicago Daily News*, December 14–15, 1971, RBL Collection, 610:6; *CQA* (1972), 904, 906. Long had proposed these ideas in a meeting with President Nixon in April 1971. John D. Ehrlichman, Notes, April 26, 1971, Nixon Presidential Materials Project, College Park, MD, John Ehrlichman Papers, Box 5, "JDE Notes of Meetings with the President 4-23-71 to 8-2-71 [1 of 5]."

36. *CQA* (1972), 899, 905, 914; *NYT*, October 18, 1972; McNown, 57, 61; Patterson, *America's Struggle*, 190; Parmet, 558. See Waddan, "A Liberal in

Wolf's Clothing," for a comparison of FAP and the Personal Responsibility and Work Opportunity Reconciliation Act of 1996.

37. Robert Mann, *Legacy to Power: Senator Russell Long of Louisiana* (New York: Paragon House, 1992), 299; RBL speech to Louisiana Police Jury Association, Lafayette, Louisiana, April 10, 1972, RBL Collection, 611:19.

38. RBL, transcript of interview for television, interviewed by Sam Shaffer, May 3, 1972, RBL Collection, 611:34.

39. RBL speech to Louisiana Police Jury Association, Lafayette, Louisiana, April 10, 1972, RBL Collection, 611:19.

40. For more on Nixon's problems of the early 1970s, see Allen J. Matusow, *Nixon's Economy: Booms, Busts, Dollars, and Votes* (Lawrence: University Press of Kansas, 1998); Stanley Kutler, *Wars of Watergate: The Last Crisis of Richard Nixon* (New York: Knopf, 1990); and Stanley Kutler, *Abuse of Power: The New Nixon Tapes* (New York: Simon and Schuster, 1997).

41. *CQA* (1973), 4-S; Mann, 312–313.

42. *CR*: September 4, 1974, 30230–30233; *CQA* (1974), 823, 825, 56-S, 80-S; Gerald R. Ford, *A Time to Heal: The Autobiography of Gerald R. Ford* (New York: Harper and Row, 1979), 226; Woods, *Quest for Identity*, 349.

43. *CQA* (1974), 83-S; *CR*: December 16, 1974, 40099; Patterson, *Grand Expectations*, 783–784.

44. *CQA* (1974), 78-S; Ford, *A Time to Heal*, 224; *CR*: December 12, 1974, 39503, 39507; Ibid.: December 13, 1974, 39858; *CQA* (1975), 90-S; Woods, *Quest for Identity*, 393.

45. Mann, 320–326; *CQA* (1975), 95; Ford, *A Time to Heal*, 340; *CR*: March 18, 1975, 7229–7330; Ibid.: March 21, 1975, 8133; March 26, 1975, 8861, 8878–8879.

46. RBL, transcript of interview for television, interviewed by Sam Shaffer, May 3, 1972, RBL Collection, 611:34.

47. Louis O. Kelso and Patricia Hetter, *Two-Factor Theory: The Economics of Reality, How to Turn Eighty Million Workers into Capitalists on Borrowed Money and Other Proposals* (1967; New York: Vintage Books, 1968), 3, 7, 41; Louis O. Kelso and Mortimer Adler, *Capitalist Manifesto* (Westport, CT: Greenwood Press, 1958), 27–29, 82, 107, 139, 145, 169–170, 176–189; Louis O. Kelso and Mortimer Adler, *The New Capitalists: A Proposal to Free Economic Growth from the Slavery of Savings* (New York: Random House, 1961), 28; Louis O. Kelso and Patricia Hetter Kelso, *Democracy and Economic Power: Extending the ESOP Revolution* (Cambridge, MA: Ballinger, 1986), 59.

48. *Barron's*, July 21, 1975, 3; *Fortune*, March 1976, 129–130; Kelso and Hetter, 79, 84, 88–89, 91–92; Kelso and Kelso, 60–64; Kelso and Adler, *The New Capitalists*, 60; *Barron's*, July 21, 1973, 3. ESOPs came under a variety

of terminologies as Kelso's theories developed: Financed Capitalist Plans, Second Income Plan Trusts, Employed Stockholders Ownership Trusts. Employee Stock Ownership Plan was the term most common after the mid-1970s.

49. RBL to Lee Rosler, August 7, 1975, RBL Collection, 561:16.

50. Louis Kelso, Russell Long, and William Simon, Panel Discussion, "Financing Self-Sufficiency and Energy Production," January 28, 1974, RBL Collection, 561:35; *Barron's*, 21 July 1975, 18.

51. RBL to Warren G. Magnuson, November 29, 1973, RBL Collection, 564:10.

52. *Barron's*, July 21, 1975, 18; *Washington Post*, August 4, August 5, 1976; *Time*, October 4, 1976, 80; *Wall Street Journal*, January 4, 1982; Mann, 409.

53. RBL to Scott O'Neal, May 8, 1975, RBL Collection, 561:20.

54. Ibid.

55. Press Release, August 4, 1976, RBL Collection, 565:30.

56. Russell Long, "ESOP Council Speech," n.d. (May 1979), RBL Collection, 625:1.

57. RBL, Remarks before the ESOP Council Second Annual Meeting, May 7, 1979, RBL Collection, 625:1.

58. *CR*: September 29, 1976, 33261, 33305; *CQA* (1976), 91-S, 82-S; *CR*: June 16, 1976: 18541.

59. Woods, *Quest for Identity*, 396–397;

60. Gould, *Most Exclusive Club*, 273–273; Mann, 352, 371.

61. On Carter's administration, see Zbigniew Brzezinski, *Power and Principle: Memoirs of the National Security Advisor* (New York: Farrar, Straus, Giroux, 1983); Burton I. Kaufman, *The Presidency of James Earl Carter* (Lawrence: University Press of Kansas, 1993); Gaddis Smith, *Morality, Reason, and Power: American Diplomacy in the Carter Years* (New York: Hill and Wang, 1986).

62. Mann, 342–348; *CQA* (1977), 711, 740.

63. Richard N. Cooper, "A Note on Deregulation of Natural Gas Prices," *Brookings Papers on Economic Activity* 2 (1982), 373; *CQA* (1977), 75-S, 114, 116.

64. *CQA* (1978), 637, 235, 243; Ibid. (1979), 612, 618, 619.

65. Jack Bass and Walter DeVries, *The Transformation of Southern Politics: Social Change and Political Consequence since 1945* (New York: Basic Books, 1976), 163; Erwin Knoll, "The Oil Lobby Is Not Depeleted," *New York Times Magazine*, March 8, 1970, 109; Martin Tolchin and Susan Tolchin, *To the Victor: Political Patronage from the Clubhouse to the White House and Beyond* (New York: Random House, 1971), 246–247; Ronnie Duggar, "Oil and Politics," *Atlantic Monthly*, September 1969, 73.

66. RBL to President Jimmy Carter, December 21, 1978, RBL Collection, 565:43; Margaret Thatcher to RBL, August 31, 1979, RBL Collection, 625:66.

67. Margaret Thatcher to RBL, August 31, 1979, RBL Collection, 625:66.

68. Ibid.

69. Ibid.

70. *Barron's*, November 18, 1985.

71. *New York Times*, January 2, 1980, D2.

72. Edward Greelegs, *Russell B. Long: Democratic Senator from Louisiana*, Ralph Nader Congress Project, Citizens Look at Congress (New York: Grossman Publishers, 1972), 4, 5.

Conclusion

1. "Ronald Reagan's Announcement for Presidential Candidacy, 11/13/1979," Ronald Reagan's Major Speeches, 1964–89, Ronald Reagan Presidential Library Archives, Simi Valley, California, available online at http://www.reagan.utexas.edu/archives/reference/11.13.79.html (retrieved August 10, 2012).

2. *Congressional Quarterly Almanac* (hereafter *CQA*) (Washington, DC: Congressional Quarterly New Features, 1981), 33-S, 42-S; M. Stephen Weatherford and Lorraine M McDonnell, "Ronald Reagan as Legislative Advocate: Passing the Reagan Revolution's Budgets in 1981 and 1983," *Congress & The Presidency* 32 (Spring 2005), 4; Randall B. Woods, *Quest for Identity: America since 1945* (Fort Worth, TX: Harcourt College Publishers, 2001), 436; William H. Chafe, *The Unfinished Journey: America since World War II*, 6th ed. (New York: Oxford University Press, 2007), 453.

3. Weatherford and McDonnell, 4; *CQA* (1981), 33-S, 42-S; Robert Mann, *Legacy to Power: Senator Russell Long of Louisiana* (New York: Paragon House, 1992), 409.

4. Mann, *Legacy to Power*, 370–374; *Times-Picayune* (New Orleans), July 31, 1980.

5. Glen Jeansonne, *Time of Paradox: America from the Cold War to the Third Millenium* (Lanham, MD: Rowman and Littlefield, 2006), 175; Woods, *Quest for Identity*, 437; Chafe, *Unfinished Journey*, 453.

6. *CQA* (1981), 76-S; Ibid. (1983), 55-S, 23-S; Ibid. (1985), 121.

7. "The Long View on Tax Reform," *CQ Weekly*, April 12, 1986, 799; Mann, 399–400, 409.

8. "The Long Goodbye Sets Off Louisiana Scramble," *CQ Weekly*, March 2, 1985, 391; "Russell Long: Tax Master and Senate Mentor," *CQ Weekly*, April 12, 1986, 797.

9. *Times-Picayune*, October 19, 1992; Ibid., July 8, 1990; *NYT*, May 11, 2003; *Washington Post*, May 11, 2003; *CQ Weekly*, May 17, 2003, 1187.

10. *Times-Picayune*, July 8, 1990; *NYT*, May 11, 2003; *Washington Post*, May 11, 2003; *CQ Weekly*, May 17, 2003, 1187.

11. *Times-Picayune*, January 23, 1980.

12. Ibid., July 8, 1990; Prime Time Radio Program (KPEL), PT 266, September 4, 1993: Sonny Mouton, guest; tape 2, side 1, Collection 150, Southwestern Archives and Manuscript Collection, University of Louisiana at Lafayette.

BIBLIOGRAPHY

PRIMARY SOURCES

Manuscript Collections

Russell B. Long Collection. Louisiana and Lower Mississippi Valley Collections. LSU Libraries. Louisiana State University. Baton Rouge.

Collections of the John F. Kennedy Presidential Library. Boston, Massachusetts.

Richard M. Nixon Presidential Materials Project. National Archives II. College Park, Maryland.

Printed Sources

Congressional Quarterly Almanac. Volumes 5–42. Washington, DC: Congressional Quarterly News Features, 1949–1986.

Congressional Record—Senate. 1949–1986. Volumes 95–132. Washington, DC: U.S. Government Printing Office, 1949–1986.

Executive Sessions of the Senate Foreign Relations Committee together with Joint Sessions with the Senate Armed Services Committee (Historical Series). Volume 9, 58th Congress, First Session. Washington, DC: U.S. Government Printing Office, 1979.

Public Papers of the Presidents of the United States: Richard Nixon, Containing the Public Messages, Speeches, and Statements of the President, 1969. Washington, D. C.: U.S. Government Printing Office, 1971.

Public Papers of the Presidents of the United States: Richard Nixon, Containing the Public Messages, Speeches, and Statements of the President, 1970. Washington, DC: U.S. Government Printing Office, 1971.

Oral History Interviews

Chubbuck, Jim. Interview by Jack Bass and Walter DeVries. January 7, 1974. Transcription. Interview 84, Southern Oral History Program #4007, Southern Historical Collection. Wilson Library. University of North Carolina at Chapel Hill.

Gravelle, Camille. Interview by John Stewart. May 23, 1967. Transcription. John F. Kennedy Presidential Library. Boston, Massachusetts.

Long, Russell B. Interview by Hugh Cates. April 23, 1971. Transcription. Oral History #61. Richard B. Russell Jr. Oral History Collection. Richard B. Russell Library for Political Research and Studies. University of Georgia Libraries. Athens, Georgia.

Long, Russell B. Interview by T. Harry Williams. November 26, 1956. Transcription. Interview 322, Southern Oral History Program #4007. Southern Historical Collection. Wilson Library. University of North Carolina at Chapel Hill.

Nichols, Jesse R. Interview by Donald A. Ritchie. Transcription. United States Senate Historical Office—Oral History Project. Available at http://www.senate.gov/artandhistory/history/oral_history/Jesse_R_Nichols.htm.

Shuman, Howard E. Interview by Donald A. Ritchie. Transcription. United States Senate Historical Office—Oral History Project. Available at http://www.senate.gov/artandhistory/history/oral_history/Howard_E_Shuman.htm.

Smathers, George A. Interview by Donald A. Ritchie. Transcription. United States Senate Historical Office—Oral History Project. Available at http://www.senate.gov/artandhistory/history/oral_history/George_A_Smathers.htm.

Newspapers

Baton Rouge *Morning Advocate.*

Fort Worth (Texas) *Star-Telegram.*

New Orleans *Times-Picayune.*

New York Times.

New York Times Book Review.

Wall Street Journal.

Washington Post.

Winn Parish (Louisiana) *Enterprise.*

Magazines

Barron's.

Fortune.

Newsweek.

Time.

SECONDARY WORKS

Electronic Resources

"BOGGS, Thomas Hale, Sr., 1914–1972." *Biographical Directory of the United States Congress.* Available at http://bioguide.congress.gov/scripts/biodisplay.pl?index=B000594.

Editorial Research Reports. CQ Electronic Library. CQ Researcher Online. Washington: CQ Press. Available at http://library.cqpress.com/cqresearcher/.

Books

Ambrose, Stephen E. *Nixon*. Volume 2. *The Triumph of a Politician, 1962–1972*. New York: Simon and Schuster, 1989.

Anderson, Martin. *Welfare: The Political Economy of Welfare Reform in the United States*. Stanford, CA: Hoover Institution, Stanford University Press, 1978.

Badger, Anthony J. *The New Deal: The Depression Years, 1933–1940*. Chicago: Ivan R. Dee, 1989.

———. *New South/New Deal: An Anthony J. Badger Reader*. Fayetteville, AR: University of Arkansas Press, 2007.

Baker, Liva. *The Second Battle of New Orleans: The Hundred-Year Struggle to Integrate the Schools*. New York: HarperCollins, 1996.

Bartley, Ernest R. *The Tidelands Oil Controversy: A Legal and Historical Analysis*. Austin: University of Texas Press, 1953.

Bartley, Numan V. *The New South, 1945–1980*. Volume 11. *A History of the South*. Baton Rouge: Louisiana State University Press, 1995.

Bass, Jack, and Walter DeVries. *The Transformation of Southern Politics: Social Change and Political Consequence since 1945*. New York: Basic Books, 1976.

Beals, Carleton. *The Story of Huey P. Long*. Philadelphia: J. B. Lippincott Co., 1935.

Becnel, Thomas. *Senator Allen Ellender of Louisiana: A Biography*. Baton Rouge: Louisiana State University Press, 1995.

Bell, Coral. *The Reagan Paradox: American Foreign Policy in the 1980s*. New Brunswick, New Jersey: Rutgers University Press, 1989.

Berkowitz, Edward. *America's Welfare State, from Roosevelt to Reagan*. Baltimore: The Johns Hopkins University Press, 1991.

———, and Kim McQuaid. *Creating the Welfare State: The Political Economy of Twentieth Century Reform*. 2nd rev. ed. New York: Praeger, 1988.

Bernstein, Irving. *Promises Kept: John F. Kennedy's New Frontier*. New York: Oxford University Press, 1991.

Beschloss, Michael. *Reaching for Glory: Lyndon Johnson's Secret White House Tapes, 1964–1965*. New York: Touchstone, 2002.

Biographical Directory of the American Congress, 1774–1949. Washington, DC: U.S. Government Printing Office, 1950.

Black, Earl, and Merle Black. *The Rise of Southern Republicans*. Cambridge, MA: Belknap Press of Harvard University Press, 2002.

Boggs, Lindy, with Katherine Hatch. *Washington through a Purple Veil: Memoirs of a Southern Woman*. New York: Harcourt Brace, 1994.
Boulard, Garry. *The Big Lie: Hale Boggs, Lucille May Grace, and Leander Perez in 1951*. Gretna, LA: Pelican, 2001.
Brauer, Carl. *John F. Kennedy and the Second Reconstruction*. New York: Columbia University Press, 1977.
Brinkley, Alan. *Voices of Protest: Huey Long, Father Coughlin, and the Great Depression*. New York: Knopf, 1983.
Brzezinski, Zbigniew. *Power and Principle: Memoir of the National Security Advisor*. New York: Farrar, Straus, Giroux, 1983.
Cannon, James M. *Time and Chance: Gerald Ford's Appointment with History*. Ann Arbor: University of Michigan Press, 1994.
Cannon, Lou. *President Reagan: The Role of a Lifetime*. New York: Simon and Schuster, 1990.
Caro, Robert A. *The Years of Lyndon Johnson: Master of the Senate*. New York: Knopf, 2002.
Carter, Dan T. *From George Wallace to Newt Gingrich: Race in the Conservative Counterrevolution*. Baton Rouge: Louisiana State University Press, 1996.
———. *The Politics of Rage: George Wallace, the Origins of the New Conservatism, and the Transformation of American Politics*. New York: Simon and Schuster, 1995.
Carter, Doris Dorcas. *Robert Floyd Kennon: Reform Governor*. Lafayette, LA: Center for Louisiana Studies, 1998.
Chafe, William H. *The Unfinished Journey: America since World War II*. 6th ed. New York: Oxford University Press, 2007.
Cohen, Lizabeth. *A Consumer's Republic: The Politics of Consumption in Postwar America*. New York: Knopf, 2003.
Cohen, Warren I. *The Cambridge History of American Foreign Relations: Vol. 4, America in the Age of Soviet Power*. Cambridge: Cambridge University Press, 1993.
Conkin, Paul. *Big Daddy from the Pedernales: Lyndon Baines Johnson*. Boston: Twayne, 1986.
Crabb, Cecil V., and Pat M. Holt. *Invitation to Struggle: Congress, the President, and Foreign Affairs*. 4th ed. Washington, DC: CQ Press, 1992.
Dallek, Robert. *Flawed Giant: Lyndon Johnson and His Times, 1961–1973*. New York: Oxford University Press, 1998.
———. *An Unfinished Life: John F. Kennedy, 1917–1963*. Boston: Little, Brown, 2003.
Daniels, Roger. *Guarding the Golden Door: American Immigration Policy and Immigrants since 1882*. New York: Hill and Wang, 2004.

Davis, Hugh Graham. *The Civil Rights Era: Origins and Development of National Policy, 1960–1972*. New York: Oxford University Press, 1990.
Deutsch, Hermann. *The Huey Long Murder Case*. Garden City, NY: Doubleday, 1963.
Douth, George. *Leaders in Profile: The United States Senate. The Ninety-Second Congress*. New York: Sperr and Douth, 1972.
Fairclough, Adam. *Race and Democracy: The Civil Rights Struggle in Louisiana, 1915–1972*. Athens: University of Georgia Press, 1995.
Ferrell, Robert H., ed. *Off the Record: The Private Papers of Harry S. Truman*. New York: Harper and Row, 1980.
Fields, Harvey G. *A True History of the Life, Works, Assassination and Death of Huey Pierce Long*. Farmerville, LA: Fields Publishing Agency, 1945.
Finley, Keith. *Delaying the Dream: Southern Senators and the Fight against Civil Rights, 1938–1965*. Baton Rouge: Louisiana State University Press, 2008.
Ford, Gerald R. *A Time to Heal: The Autobiography of Gerald R. Ford*. New York: Harper and Row, 1979.
Fortier, James A., ed. *Huey P. Long: The Martyr of the Age*. New Orleans: T. J. Moran's Sons, 1937.
Frederickson, Kari. *The Dixiecrat Revolt and the End of the Solid South, 1932–1968*. Chapel Hill: University of North Carolina Press, 2001.
Fry, Joseph A. *Dixie Looks Abroad: The South and U.S. Foreign Relations, 1789–1973*. Baton Rouge: Louisiana State University Press, 2002.
———. *Debating Vietnam: Fulbright, Stennis, and their Senate Hearings*. Lanham, MD: Rowman & Littlefield, 2006.
Gaddis, John Lewis. *We Now Know: Rethinking Cold War History*. Oxford: Oxford University Press, 1997.
Giglio, James N. *The Presidency of John F. Kennedy*. Lawrence: University of Kansas Press, 1991.
Goldfield, David R. *Black, White, and Southern: Race Relations and Southern Culture, 1940 to the Present*. Baton Rouge: Louisiana State University Press, 1990.
Gould, Louis L. *1968: The Election that Changed America*. Chicago: Ivan R. Dee, 1993.
———. *The Most Exclusive Club: A History of the Modern United States Senate*. New York: Basic Books, 2005.
Greelegs, Edward. *Russell B. Long: Democratic Senator from Louisiana*. Ralph Nader Congress Project, Citizens Look at Congress (New York: Grossman Publishers, 1972): 1-26.
Haas, Edward F. *DeLesseps S. Morrison and the Image of Reform: New Or-*

leans Politics, 1946–1961. 1974. Baton Rouge: Louisiana State University Press, paperback ed., 1986.
———, ed. *The Age of the Longs: Louisiana 1928–1960*. Vol. 8. Louisiana Purchase Bicentennial Series in Louisiana History. Lafayette, LA: Center for Louisiana Studies, 2001.
Hair, William Ivy. *The Kingfish and His Realm: The Life and Times of Huey P. Long*. Baton Rouge: Louisiana State University Press, 1991.
Hamby, Alonzo. *Beyond the New Deal: Harry S. Truman and American Liberalism*. New York: Columbia University Press, 1973.
———. *Liberalism and Its Challengers, from F.D.R. to Bush*. 2nd ed. New York: Oxford University Press, 1992.
Harris, Thomas O. *The Kingfish: Huey P. Long, Dictator*. New Orleans: Pelican, 1938.
Havard, William C., Rudolf Heberle, and Perry H. Howard. *The Louisiana Elections of 1960*. Louisiana State University Studies, Social Science Series, no. 9. Baton Rouge: Louisiana State University Press, 1963.
Henderson, Richard B. *Maury Maverick: A Political Biography*. Austin: University of Texas Press, 1970.
Herring, George C. *America's Longest War: The United States and Vietnam, 1950–1975*. Boston: McGraw-Hill, 2002.
Hill, Dylis M., et al., eds. *The Reagan Presidency: An Incomplete Revolution?* New York: St. Martin's Press, 1990.
Howard, L. Vaughan, and David R. Deener. *Presidential Politics in Louisiana, 1952*. Tulane Studies in Political Science. Vol. 1. New Orleans: Tulane University Press, 1954.
Howard, Perry H. *Political Tendencies in Louisiana, 1812–1952*. Louisiana State University Studies. Social Science Series. No. 5. Baton Rouge: Louisiana State University Press, 1957.
———. *The Louisiana Elections of 1960*. Louisiana State University Studies, Social Science Series. No. 9. Baton Rouge: Louisiana State University Press, 1963.
Jeansonne, Glen. *Leander Perez: Boss of the Delta*. 2nd ed. Lafayette, LA: Center for Louisiana Studies, 1995.
———. *Messiah of the Masses: Huey P. Long and the Great Depression*. Library of American Biography, ed. Oscar Handlin. New York: Longman, 1993.
———. *Time of Paradox: America from the Cold War to the Third Millenium*. Lanham, MD: Rowman and Littlefield, 2006.
———, ed. *Huey at 100: Centennial Essays on Huey P. Long*. Ruston, LA: McGinty, 1995.

Jones, Jacqueline. *The Dispossessed: America's Underclass from the Civil War to the Present*. New York: Basic Books, 1992.

Kane, Harnett. *Louisiana Hayride: The American Rehearsal for Dictatorship, 1928–1940*. New York: W. Morrow, 1941.

Kaufman, Burton I. *The Presidency of James Earl Carter*. Lawrence: University Press of Kansas, 1993.

Kelso, Louis O., and Mortimer J. Adler. *The Capitalist Manifesto*. Westport, CT: Greenwood Press, 1958.

———. *The New Capitalists: A Proposal to Free Economic Growth from the Slavery of Savings*. New York: Random House, 1961.

Kelso, Louis O., and Patricia Hetter. *Two-Factor Theory: The Economics of Reality, How to Turn Eighty Million Workers into Capitalists on Borrowed Money and Other Proposals*. 1967. New York: Vintage, 1968.

Kelso, Louis O., and Patricia Hetter Kelso. *Democracy and Economic Power: Extending the ESOP Revolution*. Cambridge, MA: Ballinger, 1986.

Key, V. O. *Southern Politics in State and Nation*. New York: Knopf, 1949.

Kotlowski, Dean J. *Nixon's Civil Rights: Politics, Principle, and Policy*. Cambridge, MA: Harvard University Press, 2001.

Kurtz, Michael L., and Morgan D. Peoples. *Earl K. Long: The Saga of Uncle Earl and Louisiana Politics*. Southern Biography Series., ed. William J. Cooper. Baton Rouge: Louisiana State University Press, 1990.

Kutler, Stanley. *The Wars of Watergate: The Last Crisis of Richard Nixon*. New York: Knopf, 1990.

———. *Abuse of Power: The New Nixon Tapes*. New York: Simon and Schuster, 1997.

Lawson, Alan. *A Commonwealth of Hope: The New Deal Response to Crisis*. Baltimore: The Johns Hopkins University Press, 2006.

Lawson, Steven. *Black Ballots: Voting Rights in the South, 1944–1969*. New York: Columbia University Press, 1976.

———, and Charles Payne. *Debating the Civil Rights Movement, 1945–1968*. Lanham, MD: Rowman & Littlefield, 1998.

Leuchtenburg, William E. *Franklin D. Roosevelt and the New Deal, 1932–1940*. New York: Harper and Row, 1963.

———. *The White House Looks South: Franklin D. Roosevelt, Harry S. Truman, Lyndon B. Johnson*. Baton Rouge: Louisiana State University Press, 2005.

Liebling, A. J. *The Earl of Louisiana*. Baton Rouge: Louisiana State University Press, 1970.

Long, Huey P. *Every Man a King: The Autobiography of Huey P. Long*. New Orleans: National Book Co., 1933.

Machlup, Fritz. *The Basing-point System: An Economic Analysis of a Controversial Pricing Practice*. Philadelphia: Blakiston, 1949.

Maginnis, John. *The Last Hayride*. Baton Rouge, LA: Gris Gris Press, 1984.

Mann, Robert. *Legacy to Power: Senator Russell Long of Louisiana*. New York: Paragon House, 1992.

Martin, Thomas. *Dynasty: The Longs of Louisiana*. New York: G. P. Putnam's Sons, 1960.

Matusow, Allen. *The Unraveling of America: A History of Liberalism in the 1960s*. New York: HarperCollins, 1984.

———. *Nixon's Economy: Booms, Busts, Dollars, and Votes*. Lawrence: University Press of Kansas, 1998.

McCormick, Thomas J. *America's Half-Century: United States Foreign Policy in the Cold War and After*. 2nd ed. Baltimore: The Johns Hopkins University Press, 1995.

Moynihan, Daniel Patrick. *The Negro Family: The Case for National Action*. Washington, DC: U.S. Government Printing Office, 1965.

———. *The Politics of a Guaranteed Income: The Nixon Administration and the Family Assistance Plan*. New York: Random House, 1973.

Murray, Charles. *Losing Ground: American Social Policy, 1950–1980*. New York: Basic Books, 1984.

Opotowsky, Stan. *The Longs of Louisiana*. New York: Dutton, 1960.

Parent, Wayne. *Inside the Carnival: Unmasking Louisiana Politics*. Baton Rouge: Louisiana State University Press, 2004.

Parmet, Herbert S. *JFK: The Presidency of John F. Kennedy*. New York: Dial Press, 1983.

———. *Richard M. Nixon and His America*. Boston: Little, Brown, 1990.

Patterson, James T. *Grand Expectations: The United States, 1945–1974*. New York: Oxford University Press, 1996.

———. *America's Struggle against Poverty in the Twentieth Century*. Cambridge, MA: Harvard University Press, 2001.

———. *Brown v. Board of Education: A Civil Rights Milestone and Its Troubled Legacy*. Pivotal Moments in American History. Ed. David Hackett Fischer and James M. McPherson. Oxford: Oxford University Press, 2001.

Reed, Merl E. *Seedtime for the Modern Civil Rights Movement: The President's Committee on Fair Employment Practice,1941–1946*. Baton Rouge: Louisiana State University Press, 1991.

Schaller, Michael. *Reckoning with Reagan: America and Its President in the 1980s*. New York: Oxford University Press, 1992.

Schapsmeier, Edward L., and Frederick H. Schapsmeier. *Gerald R. Ford's Date with Destiny: A Political Biography*. New York: Peter Lang, 1989.

Schrecker, Ellen. *Many Are the Crimes: McCarthyism in America*. Boston: Little, Brown, 1998.

Schwarz, John. *America's Hidden Success: A Reassessment of Twenty Years of Public Policy*. New York: Norton, 1983.

Sindler, Allan P. *Huey Long's Louisiana: State Politics, 1920–1952*. Baltimore: The Johns Hopkins University Press, 1956.

Sloan, John W. *The Reagan Effect: Economics and Presidential Leadership*. Lawrence: University Press of Kansas, 1999.

Smith, Gaddis. *Morality, Reason, and Power: American Diplomacy in the Carter Years*. New York: Hill and Wang, 1986.

Spector, Ronald. *After Tet: The Bloodiest Year in Vietnam*. New York: Free Press, 1992.

Tolchin, Martin, and Susan Tolchin. *To the Victor: Political Patronage from the Clubhouse to the White House and Beyond*. New York: Random House, 1971.

Wall, Bennett H., et al. *Louisiana: A History*. 2nd ed. Arlington Heights, IL: Forum Press, 1990.

White, Donald W. *The American Century: The Rise and Decline of the United States as a World Power*. New Haven, CT: Yale University Press, 1996.

White, Richard. *Kingfish: The Reign of Huey P. Long*. New York: Random House, 2006.

Williams, T. Harry. *Huey Long*. New York: Knopf, 1970.

Wills, Garry. *Reagan's America: Innocents at Home*. Garden City, NY: Doubleday, 1987.

Wirls, Daniel. *Buildup: The Politics of Defense in the Reagan Era*. Ithaca, NY: Cornell University Press, 1992.

Woods, Randall B. *Quest for Identity: America since 1945*. Fort Worth, Texas: Harcourt College Publishers, 2001.

———, and Howard Jones. *Dawning of the Cold War: The United States Quest for Order*. Athens: University of Georgia Press, 1991.

Zinman, David. *The Day Huey Long Was Shot, September 8, 1935*. New York: Ivan Obolensky, 1963.

Journal Articles, Magazine Articles, Book Chapters

Abadie, Dale, et al. "Memories from the Bullpen and Lincolnand," *Louisiana History* 41 (Spring 2000): 203–215.

Amenta, Edwin, Kathleen Dunleavy, and Mary Bernstein. "Stolen Thunder? Huey Long's 'Share Our Wealth,' Political Mediation, and the Second New Deal," *American Sociological Review* 59, no. 5 (1994): 678–702.

Anderson, James E. "Poverty, Unemployment, and Economic Development: The Search for a National Anti-Poverty Policy," *Journal of Politics* 29 (February 1967): 70–93.
Asen, Robert. "Nixon's Welfare Reform: Enacting Historical Contradictions of Poverty Discourses," *Rhetoric and Public Affairs* 4 (2001): 261–279.
Baker, Ross K. "Mike Mansfield and the Birth of the Modern Senate." In *First Among Equals: Outstanding Senate Leaders of the Twentieth Century.* Ed. Richard A. Baker and Roger H. Davidson. Washington, DC: Congressional Quarterly, 1991, 264–296.
Basso, Hamilton. "The Huey Long Legend." *Life*, December 9, 1946, 106–121.
Bierman, Pearl. "The Special Problems of Low-Income Groups and the Aged: Meeting the Health Needs of Low-Income Families." *Annals of the American Academy of Political and Social Science* 37 (September 1961): 103–113.
Carleton, Mark T. "Four Anti-Longites: A Tentative Assessment." *Louisiana History* 30 (Summer 1989): 249–262.
Cooper, Richard N. "A Note on Deregulation of Natural Gas Prices." *Brookings Papers on Economic Activity* 2 (1982): 371–394.
Davis, Otto A., and John E. Jackson. "Senate Defeat of the Family Assistance Plan." *Public Policy* 22 (1974): 245–273.
Duggar, Ronnie. "Oil and Politics." *Atlantic Monthly*, September 1969, 66-90.
Ferrell, Thomas H., and Judith Haydel. "Hale and Lindy Boggs: Louisiana's National Democrats." *Louisiana History* 35 (Fall 1994): 389–402.
Giglio, James N. "John F. Kennedy and the Nation." In *Debating the Kennedy Presidency*. Ed. James N. Giglio and Stephen G. Rabe. Lanham, MD: Rowman & Littlefield, 2003, 95–166.
Graham, Hugh Davis. "The Enigma of Huey Long: A Review Essay." *Journal of Southern History* 36 (May 1970): 205–211.Gueron, Nicole L. "An Idea Whose Time Has Come: A Comparative Procedural History of the Civil Rights Acts of 1960, 1964, and 1991." *Yale Law Journal* 104 (March 1995): 1201–1234.
Haas, Edward F. "De Lesseps S. Morrison and the Governorship: A Reassessment." In *The Age of the Longs: Louisiana, 1928–1960*. Ed. Edward F. Haas. Vol. 8, The Louisiana Purchase Bicentennial Series in Louisiana History. Lafayette, LA: Center for Louisiana Studies, 2001, 419–433.
———. "'Don't Believe Any False Rumors': Mayor Victor H. Schiro, Hurricane Betsy, and Urban Myths." *Louisiana History* 45 (2004): 436-468.
Heleniak, Roman J. "Lyndon Johnson in New Orleans." In *Louisiana since*

the Longs, 1960 to Century's End. Ed. Michael L. Kurtz. Vol. 9, The Louisiana Purchase Bicentennial Series in Louisiana History. Lafayette, LA: Center for Louisiana Studies, 1998, 353–363.

Hogan, Michael J. "Corporatism." In *Explaining the History of American Foreign Relations*. Ed. Michael J. Hogan and Thomas G. Paterson. 1991. Repr. ed., Cambridge: Cambridge University Press, 1996, 226–236.

Howard, Perry. "Louisiana: Resistance and Change." In *The Changing Politics of the South*. Ed. William C. Havard. Baton Rouge: Louisiana State University Press, 1972, 525–587.

Ingram, E. Glynn. "Huey P. Long: A Synopsis; With a Selected Bibliography of Works on Huey P. Long and His Era." In *Huey at 100: Centennial Essays on Huey P. Long*. Ed. Glen Jeansonne. Ruston, LA: McGinty, 1995, 197–218.

Jeansonne, Glen. "Challenge to the New Deal: Huey P. Long and the Redistribution of National Wealth." *Louisiana History* 21 (Fall 1980): 331–339.

———. "The Long Era and Beyond." In *A Guide to the History of Louisiana*. Ed. Light Townsend Cummins and Glen Jeansonne. Westport, CT: Greenwood Press, 1982, 59–70.

———. "The Apotheosis of Huey Long." *Biography* 12 (Fall 1989): 283–301.

———. "Huey Long and Racism." *Louisiana History* 33 (Summer 1992): 265–282.

———. "De Lesseps Morrison: "Why He Couldn't Become Governor of Louisiana." In *The Age of the Longs: Louisiana, 1928–1960*. Ed. Edward F. Haas. Vol. 8. The Louisiana Purchase Bicentennial Series in Louisiana History. Lafayette, LA: Center for Louisiana Studies, 2001, 410–418.

Katz, Michael B. "The Urban 'Underclass' as a Metaphor of Social Transformation." In *The "Underclass" Debate: Views from History*. Ed. Michael B. Katz. Princeton, NJ: Princeton University Press, 1993, 3–23.

Kurtz, Michael L. "Robert F. Kennon." In *The Louisiana Governors: From Iberville to Edwards*. Ed. Joseph G. Dawson III. Baton Rouge: Louisiana State University Press, 1990, 263–267.

———. "Government by the Civics Books: The Administration of Robert F. Kennon, 1952–1956." In *The Age of the Longs: Louisiana, 1928–1960*. Ed. Edward F. Haas. Vol. 8. The Louisiana Purchase Bicentennial Series in Louisiana History. Lafayette, LA: Center for Louisiana Studies, 2001, 400–409.

Lang, Robert E., and Rebecca R. Sohmer. "Editors Introduction: Legacy of the Housing Act of 1949: The Past, Present, and Future of Federal Housing and Urban Policy." *Housing Policy Debate* 11 (2000): 291–298.

Lenkowsky, Leslie. "Welfare Reform and the Liberals." *Commentary* 67 (1979): 56–61.

Long, Russell B. "Foreword." In *Uncle Earl Deserved Better*. By Jack B. McGuire. New Orleans: Good Reading Books, 1995.

Martin, Michael S. "Insiders and Outsiders: Earl K. Long and the Media, May–July 1959." *Louisiana History* 40 (Spring 1999): 197–209.

———. "'High Time We Put Behind Us the Blind Prejudice of the Past': Russell Long and Louisiana Politics, 1948–1952." *Louisiana History* 46 (Spring 2005): 133–153.

———. "New Orleans Becomes a Big-League City: The NFL-AFL Merger and the Creation of the New Orleans Saints." In *Horsehide, Pigskin, Oval Tracks, and Apple Pie: Essays on Sports and American Culture*. Ed. Jim Vlasich. Jefferson, NC: McFarland, 2006, 119–131.

McNown, Robert F. "The Story of the Family Assistance Plan." *Current History* 65 (1973): 57–61, 86.

Miller, Gregory Blaine. "Louisiana's Tidelands Controversy: *The United States of America v. State of Louisiana* Maritime Boundary Cases." *Louisiana History* 38 (Spring 1997): 203–221.

Neustadt, Richard E. "Congress and the Fair Deal: A Legislative Balance Sheet." In *Harry S. Truman and the Fair Deal*. Ed. Alonzo Hamby. Lexington, MA: D.C. Heath and Company, 1974, 15–42.

O'Neill, William L. "Eisenhower and American Society." In *Eisenhower: A Centenary Assessment*. Ed. Gunter Bischoff and Stephen E. Ambrose. Baton Rouge: Louisiana State University Press, 101–107.

Patterson, James. Review of *Huey Long*. *Journal of American History* 57 (June 1970): 201–203.

Quadagno, Jill. "Race, Class, and Gender in the U.S. Welfare State: Nixon's Failed Family Assistance Plan." *American Sociological Review* 55 (1990): 11–28.

Reedy, George. "The True Dawn of the Civil Rights Movement." *Washington Monthly* 14 (1982): 46–51.

Reeves, Thomas C. "Introduction." In *McCarthyism*. Ed. Thomas C. Reeves. Huntington, NY: Robert E. Krieger, 1978, 1–7.

Rovere, Richard. "McCarthyism as a Bipartisan Doctrine." In *McCarthyism*. Ed. Thomas C. Reeves. Huntington, NY: Robert E. Krieger, 1978, 93–96.

Schlesinger, Arthur, Jr. "Messiah of the Rednecks." In his *The Age of Upheaval*. New York: Houghton Mifflin, 1960, 42–68.

Schott, Matthew. "Huey Long, the Biographer, and the Question of Character." In *Huey at 100: Centennial Essays on Huey P. Long*. Ed. Glen Jeansonne. Ruston, LA: McGinty Publications, 1995, 77–98.

Shalowitz, Aaron L. "Boundary Problems Raised by the Submerged Lands Act." *Columbia Law Review* 54 (November 1954): 1021–1048.

Silbey, Joel H. "Current Historiographic Trends in the Study of the Twentieth-Century Congress." *Social Science History* 24 (2000): 317–331.

Thornton III, J. Mills. "First among Equals: The Montgomery Bus Boycott." In *The Walking City: The Montgomery Bus Boycott, 1955–1956*. Ed. David J. Garrow. Brooklyn, NY: Carlson, 1989, xvii–xxiv.

Tindall, George Brown. Review of *Huey Long*. *American Historical Review* 75 (October 1970): 1792–1794.

Wadden, Alex. "A Liberal in Wolf's Clothing: Nixon's Family Assistance Plan in the Light of 1990s Welfare Reform." *Journal of American Studies* 32 (1998): 203–218.

Weatherford, M. Stephen, and Lorraine M. McDonnell. "Ronald Reagan as Legislative Advocate: Passing the Reagan Revolution's Budgets in 1981 and 1983." *Congress & the Presidency* 32 (Spring 2005): 1–29.

Wiley, Bell I. "T. Harry Williams, As I Knew Him." *Military Affairs* 44 (1980): 33.

Williams, Estelle. "A Biographical Introduction by Estelle Williams." In *The Selected Essays of T. Harry Williams.* Baton Rouge: Louisiana State University Press, 1983.

Williams, T. Harry. "The Gentleman from Louisiana: Demagogue or Democrat?" *Journal of Southern History* 26 (February 1960): 3–21.

Wynne, Michael. "Annotated Bibliography on Huey Long." In *Huey at 100: Centennial Essays on Huey P. Long*. Ed. Glen Jeansonne. Ruston, LA: McGinty, 1995, 219–225.

Yergin, Dan, Senator Bennett Johnston, and John Deutch. "Oil Lessons from the 1970s." *The International Economy* 23 (Fall 2009): 26–29, 58–64.

Zelizer, Julian E. "Introduction to Roundtable: The U.S. Congress in the Twentieth Century." *Social Science History* 24 (2000): 307–316.

INDEX